Dept
Mic
Eas

The Structuralists:

FROM MARX TO LÉVI-STRAUSS

RICHARD T. DE GEORGE is Professor of Philosophy at The University of Kansas. He received his Ph.D. from Yale University in 1959. He is the editor of *Ethics and Society,* and his books include *Patterns of Soviet Thought* (1966), *The New Marxism* (1968), and *Soviet Ethics and Morality* (1969).

FERNANDE M. DE GEORGE received her M.A. from Yale University in 1956 and her M. Phil. in French literature from The University of Kansas in 1970. A former Fulbright Fellow to France, she is presently completing her doctoral dissertation on Baudelaire.

The Structuralists:

FROM MARX TO LÉVI-STRAUSS

Edited with an Introduction

by

RICHARD T. DE GEORGE

and

FERNANDE M. DE GEORGE

ANCHOR BOOKS

Doubleday & Company, Inc.

GARDEN CITY, NEW YORK

This anthology has been especially prepared for Anchor Books
and has never before appeared in book form.
Anchor Books edition: 1972
Library of Congress Catalog Number 76–175409
Copyright © 1972 by Richard T. and Fernande M. De George
All Rights Reserved
Printed in the United States of America

TO

REBECCA, ANNE MARIE, AND CATHERINE

PREFACE

"Structuralism" is a term used to refer to a variety of different kinds of endeavors, all more or less interrelated. It cuts across traditional disciplinary boundaries, and bibliographies on structuralism can be virtually endless if one succumbs to the temptation to include everything related to the topic. The first purpose of the present volume is to make easily available representative writings from a relatively small number of modern thinkers and writers who are almost certain to be included in any list of structuralists. They represent a variety of fields; in each case the structuralist methodology employed is dictated by the subject matter and intent of the author. Each of these writers is in some sense a pioneer in his field who has forged a new approach in his area, generated a considerable stir therein, and drawn an appreciable following.

A second purpose of this volume is to help place structuralism in some kind of historical perspective. It is too frequently presented as if it were a spontaneous phenomenon of the 1960s, owing no debt to the past. Both the term "structure" and many of the basic ideas behind structuralism are not new to Western intellectual thought. Marx, Freud, and Saussure are clearly precursors of present-day structuralism. Not only are all three cited and explicitly credited by contemporary structuralists for having raised the basic problems and suggested the basic approach for many structuralist investigations, but they also developed many of the techniques which have been honed since their death and are being combined and adapted in original ways by contemporary structuralists.

The choice of material for an anthology such as this was a difficult one because of the wealth, diversity, and sometimes the length and technicality of the available material. We have tried to avoid the very esoteric and the very technical pieces which in some instances might interest the specialist in a field more than some of the programmatic and summary statements which we have included. Each item included is understandable in its own right to an intelligent reader who is not a specialist in the field; each is representative of a position; and almost all of the items are historically important in the development of structuralism.

A short prefatory note precedes each selection. The purpose of these notes is simply to identify the author of the particular piece, indicate some of his other writings, and help place the reprinted material in the proper context. Where English translations of a work originally published in another language are available, the English translation rather than the original title has been cited. No attempt has been made to mention all of the works, or even all of the important works, of any author.

CONTENTS

INTRODUCTION

Structuralism has been described as a method, a movement, an intellectual fad, and an ideology. Each of these characterizations is in part valid. For structuralism is a loose, amorphous, many-faceted phenomenon with no clear lines of demarcation, no tightly knit group spearheading it, no specific set of doctrines held by all those whom one usually thinks of as being associated with it. It cuts across many disciplines—linguistics, anthropology, literary criticism, psychology, philosophy. For some it gives hope of uncovering or developing a common basic approach to the social sciences, literature, and art which would unify them and put them on a scientific footing, much as the "scientific method" grounds and unifies the physical sciences.

To the extent that structuralism is a movement, it is multidimensional with several independent leaders, each disowning any relation to the others and each carrying along with him a group of devoted and enthusiastic followers. Claude Lévi-Strauss is the undisputed high priest whose impressive and highly controversial work in anthropology made "structuralism" an everyday word first among French intellectuals and now among large numbers throughout the world. Roland Barthes in literary criticism, Jacques Lacan in psychoanalysis, Michel Foucault in philosophy, and Louis Althusser in Marxist theory are the major, acknowledged, dominant, "first-generation" structuralists who are frequently grouped together as the leaders of the movement by non-structuralists. If each disowns the others as brothers-in-arms and struggles to get free of invidious labels, scores of lesser figures fight to be included in the group, to learn the terminology, and to apply and misapply the techniques at random and at will in order to be associated with the fashionable successor of existentialism.

As with all such phenomena, there is an attempt by some expositors to capture structuralism in slogans, to popularize complex and subtle doctrines, to codify, rigidify, and mechanically apply its method or methods, and to impose it upon others. Thus, for some critics it has tended to become an ideology; for others, its inherently antihumanistic (or a-humanistic) tendencies make it less a value-free approach to the human sciences than a value-drenched assumption about them.

Structuralism as an intellectual movement is sparked by new techniques and impressive results in linguistics, anthropology, and literary and art criticism. Though concern with structure is no innovation in the history of Western thought and can be traced back to ancient times, the more proximate roots of structuralism date from the nineteenth century. Among the precursors of the movement, three figures stand out clearly both for having foreshadowed and for having directly influenced the major structuralists of today. The three are Karl Marx, Sigmund Freud, and Ferdinand de Saussure. The techniques, insights, and methodology of all three have been continued, refined, and combined in various ways by the contemporary practitioners and theoreticians.

What Marx, Freud, and Saussure have in common, and what they share with present-day structuralists, is a conviction that surface events and phenomena are to be explained by structures, data, and phenomena below the surface. The explicit and obvious is to be explained by and is determined—in some sense of the term—by what is implicit and not obvious. The attempt to uncover deep structures, unconscious motivations, and underlying causes which account for human actions at a more basic and profound level than do individual conscious decisions, and which shape, influence, and structure these decisions, is an enterprise which unites Marx, Freud, Saussure, and modern structuralists.

Marx

One of the basic thrusts of Marx's position is neatly summarized in a sentence from *The German Ideology:* "Life is not determined by consciousness, but consciousness by life."

According to Marx, men must live before they can think, and how and what they think is closely related to how they live. For what men are and the ways in which they express themselves depend on what and how they live. The distinguishing characteristic of man is that, as opposed to other animals, he produces the means of his own subsistence. How he does this depends on his physical organization and on what he finds available to him. What he does and how he does it depend in large part on the conditions determining his production.

According to Marx, it is a mistake to think either that consciousness is something that man always had in its full flower or that man was intellectually able to determine his conditions of life. Consciousness, like man himself, developed as his needs developed. Thinking and ideas developed together with human activity and life. Intellectual activity came to appear separate from man's practical activity only when the division of labor had progressed sufficiently far for some men to become "thinkers," their practical physical needs being taken care of by the productive activity of other men in their society. But the claim that the ideas or thoughts of such men, that philosophy, morality, or any other body of thought can be separated from the society of which it is a part, is a mistake. It is a mistake which becomes plausible only because of the complexity of modern society which hides the real links and connections between the physical conditions of life in a society and the ideas and institutions prevalent in that society.

Marx maintains that the social structure of a society, as well as the structure of its institutions, its morality, its philosophy, and its religion, are ultimately determined by the conditions of life—especially the productive conditions of that society. He thus divides society into its infrastructure or economic base, and the superstructure which is built upon it.

In Marx's model the economic base consists of the means, the modes, and the relations of production. The means of production can be roughly equated with the materials available for the productive process; the modes of production with the techniques available; and the relations of production with the type of ownership prevalent, together with the concomitant division between owners and workers in a class society, and the relations among all those engaged in the productive process. Each of these has a structure, and since the productive process is not static but dynamic, the structures themselves develop and conflict one with another, producing tensions which are resolved only to be replaced by new tensions. The history of mankind is ultimately the result of this development: primitive communal society gives way to a slaveholding society, which in its turn develops into feudalism, only to yield in turn to capitalism.

Each epoch is characterized and structured by the types of production and ownership corresponding to it. The division of a society into masters and slaves, lords and serfs, entrepreneurs and proletarians does not end with production but carries over into all other areas of life. A society which is basically divided by its productive relations continues to be divided in its other social relations. Hence the social relations, institutions, laws, religion, philosophy, literature—the superstructure of a society—reflect and are ultimately determined by the infrastructure of the society. The masters rule not only over production but over the rest of society as well. They, rather than the slaves, are the lawmakers and the law enforcers. The laws they make reflect their position and status, and consciously or not, the laws are framed to protect their interests and property. The institutions which develop are closely tied to the economic divisions present in society; what is taught in the schools and preached in the churches reflects the views, values, and needs of the ruling class. The public morality which is developed and imposed similarly reflects the interests of the ruling class; and philosophers, writers, theoreticians of every kind—having been formed by the society in which they grew up—reflect that society and are representatives of their class. This does not mean that they are insincere or that they consciously attempt to dupe the masses. Marx simply claims that what they believe is determined by their social situation, whether they realize it or not.

The needs of the workers in a class society are not the same as those of the owners of the means of production, nor are their interests and the actual conditions in which they live their lives. Their values, their attitude toward property, their style of life consequently differ from those of the rulers of society. Though educated in schools which reflect the views of the rulers of society, though subject to the laws made by those rulers, their own conditions of life sooner or later force them to see things differently from the rulers and to reflect their different conditions.

The development of society is of course a complicated matter. Exactly how thoughts are determined by the conditions of life is not always clear; and of course the thoughts of earlier periods condition and influence to some extent the thoughts of a later period. For Marx this relative independence of the superstructure, or of parts of it, does not negate the ultimate determining role of the economic base on the superstructure.

In *Capital* Marx attempted to demonstrate his thesis by a detailed analysis of the productive forces operative in what he called "modern bourgeois society." He sought to uncover the contradictions and tensions inherent in capitalist production so that he could chart its movement and "lay bare the economic law of motion of modern society." The accuracy of his description and the validity of the laws which he describes are not at issue here. And it can be readily admitted that Marx did not make any attempt to produce all the connecting links which would show how particular theories or doctrines are determined by the societies in which they appear.

The similarities between Marx's view and that held by many structuralists are striking. They, like Marx, seek to explain consciousness by life and not life by consciousness. In general, they give up any claim to privileged status which might be made on the part of consciousness or of the conscious individual. The primacy of the individual ego, which found its most eloquent spokesman in Descartes and which through the history of modern European thought has continued to be a central theme, is denied by both Marx and the structuralists. Foucault, like Marx, is more concerned with the thought of an age than with the thought of individuals in their individuality. Lévi-Strauss, like Marx, sees a close relation between man's life and his thought and defends the "savage mind" which he sees as being as human as that of the contemporary Western thinker.

Of all the structuralists, Althusser has most explicitly developed Marx's thought along what has been called structuralist lines. In his reading of Marx he sees and emphasizes the structures, levels, and dialectical interactions which are present in Marx's model of society. Althusser underscores how

Marx turned the study of political economy into a science by supplying the theoretical concepts and constructs necessary to account for the surface phenomena, and by searching out the general laws operative behind the economic scene. Althusser's reading of Marx is not always acceptable to other Marxists; but he claims both to be faithful to Marx and to continue in a contemporary mode what Marx began.

That social thought can be explained and accounted for in terms other than that of conscious thought itself is a basic insight which Marx shares with the structuralists.

Freud

Though Marx claimed to have uncovered the relationship between the economic conditions of a society and the thought and institutions of that society, he made no attempt to treat individual thought. His concern was primarily with social classes and with the ideology of those classes. Individual exceptions, if explained at all, were explained by the fact that the member of one class could identify with another class. Why one particular individual rather than another identifies himself with a class other than his own is a question which Marx never attempted to answer and which his techniques gave him no means of answering.

Freud's concern, on the other hand, was not so much with social consciousness as with individual consciousness. He was no less deterministic in his approach than was Marx, and like Marx he looked below the surface to explain and account for the seemingly accidental. He was less interested in the conscious reasons or rationalizations given for conduct than in the really determining factors which he found in the subconscious or unconscious life of man.

Though he was interested in psychopathology, Freud's theories range beyond the pathological to include many facets of what can be called normal mental activity. For, he claimed, the same psychic mechanisms were operative in both cases, though in different degrees. The techniques and theories which he developed for the study of unconscious mental processes constitute the field of depth psychology, many of the terms of which have become parts of our ordinary speech.

Among Freud's best-known writings are *The Interpretation*

of Dreams and *The Psychopathology of Everyday Life.* Both underline the claim that even the smallest detail of mental life is determined and that the determining psychical factors are in principle discoverable. In working with dreams he developed the technique of free association in order to uncover their meaning, convinced that word associations are not really "free" or arbitrary. They can thus be used to uncover wishes and desires repressed and hidden from one's own conscious thoughts. Basic to his interpretation of dreams is the assumption that the dream in all its facets, in its very distortions, can in fact be accounted for. In order to trace the transformation of the latent dream material into manifest dream content, he takes into account such factors as condensation, displacement, representation, and transference. In dreams the critical censor, which inhibits certain wishes from entering our consciousness and impelling us to forbidden actions, relaxes and allows our unconscious impulses to achieve expression. Freud tells us, "for all practical purposes in judging human character, a man's actions and conscious expressions of thought are in most cases sufficient," but the study of dreams gives knowledge "of the structure and functions of the psychic apparatus" which will help our understanding of both neuroses and "normal" psychic activity.

In his perceptive analyses of such common occurrences as slips of the tongue or the forgetting of proper names, foreign words, or the order of words, Freud took the obvious and, instead of dismissing it as accidental, looked for the reasons why we make the everyday mistakes we do. Once again the basic presupposition is that the smallest detail of psychic activity is determined and can be accounted for. The difference between the neurotic and the normal person is one of degree; but in both of them actions and inadequacies which seem accidental and unintentional turn out to be strictly determined by unconscious motives or mechanisms.

Despite the controversy which still surrounds much of Freud's psychoanalytic theories, his attempt to explain both neurotic and normal activity in terms of unconscious motivations and factors has been enormously suggestive and influential not only in psychology and psychiatry but also in the interpretation of literature, mythology, and art. Lévi-Strauss refers to Freud as one of his "three mistresses" (together with Marx and geology).

Jacques Lacan, among contemporary structuralists, has underlined the structuralist aspects of Freud's work, which he claims to be continuing. He has drawn attention to Freud's emphasis on the analysis of language in word associations, slips of the tongue, puns, and the analysis of dreams. He has pointed out Freud's concern with uncovering the structures of the language of the unconscious and Freud's attempt to find the transformation laws which link them to the language of conscious life. In continuing what he sees as Freud's basic message and work, Lacan has recast and developed Freud's theory making use of the terms and concepts of structural linguistics, which were not available to Freud but the importance of which, Lacan claims, is enormous for the structural analyses with which Freud was concerned. For, Lacan insists, man's mental apparatus clusters around the linguistic mode, and the key to the unconscious depends on its being seen as a language system and its being analyzed accordingly.

Saussure and Linguistics

A key to the techniques of structuralism is to be found in linguistics, and the influence on structuralism of the "Father of Modern Linguistics," Ferdinand de Saussure, can scarcely be exaggerated. It was Saussure who was the first to treat language as a system of signs, and to include it within what he called *semiology* or the science which studies signs within society. Not only did he significantly change the standard approach to linguistics, but his suggestion that rites, customs, and similar social phenomena could be treated as systems of signs and studied in ways similar to the ways in which language is studied opened up an approach to the investigation of society which has been fruitfully mined by structuralists in many disciplines. As Saussure correctly foresaw, linguistics has "become the master-pattern for all branches of semiology."

Saussure's contributions to linguistics were many, and even where his views have not been followed they have led to many of the developments which came after his death. He pointed out the arbitrary nature of the linguistic sign, he distinguished the *signified* (concept) and the *signifier* (sound-image), which together make up the sign, he emphasized the social aspect of language, and he divided synchronic from diachronic linguistics.

Saussure laid emphasis on the functional and structural aspects of language. In a broad sense both he and most modern schools of linguistics can be grouped together as being concerned with "structural linguistics," although the term is also more narrowly applied to refer to the American Bloomfieldian school of linguistics, as opposed to the "transformational school" of which Noam Chomsky is the most notable figure.

It is characteristic of structural linguistics (taken in the broad sense) to approach language as a system and to attempt to uncover its structure, that is, the general laws or rules governing its operation. The laws operate on a number of levels and govern various facets of language.

Phonemes are the smallest distinctive sound unit of a system of language, and the study of phonemes is the lowest or most elementary level at which structural laws of language can be formulated. In 1928 at the First International Congress of Linguistics, N. S. Trubetzkoy, R. Jakobson, and S. Karcevskij called for the study of the structural laws of phonological systems. Trubetzkoy's *Principles of Phonology* became a classic in the field of structural linguistics, detailing the rules for the determination, classification, and combination of phonemes. Jakobson further reduced all phonemic oppositions to binary oppositions, and his emphasis on dichotomous relations and binary terms and oppositions—though it has recently come under attack—has been remarkably influential not only on linguists but also in other realms such as anthropology. Lévi-Strauss, following Jakobson's model, has sought to reduce much ethnological data to binary oppositions.

Morphemes are the next larger linguistic unit and constitute the smallest individually meaningful element of language. The study of the phonemic structure of the morpheme, and how the morphemic structure varies constitute the next level at which structural linguistics attempts to uncover the structural laws of language. The study of the grammatical forms of a language yields another level of rules or laws, followed by the study of syntax, or the proper ordering of words in an utterance or a sentence. At each level, different languages are structured, at least superficially, in different ways. The task of the structural linguist is to uncover these structures for individual languages, groups of languages, or, if possible, for all languages.

The uncovering of syntactic rules has been given special prominence by the transformational grammarians. Children learn the grammatical rules—the structure—of their native language from the speech of the adults around them, and they are able to use these rules creatively to produce new, well-formed sentences. Though the surface structures of languages differ, Noam Chomsky and others claim that the "deep structure" underlying them is to a large extent common. Transformational grammar has as its task the uncovering of the deep structure of language and the rules according to which this structure is transformed into the surface structures of various languages.

The techniques for uncovering the general grammar of language can serve as a model for similar analysis in other areas of social human endeavor. Furthermore, if a common deep structure of languages can be unfolded, it may well help uncover the structure of the human mind. It is along lines similar to these that Lévi-Strauss in his work on mythology and Roland Barthes in his analyses of modes of dress have been pushing their research and investigations.

Literary Criticism

Roman Jakobson, by his breadth of interest and the scope and originality of his work, has been a key figure in the development of structuralism. A member of the Russian Formalist School and of the Prague Linguistic Circle, as well as a professor at Columbia University, Harvard University, and M.I.T., he has served as a bridge between European and American schools of linguistics. By his interest in poetry, folklore, and literature he has helped relate linguistics and linguistic techniques with literary criticism; and in the realm of literary criticism itself he was instrumental in bringing about the transition from formalism to structuralism.

Formalism, as found in the Russian Formalist School of the 1920s, focused on the form of the work of art, on the craft of the artist, and on his use of the tools of his trade, in reaction to the traditional emphasis on the content of the work and on matters external to the work itself. The rise of formalism was closely related to the appearance of futurist and surrealist writers, who were fascinated with the almost limitless possibilities of a word, and the multiplication of possibilities in putting together a combination of words. These possibilities in turn were multiplied by what the reader himself brought to the poem. As a result, no one interpretation was possible any longer, and traditional ways of looking at art (in terms of literary movements, biographies of the writer, the psychology of the hero, etc.) had to be altered. Thus linguists, critics, and writers of the period all became intrigued by the same question: how do words become literature?

The importance of the word, broken down into a series of sounds and put together in a poetic way, was of central interest to the formalists. Poetry should, according to them, be enjoyed as poetry, i.e., as a poetic, conscious, artificial, and artful use of words combined in such a way that they produce a desired esthetic effect.

The move to structuralism consisted in part in recognizing that it was not possible to study words alone, divorced of meaning. The traditional dichotomy, content and form, was found unsatisfactory for the study of the work as an integrated, esthetic unity. Instead, the early structuralists developed the concept of structure, that is, of the systems within the work (the words, syntax, ideas, plot, etc.) which together help produce a given esthetic effect and make an integral whole. These systems interact through "equivalences," i.e., relationships which are similar or dissimilar, to bring about the desired effect. The skill of the artist consists in his ability to unite all these factors, each of which has its own structure and forms a system, into a total, structured larger system, the work as a whole. The invariant structures which certain kinds or types of literature or poetry or folktales have, and the variants of a particular work of art, are the concern of structural analysis. The work itself is to be studied as a totality or system before it is to be related to other systems—historical, social, biographical, or other.

Vladimir Propp, one of the Russian formalists, in his *Mor-*

phology of the Folk-Tale made an important contribution to the field of literary criticism. He significantly influenced studies in the field, and Lévi-Strauss recognizes Propp as a precursor of his own work on mythology. Propp's method consisted in breaking the folktale down into its component parts and analyzing the relation of one part to the others and to the whole. He was thus able to reduce the apparently limitless number of folktales to a limited number of types. For although he found an unlimited number of names of characters, he discovered that they perform a limited number of typical actions or functions. This technique, when joined with others developed by Jakobson, closely resembles that which has been adopted by Lévi-Strauss in his structural study of myths.

If Jakobson has blazed the widest trail in uniting linguistic techniques with the study of literature, Roland Barthes has become the most prominent and articulate expositor and practitioner of structural criticism among France's "new critics." Barthes, in his article "Les Deux Critiques," is reminiscent of the Russian formalists in his insistence on the preeminent importance of an immanent analysis which locates itself within the work. Only after the function and structure of the work itself have been studied should the more traditional tasks of relating it to history or psychology or of establishing its connections with other disciplines or with the world be undertaken.

Barthes is writing for an audience which has been nurtured on symbolism, surrealism, the theater of the absurd, and the new novel. This non-traditional literature demands a new approach to criticism. Barthes has developed his structuralist approach at least in part as a response to this demand, though his criticism covers a broad range of literary interests, from the classical theater (*Sur Racine*) to the "nouveau roman" (Robbe-Grillet). He is interested primarily in language—how it is used and how it functions—and in probing what writing, literature, language, and style are. For, as Barthes notes, the critic, like the author whose work he criticizes, is a writer. The enterprise of writing, whether as author or critic, is creative, and the structuralist approach to both, which he has analyzed more clearly than any other literary critic within the movement, is similar in both kinds of endeavor.

Barthes' works do not end with criticism, however. He has developed Saussure's notion of semiology, not only elaborating it theoretically in his *Elements of Semiology,* but applying it in his *Mythologies* and *Système de la Mode.* In the latter he treats styles of dress as described in fashion magazines as a system, a cultural set of signs by which society expresses itself and which Barthes makes the object of a structural analysis. He has thus initiated a structural investigation of contemporary social systems somewhat comparable to Lévi-Strauss' structural studies of primitive societies and myths.

Structural Anthropology

For some, structuralism is synonymous with the writings of Claude Lévi-Strauss. There can be no doubt that he is the central figure in the movement and that his writings have sparked more interest and inspired more followers than anyone else's connected with it. The reason perhaps is that his views are more encompassing, his hypotheses more daring, his generalizations more sweeping than those of any of the other structuralists.

His aim, ultimately, is to uncover the structure of human nature itself, to discover the universal, basic structure of man which is hidden below the surface and which manifests itself in language, cooking, dress, table manners, art, myths, and all the other expressions of social life. Like both Marx and Freud he believes that much of what is generally considered arbitrary and accidental is in fact determined, and that seemingly gratuitous customs and beliefs are but surface manifestations of deeper realities and of a deeper order. He implicitly agrees with Marx's claim both that as an individual acts, so he is, and that man is the ensemble of his social relations. He thus seeks to discover what man basically is by analyzing the forms of his social activities.

Underlying Lévi-Strauss' search are two fundamental assumptions which can be taken as heuristic principles guiding his research. The first is that the basic or deep structure of a set of different activities in a given society will be the same for them all. Since the table manners, cooking customs, kinship system, and so on of a given society are all ways in which that society expresses itself, they should all, as manifestations of that society, have something in common. What is common is not to be found on the surface. Rather, if each is seen as a type of manifestation of the society, and if the structure of each is laid bare, there will be, if Lévi-Strauss is correct, fundamental similarities in their structures, which in fact will constitute the deep structure underlying them all. Second, if we go on to compare two different societies, each of which has its own myths, table manners, cooking customs, kinship system, etc., Lévi-Strauss postulates that there will be a basic similarity between them, such that if one could uncover the proper rules of transformation, one could transpose the one set of systems into the other set. If one were able to bring to light the deeper structure common to the deep structures of each of the systems, one would be well advanced toward the goal of discovering the structure of human nature itself. Of course Lévi-Strauss has not yet discovered all this. The undertaking is a vast one. But he has made a start in this direction, he has charted the course one must take in its broad outlines, and he has begun the task of working through some of the details.

His most impressive results have been in the realm of mythology. Three large volumes on the logic of mythology have already appeared, with more still to come. Lévi-Strauss has taken a vast number of myths which have appeared to previous investigators to be related only by the fact that they were held by a particular Indian tribe. Working primarily with the myths of the Bororo Indians of central Brazil he brought order out of the previous chaos by treating the myths not as discrete units but as interconnected parts forming a system. In analyzing the myths he has grouped them into sets, and has submitted them to a structural analysis. He claims that the structure of the various sets are homologous, and that one set can be transformed into another set by making certain substitutions throughout. He claims further that by applying certain binary relations he can transform one set of Bororo myths which express the Bororo view of the transition from nature to culture into an apparently quite different set of myths of the Sherente tribe. This, he claims, is evidence that the structure underlying both sets is the same.

Structural linguistics provides the methodological model which Lévi-Strauss has adapted to his anthropological analyses.

He treats cooking, music, art, modes of dress, table manners, and other forms of social activity as if each were a language, since each is a method of social expression. Like language, each is a type of communication, a form of expression, and a system of behavior which is structured by unconscious laws. The structure of each corresponds to the grammar of a language. As the grammar of English is to spoken English, so the grammar or structure of each of these activities is to that activity. Just as a native English speaker is not conscious of the rules of grammar in forming each sentence he utters, despite the fact that the sentence is well-formed and conforms to and exemplifies the grammar, so with these other activities. That we are unconscious of the structure of our culinary customs or modes of dress does not mean that they are unstructured; their structure is both within them and underlies them, and if we are to see it, it must be made explicit in much the same way that English grammar has over the course of years been made explicit. This is precisely the primary task which structural anthropology has taken as its own. Cultural phenomena are not simply to be described and classified, but explained in terms of general laws and unconscious structures.

According to Lévi-Strauss, a structure "consists of a model meeting with several requirements. First, the structure exhibits the characteristics of a system. It is made up of several elements, none of which can undergo a change without effecting changes in all the other elements. Second, for any given model there should be a possibility of ordering a series of transformations resulting in a group of models of the same type. Third, the above properties make it possible to predict how the model will react if one or more of its elements are submitted to certain modifications. Finally, the model should be constituted so as to make immediately intelligible all the observed facts." It is in this fairly formal sense that Lévi-Strauss uses the term "structure," and his structural analyses consist in producing such models of systems.

Societies are of course complex in their total structure and encompass a multiplicity of levels. Following Marx's lead, Lévi-Strauss states that both the economic base and the social superstructure of society is made up of multiple levels, with various types of transformations operative from one level to another. Different types of societies can be characterized by the different types of transformations. Structural anthropology can carry further the task initiated by Marx by continuing to uncover the multiplicity of structures at all levels of society, and by showing in detail how they are homologous one to another. Marx correctly saw that the art, law, religion, philosophy, and morality of a society were the result of and were determined by its economic structure. But he left unfinished the job of showing just how they were transformations the one of the other, and just how each was structured.

Two results follow from the work of Lévi-Strauss which have consequences far beyond the realm of anthropology. The first is that the divisions between the various humanistic disciplines are seen as arbitrary, and Lévi-Strauss suggests a means of joining and uniting them. For art, literature, myth, religion, table manners are all ways of social expression, all are structured by similar unconscious processes of the human mind. If each of the different disciplines builds its models applicable to its type of phenomena and its level, each, if pushed far enough, should come to a similar common basis in the structuring mind of man. Not only can all of them be seen as related and interconnected, but the principles and unconscious structure of any one type of institution or custom, such as cooking, should serve as a valid principle of interpretation for other institutions or customs, such as religion or law. Second, just as the divisions between disciplines give way to their underlying common structures, so the divisions between men should give way once mind is seen to be common for all men, whether primitive or civilized, Western or Eastern, modern or ancient. The difference lies not in differing intellectual qualities of mind or in its constraining structures, which are everywhere the same, but in the differing nature of the things to which the human mind has been put. There are no higher and lower societies; there are simply societies which differ one from another in ways similar to the manner in which the surface grammars of languages differ one from another. Ultimately human nature is common wherever it is found. What remains to be clarified is the nature of its basic structure, which is in fact the nature of the basic ways it structures the reality with which it comes in contact. This is the final goal of Lévi-Strauss' endeavor.

The Structuralist Phenomenon

Michel Foucault, the French philosopher, has been included by commentators among structuralism's inner circle from the beginning of its rise to popularity in France. Yet "structuralist" is a label he has sought to avoid, correctly claiming that he does not use the techniques and key terms borrowed from linguistics which characterize the work of Lévi-Strauss, Barthes, and Lacan. His inclusion in the structuralist camp is in itself instructive.

In *The Order of Things,* Foucault presents us with what he calls "an archaeology of the human sciences." Though his particular techniques are not those employed by the other structuralists, he nonetheless shares with them a number of important presuppositions and concerns. His first hypothesis, he tells us, is that non-formal knowledge (e.g., that concerned with living beings, languages, or economic facts) itself has a system. In working this hypothesis through the modern period beginning with the seventeenth century he described not the genesis of the various sciences but the "epistemological space specific to a particular period." His particular focus became the underside of science, or what he calls the "positive unconscious of knowledge." And a major focus throughout his work concerns the language of the periods he investigates: the problems of writing, the being of language, the questions of speaking, classifying, representing, and the place and function of the human sciences.

Not only does Foucault look below the surface of society, focus on its language, and attempt to find system where others have traditionally found chaos, but he also uncovers levels and structures in the material he analyzes. It is thus not without reason that he is considered a structuralist. He comes to the conclusion that "man is an invention of recent date. And one perhaps nearing its end." The conclusion, as well as the denial throughout the work of the importance or primacy of the individual ego, is typical of the structuralist approach in general.

Structuralism is not a consciously formed school, and is

not a consciously united movement. But on its own presuppositions, the conscious claims or denials of its practitioners are somewhat beside the point. The fact that a group of writers and scholars is seen as a movement by others, the fact that they and the movement itself have attracted followers, have sparked interest, and have excited controversy, the fact that the so-called structuralist writings are expressive of the feelings, emotions, and the outlook on life of its adherents, and the fact that as a movement it represents the convergence of a variety of trends and disciplines are an indication that structuralism is a social phenomenon and that it is more than simply the writings of a few men.

Structuralism has given rise to new hopes and promised new life to a large area of the often staid humanities and social sciences. Just as Lévi-Strauss has brought order to a large mass of ethnological data and attempted to make anthropology not simply a descriptive but a theoretical science, so he has given a model for others in other fields to follow. Linguistics has come of age since the days of Saussure, and structuralist criticism has given some the hope that literary criticism might become an objective discipline. Semiotics has opened up large areas of human activity to disciplined, systematic investigation. Structuralism, as encompassing all of this, has given respectability to the practice of crossing disciplinary boundaries, which had begun before the advent of structuralism, but which needed a firmer underpinning than it previously had. It has also drawn together diverse strains of contemporary thought—Marxism, Freudianism, and rationalism, among others.

In a world in search of meaning and an understanding of itself, structuralism has given voice to a new view, a new "myth" which has been recognized and seized by many people, each in his own way. If viewed as a myth, it is beside the point to ask whether it is valid or invalid, though this question should certainly be raised if it is considered as a science. It can itself be viewed, like cooking, as an expression of the human mind, and as a means by which a large number of intellectuals have chosen to express themselves. As such, it can scarcely be legitimately ignored by anyone interested in contemporary society.

Lévi-Strauss has attempted to uncover the structure of human nature. The task, if it can be achieved, will certainly take a long time before it is completed. But already Lévi-Strauss has suggested new ways for man to understand himself and his world, he has argued against cultural parochialism, he has insisted that no society or people is inherently better than any other, he has expressed an appreciation of non-verbal types of behavior, and he has postulated a type of transcendent unity of man and nature.

Structuralism promises an intellectual revolution in the social sciences, the humanities, and the arts. Whether the revolution will be successful, only time will tell. It is at present a promise in search of its fulfillment.

KARL MARX

Marx was born in 1818 in Trier, Prussia, and died in 1883 in London. Though he received a doctorate in philosophy in 1841, he was precluded by circumstances from pursuing an academic career. He turned to practical political studies, and soon recognized the need for the study of political economy. His early works include *Economic and Philosophic Manuscripts of 1844* which contains his most detailed account of alienation, and *The German Ideology* in which he (together with Frederick Engels) outlines a materialist interpretation of history. The most succinct statement of how the economic base of society determines the cultural and intellectual superstructure is contained in Marx's "Preface" to *A Contribution to the Critique of Political Economy,* which is a precursor of his *Capital.*

Capital is Marx's most famous work. In it he attempted to lay bare the economic law of motion of modern society. It is not only an economic study but also an analysis and critique of capitalist society. In his prefaces to *Capital* Marx both set forth the general program of the work and clarified the dialectical method which he used therein. Chapter XXXII is the next to last chapter of the first volume. It illustrates something of Marx's method, some of the categories of his analysis, and the thrust of the work as a whole.

1

Preface to *A Contribution to the Critique of Political Economy*

I consider the system of bourgeois economy in the following order: *Capital, landed property, wage labor; state, foreign trade, world market.* Under the first three heads I examine the conditions of the economic existence of the three great classes, which make up modern bourgeois society; the connection of the three remaining heads is self evident. The first part of the first book, treating of capital, consists of the following chapters: 1. Commodity; 2. Money, or simple circulation; 3. Capital in general. The first two chapters form the contents of the present work. The entire material lies before me in the form of monographs, written at long intervals not for publication, but for the purpose of clearing up those questions to myself, and their systematic elaboration on the plan outlined above will depend upon circumstances.

I omit a general introduction which I had prepared, as on second thought any anticipation of results that are still to be proven, seemed to me objectionable, and the reader who wishes to follow me at all, must make up his mind to pass from the special to the general. On the other hand, some remarks as to the course of my own politico-economic studies may be in place here.

The subject of my professional studies was jurisprudence, which I pursued, however, in connection with and as secondary to the studies of philosophy and history. In 1842-43, as editor of the "Rheinische Zeitung," I found myself embarrassed at

This selection is from *A Contribution to the Critique of Political Economy* by Karl Marx, translated by N. I. Stone, Chicago: Charles H. Kerr & Co., © 1904 by the International Library Publishing Company.

first when I had to take part in discussions concerning so-called material interests. The proceedings of the Rhine Diet in connection with forest thefts and the extreme subdivision of landed property; the official controversy about the condition of the Mosel peasants into which Herr von Schaper, at that time president of the Rhine Province, entered with the "Rheinische Zeitung;" finally, the debates on free trade and protection, gave me the first impulse to take up the study of economic questions. At the same time a weak, quasi-philosophic echo of French socialism and communism made itself heard in the "Rheinische Zeitung" in those days when the good intentions "to go ahead" greatly outweighed knowledge of facts. I declared myself against such botching, but had to admit at once in a controversy with the "Allgemeine Augsburger Zeitung" that my previous studies did not allow me to hazard an independent judgment as to the merits of the French schools. When, therefore, the publishers of the "Rheinische Zeitung" conceived the illusion that by a less aggressive policy the paper could be saved from the death sentence pronounced upon it, I was glad to grasp that opportunity to retire to my study room from public life.

The first work undertaken for the solution of the question that troubled me, was a critical revision of Hegel's "Philosophy of Law"; the introduction to that work appeared in the "Deutsch-Französische Jahrbücher," published in Paris in 1844. I was led by my studies to the conclusion that legal relations as well as forms of state could neither be understood by themselves, nor explained by the so-called general progress of the human mind, but that they are rooted in the material conditions of life, which are summed up by Hegel after the fashion of the English and French of the eighteenth century under the name "civic society;" the anatomy of that civic society is to be sought in political economy. The study of the latter which I had taken up in Paris, I continued at Brussels whither I emigrated on account of an order of expulsion issued by Mr. Guizot. The general conclusion at which I arrived and which, once reached, continued to serve as the leading thread in my studies, may be briefly summed up as follows: In the social production which men carry on they enter into definite relations that are indispensable and independent of their will; these relations of production correspond to a definite stage of development of their material powers of production. The sum total of these relations of production constitutes the economic structure of society—the real foundation, on which rise legal and political superstructures and to which correspond definite forms of social consciousness. The mode of production in material life determines the general character of the social, political and spiritual processes of life. It is not the consciousness of men that determines their existence, but, on the contrary, their social existence determines their consciousness. At a certain stage of their development, the material forces of production in society come in conflict with the existing relations of production, or—what is but a legal expression for the same thing—with the property relations within which they had been at work before. From forms of development of the forces of production these relations turn into their fetters. Then comes the period of social revolution. With the change of the economic foundation the entire immense superstructure is more or less rapidly transformed. In considering such transformations the distinction should always be made between the material transformation of the economic conditions of production which can be determined with the precision of natural science, and the legal, political, religious, aesthetic or philosophic—in short ideological forms in which men become conscious of this conflict and fight it out. Just as our opinion of an individual is not based on what he thinks of himself, so can we not judge of such a period of transformation by its own consciousness; on the contrary, this consciousness must rather be explained from the contradictions of material life, from the existing conflict between the social forces of production and the relations of production. No social order ever disappears before all the productive forces, for which there is room in it, have been developed; and new higher relations of production never appear before the material conditions of their existence have matured in the womb of the old society. Therefore, mankind always takes up only such problems as it can solve; since, looking at the matter more closely, we will always find that the problem itself arises only when the material conditions necessary for its solution already exist or are at least in the process of formation. In broad outlines we can designate the Asiatic, the ancient, the feudal, and the modern bourgeois methods of production as so many epochs in the progress of the economic formation of society. The bourgeois relations of production are the last antagonistic form of the social process of production—antagonistic not in the sense of individual antagonism, but of one arising from conditions surrounding the life of individuals in society; at the same time the productive forces developing in the womb of bourgeois society create the material conditions for the solution of that antagonism. This social formation constitutes, therefore, the closing chapter of the prehistoric stage of human society.

Frederick Engels, with whom I was continually corresponding and exchanging ideas since the appearance of his ingenious critical essay on economic categories (in the "Deutsch-Französische Jahrbücher"), came by a different road to the same conclusions as myself (see his "Condition of the Working Classes in England"). When he, too, settled in Brussels in the spring of 1845, we decided to work out together the contrast between our view and the idealism of the German philosophy, in fact to settle our accounts with our former philosophic conscience. The plan was carried out in the form of a criticism of the post-Hegelian philosophy. The manuscript in two solid octavo volumes had long reached the publisher in Westphalia, when we received information that conditions had so changed as not to allow of its publication. We abandoned the manuscript to the stinging criticism of the mice the more readily since we had accomplished our main purpose—the clearing up of the question to ourselves. Of the scattered writings on various subjects in which we presented our views to the public at that time, I recall only the "Manifesto of the Communist Party" written by Engels and myself, and the "Discourse on Free Trade" written by myself. The leading points of our theory were first presented scientifically, though in a polemic form, in my "Misère de la Philosophie, etc." directed against Proudhon and published in 1847. An essay on "Wage Labor," written by me in German, and in which I put together my lectures on the subject delivered before the German Workmen's Club at Brussels, was prevented from leaving the hands of the printer by the February revolution and my expulsion from Belgium which followed it as a consequence.

The publication of the "Neue Rheinische Zeitung" in 1848 and 1849, and the events which took place later on, interrupted my economic studies which I could not resume before 1850 in London. The enormous material on the history of political economy which is accumulated in the British Museum; the favorable view which London offers for the observation of bourgeois society; finally, the new stage of development upon which the latter seemed to have entered with the discovery of gold in California and Australia, led me to the decision to resume my studies from the very beginning and work up critically the new material. These studies partly led to what might seem side questions, over which I nevertheless had to stop for longer or shorter periods of time. Especially was the time at my disposal cut down by the imperative necessity of working for a living. My work as contributor on the leading Anglo-American newspaper, the "New York Tribune," at which I have now been engaged for eight years, has caused very great interruption in my studies, since I engage in newspaper work proper only occasionally. Yet articles on important economic events in England and on the continent have formed so large a part of my contributions that I have been obliged to make myself familiar with practical details which lie outside the proper sphere of political economy.

This account of the course of my studies in political economy is simply to prove that my views, whatever one may think of them, and no matter how little they agree with the interested prejudices of the ruling classes, are the result of many years of conscientious research. At the entrance to science, however, the same requirement must be put as at the entrance to hell:

> Qui si convien lasciare ogni sospetto
> Ogni viltà convien che qui sia morta.

London, January, 1859.

2

Capital

PREFACE TO THE FIRST EDITION

The work, the first volume of which I now submit to the public, forms the continuation of my "Zur Kritik der Politischen Oekonomie" (A Contribution to the Critique of Political Economy) published in 1859. The long pause between the first part and the continuation is due to an illness of many years' duration that again and again interrupted my work.

The substance of that earlier work is summarised in the first three chapters of this volume. This is done not merely for the sake of connection and completeness. The presentation of the subject-matter is improved. As far as circumstances in any way permit, many points only hinted at in the earlier book are here worked out more fully, whilst, conversely, points worked out fully there are only touched upon in this volume. The sections on the history of the theories of value and of money are now, of course, left out altogether. The reader of the earlier work will find, however, in the notes to the first chapter additional sources of reference relative to the history of those theories.

Every beginning is difficult, holds in all sciences. To understand the first chapter, especially the section that contains the analysis of commodities, will, therefore, present the greatest difficulty. That which concerns more especially the analysis

Reprinted here are the prefaces to the first and second editions and Chapter XXXII of *Capital*, translated from the third German edition by Samuel Moore and Edward Aveling, and edited by Frederick Engels, London: Swan Sonnenschein and Co., 1889.

of the substance of value and the magnitude of value, I have, as much as it was possible, popularised.[1] The value-form, whose fully developed shape is the money-form, is very elementary and simple. Nevertheless, the human mind has for more than 2000 years sought in vain to get to the bottom of it, whilst on the other hand, to the successful analysis of much more composite and complex forms, there has been at least an approximation. Why? Because the body, as an organic whole, is more easy of study than are the cells of that body. In the analysis of economic forms, moreover, neither microscopes nor chemical reagents are of use. The force of abstraction must replace both. But in bourgeois society the commodity-form of the product of labor—or the value-form of the commodity—is the economic cell-form. To the superficial observer, the analysis of these forms seems to turn upon minutiæ. It does in fact deal with minutiæ, but they are of the same order as those dealt with in microscopic anatomy.

With the exception of the section on value-form, therefore, this volume cannot stand accused on the score of difficulty. I pre-suppose, of course, a reader who is willing to learn something new and therefore to think for himself.

The physicist either observes physical phenomena where they occur in their most typical form and most free from disturbing influence, or, wherever possible, he makes experiments under conditions that assure the occurrence of the phenomenon in its normality. In this work I have to examine the capitalist mode of production, and the conditions of production and exchange corresponding to that mode. Up to the present time, their classic ground is England. That is the

---

[1] This is the more necessary, as even the section of Ferdinand Lassalle's work against Schulze-Delitzsch, in which he professes to give "the intellectual quintessence" of my explanations on these subjects, contains important mistakes. If Ferdinand Lassalle has borrowed almost literally from my writings, and without any acknowledgment, all the general theoretical propositions in his economic works, *e.g.*, those on the historical character of capital, on the connection between the conditions of production and the mode of production, &c., &c., even to the terminology created by me, this may perhaps be due to purposes of propaganda. I am here, of course, not speaking of his detailed working out and application of these propositions, with which I have nothing to do.

reason why England is used as the chief illustration in the development of my theoretical ideas. If, however, the German reader shrugs his shoulders at the condition of the English industrial and agricultural laborers, or in optimist fashion comforts himself with the thought that in Germany things are not nearly so bad, I must plainly tell him, *"De te fabula narratur!"*

Intrinsically, it is not a question of the higher or lower degree of development of the social antagonisms that result from the natural laws of capitalist production. It is a question of these laws themselves, of these tendencies working with iron necessity towards inevitable results. The country that is more developed industrially only shows, to the less developed, the image of its own future.

But apart from this. Where capitalist production is fully naturalised among the Germans (for instance, in the factories proper) the condition of things is much worse than in England, because the counterpoise of the Factory Acts is wanting. In all other spheres, we, like all the rest of Continental Western Europe, suffer not only from the development of capitalist production, but also from the incompleteness of that development. Alongside of modern evils, a whole series of inherited evils oppress us, arising from the passive survival of antiquated modes of production, with their inevitable train of social and political anachronisms. We suffer not only from the living, but from the dead. *Le mort saisit le vif!*

The social statistics of Germany and the rest of Continental Western Europe are, in comparison with those of England, wretchedly compiled. But they raise the veil just enough to let us catch a glimpse of the Medusa head behind it. We should be appalled at the state of things at home, if, as in England, our governments and parliaments appointed periodically commissions of enquiry into economic conditions; if these commissions were armed with the same plenary powers to get at the truth; if it was possible to find for this purpose men as competent, as free from partisanship and respect of persons as are the English factory-inspectors, her medical reporters on public health, her commissioners of enquiry into the exploitation of women and children, into housing and food. Perseus wore a magic cap that the monsters he hunted down might not see him. We draw the magic cap down over eyes and ears as a make-believe that there are no monsters.

Let us not deceive ourselves on this. As in the 18th century, the American war of independence sounded the tocsin for the European middle-class, so in the 19th century, the American civil war sounded it for the European working-class. In England the progress of social disintegration is palpable. When it has reached a certain point, it must re-act on the continent. There it will take a form more brutal or more humane, according to the degree of development of the working-class itself. Apart from higher motives, therefore, their own most important interests dictate to the classes that are for the nonce the ruling ones, the removal of all legally removable hindrances to the free development of the working-class. For this reason, as well as others, I have given so large a space in this volume to the history, the details, and the results of English factory legislation. One nation can and should learn from others. And even when a society has got upon the right track for the discovery of the natural laws of its movement—and it is the ultimate aim of this work, to lay bare the economic law of motion of modern society—it can neither clear by bold leaps, nor remove by legal enactments, the obstacles offered by the successive phases of its normal development. But it can shorten and lessen the birth-pangs.

To prevent possible misunderstanding, a word. I paint the capitalist and the landlord in no sense *couleur de rose*. But here individuals are dealt with only in so far as they are the personifications of economic categories, embodiments of particular class-relations and class-interests. My stand-point, from which the evolution of the economic formation of society is viewed as a process of natural history, can less than any other make the individual responsible for relations whose creature he socially remains, however much he may subjectively raise himself above them.

In the domain of Political Economy, free scientific enquiry meets not merely the same enemies as in all other domains. The peculiar nature of the material it deals with, summons as foes into the field of battle the most violent, mean and malig-

nant passions of the human breast, the Furies of private interest. The English Established Church, *e.g.*, will more readily pardon an attack on 38 of its 39 articles than on $\frac{1}{39}$ of its
income. Now-a-days atheism itself is *culpa levis*, as compared
with criticism of existing property relations. Nevertheless, there
is an unmistakable advance. I refer, *e.g.*, to the bluebook published within the last few weeks: "Correspondence with Her
Majesty's Missions Abroad, regarding Industrial Questions and
Trades' Unions." The representatives of the English Crown in
foreign countries there declare in so many words that in Germany, in France, to be brief, in all the civilised states of the
European continent, a radical change in the existing relations
between capital and labor is as evident and inevitable as in
England. At the same time, on the other side of the Atlantic
Ocean, Mr. Wade, vice-president of the United States, declared
in public meetings that, after the abolition of slavery, a radical
change of the relations of capital and of property in land is
next upon the order of the day. These are signs of the times,
not to be hidden by purple mantles or black cassocks. They
do not signify that to-morrow a miracle will happen. They
show that, within the ruling-classes themselves, a foreboding
is dawning, that the present society is no solid crystal, but an
organism capable of change, and is constantly changing.

The second volume of this work will treat of the process of
the circulation of capital (Book II.), and of the varied forms
assumed by capital in the course of its development (Book
III.), the third and last volume (Book IV.), the history of the
theory.

Every opinion based on scientific criticism I welcome. As to
the prejudices of so-called public opinion, to which I have
never made concessions, now as aforetime the maxim of the
great Florentine is mine:

"Segui il tuo corso, e lascia dir le genti."

London, July 25, 1867.

PREFACE TO THE SECOND EDITION

To the present moment Political Economy, in Germany, is a foreign science. Gustav von Gülich in his "Historical description of Commerce, Industry," &c.,[2] especially in the two first volumes published in 1830, has examined at length the historical circumstances that prevented, in Germany, the development of the capitalist mode of production, and consequently the development, in that country, of modern bourgeois society. Thus the soil whence Political Economy springs was wanting. This "science" had to be imported from England and France as a ready-made article; its German professors remained schoolboys. The theoretical expression of a foreign reality was turned, in their hands, into a collection of dogmas, interpreted by them in terms of the petty trading world around them, and therefore misinterpreted. The feeling of scientific impotence, a feeling not wholly to be repressed, and the uneasy consciousness of having to touch a subject in reality foreign to them, was but imperfectly concealed, either under a parade of literary and historical erudition, or by an admixture of extraneous material, borrowed from the so-called "Kameral" sciences, a medley of smatterings, through whose purgatory the hopeless candidate for the German bureaucracy has to pass.

Since 1848 capitalist production has developed rapidly in Germany, and at the present time it is in the full bloom of speculation and swindling. But fate is still unpropitious to our professional economists. At the time when they were able to deal with Political Economy in a straightforward fashion, modern economic conditions did not actually exist in Germany. And as soon as these conditions did come into existence, they did so under circumstances that no longer allowed of their being really and impartially investigated within the bounds of the bourgeois horizon. In so far as Political Economy remains within that horizon, in so far, *i.e.*, as the capitalist régime is looked upon as the absolutely final form of social

[2] Geschichtliche Darstellung des Handels, der Gewerbe und des Ackerbaus, &c., von Gustav von Gülich. 5 vols., Jena, 1830–45.

production, instead of as a passing historical phase of its evolution, Political Economy can remain a science only so long as the class-struggle is latent or manifests itself only in isolated and sporadic phenomena.

Let us take England. Its political economy belongs to the period in which the class-struggle was as yet undeveloped. Its last great representative, Ricardo, in the end, consciously makes the antagonism of class-interests, of wages and profits, of profits and rent, the starting-point of his investigations, naïvely taking this antagonism for a social law of nature. But by this start the science of bourgeois economy had reached the limits beyond which it could not pass. Already in the lifetime of Ricardo, and in opposition to him, it was met by criticism, in the person of Sismondi.[3]

The succeeding period, from 1820 to 1830, was notable in England for scientific activity in the domain of Political Economy. It was the time as well of the vulgarising and extending of Ricardo's theory, as of the contest of that theory with the old school. Splendid tournaments were held. What was done then, is little known to the Continent generally, because the polemic is for the most part scattered through articles in reviews, occasional literature and pamphlets. The unprejudiced character of this polemic—although the theory of Ricardo already serves, in exceptional cases, as a weapon of attack upon bourgeois economy—is explained by the circumstances of the time. On the one hand, modern industry itself was only just emerging from the age of childhood, as is shown by the fact that with the crisis of 1825 it for the first time opens the periodic cycle of its modern life. On the other hand, the class-struggle between capital and labor is forced into the background, politically by the discord between the governments and the feudal aristocracy gathered around the Holy Alliance on the one hand, and the popular masses, led by the bourgeoisie on the other; economically by the quarrel between industrial capital and aristocratic landed property—a quarrel that in France was concealed by the opposition between small and large landed property, and that in England broke out openly after the Corn Laws. The literature of Political Econ-

[3] See my work "Critique, &c.," p. 70.

omy in England at this time calls to mind the stormy forward movement in France after Dr. Quesnay's death, but only as a Saint Martin's summer reminds us of spring. With the year 1830 came the decisive crisis.

In France and in England the bourgeoisie had conquered political power. Thenceforth, the class-struggle, practically as well as theoretically, took on more and more outspoken and threatening forms. It sounded the knell of scientific bourgeois economy. It was thenceforth no longer a question, whether this theorem or that was true, but whether it was useful to capital or harmful, expedient or inexpedient, politically dangerous or not. In place of disinterested enquirers, there were hired prize-fighters; in place of genuine scientific research, the bad conscience and the evil intent of apologetic. Still, even the obtrusive pamphlets with which the Anti-Corn Law League, led by the manufacturers Cobden and Bright, deluged the world, have a historic interest, if no scientific one, on account of their polemic against the landed aristocracy. But since then the Free Trade legislation, inaugurated by Sir Robert Peel, has deprived vulgar economy of this its last sting.

The Continental revolution of 1848-9 also had its reaction in England. Men who still claimed some scientific standing and aspired to be something more than mere sophists and sycophants of the ruling-classes, tried to harmonise the Political Economy of capital with the claims, no longer to be ignored, of the proletariat. Hence a shallow syncretism, of which John Stuart Mill is the best representative. It is a declaration of bankruptcy by bourgeois economy, an event on which the great Russian scholar and critic, N. Tschernyschewsky, has thrown the light of a master mind in his "Outlines of Political Economy according to Mill."

In Germany, therefore, the capitalist mode of production came to a head, after its antagonistic character had already, in France and England, shown itself in a fierce strife of classes. And meanwhile, moreover, the German proletariat had attained a much more clear class-consciousness than the German bourgeoisie. Thus, at the very moment when a bourgeois science of political economy seemed at last possible in Germany, it had in reality again become impossible.

Under these circumstances its professors fell into two

groups. The one set, prudent, practical business folk, flocked to the banner of Bastiat, the most superficial and therefore the most adequate representative of the apologetic of vulgar economy; the other, proud of the professorial dignity of their science, followed John Stuart Mill in his attempt to reconcile irreconcilables. Just as in the classical time of bourgeois economy, so also in the time of its decline, the Germans remained mere schoolboys, imitators and followers, petty retailers and hawkers in the service of the great foreign wholesale concern.

The peculiar historic development of German society therefore forbids, in that country, all original work in bourgeois economy; but not the criticism of that economy. So far as such criticism represents a class, it can only represent the class whose vocation in history is the overthrow of the capitalist mode of production and the final abolition of all classes—the proletariat.

The learned and unlearned spokesmen of the German bourgeoisie tried at first to kill "Das Kapital" by silence, as they had managed to do with my earlier writings. As soon as they found that these tactics no longer fitted in with the conditions of the time, they wrote, under pretence of criticising my book, prescriptions "for the tranquillisation of the bourgeois mind." But they found in the workers' press—see, *e.g.*, Joseph Dietzgen's articles in the "Volksstaat"—antagonists stronger than themselves, to whom (down to this very day) they owe a reply.[4]

[4] The mealy-mouthed babblers of German vulgar economy fell foul of the style of my book. No one can feel the literary shortcomings in "Das Kapital" more strongly than I myself. Yet I will for the benefit and the enjoyment of these gentlemen and their public quote in this connection one English and one Russian notice. The "Saturday Review," always hostile to my views, said in its notice of the first edition: "The presentation of the subject invests the driest economic questions with a certain peculiar charm." The "St. Petersburg Journal" (Sankt-Peterburgskie Viedomosti), in its issue of April 20, 1872, says: "The presentation of the subject, with the exception of one or two exceptionally special parts, is distinguished by its comprehensibility by the general reader, its clearness, and in spite of the scientific intricacy of the subject, by an unusual liveliness. In this respect the author in no way resembles . . . the majority of German scholars who . . . write their books in a language so dry and obscure that the heads of ordinary mortals are cracked by it."

An excellent Russian translation of "Das Kapital" appeared in the spring of 1872. The edition of 3000 copies is already nearly exhausted. As early as 1871, A. Sieber, Professor of Political Economy in the University of Kiev, in his work "David Ricardo's Theory of Value and of Capital," referred to my theory of value, of money and of capital, as in its fundamentals a necessary sequel to the teaching of Smith and Ricardo. That which astonishes the Western European in the reading of this excellent work, is the author's consistent and firm grasp of the purely theoretical position.

That the method employed in "Das Kapital" has been little understood, is shown by the various conceptions, contradictory one to another, that have been formed of it.

Thus the Paris *Revue Positiviste* reproaches me in that, on the one hand, I treat economics metaphysically, and on the other hand—imagine!—confine myself to the mere critical analysis of actual facts, instead of writing recipes (Comtist ones?) for the cook-shops of the future. In answer to the reproach *in re* metaphysics, Professor Sieber has it: "In so far as it deals with actual theory, the method of Marx is the deductive method of the whole English school, a school whose failings and virtues are common to the best theoretic economists." M. Block —"Les théoriciens du socialisme en Allemagne, Extrait du Journal des Economistes, Juillet et Août 1872"—makes the discovery that my method is analytic and says: "Par cet ouvrage M. Marx se classe parmi les esprits analytiques les plus éminents." German reviews, of course, shriek out at "Hegelian sophistics." The *European Messenger* of St. Petersburg, in an article dealing exclusively with the method of "Das Kapital" (May number, 1872, pp. 427-436), finds my method of inquiry severely realistic, but my method of presentation, unfortunately, German-dialectical. It says: "At first sight, if the judgment is based on the external form of the presentation of the subject, Marx is the most ideal of ideal philosophers, always in the German, *i.e.*, the bad sense of the word. But in point of fact he is infinitely more realistic than all his forerunners in the work of economic criticism. He can in no sense be called an idealist." I cannot answer the writer better than by aid of a few extracts from his own criticism, which may interest some of my readers to whom the Russian original is inaccessible.

After a quotation from the preface to my "Critique of Political Economy," Berlin, 1859, pp. 11–13, where I discuss the materialistic basis of my method, the writer goes on: "The one thing which is of moment to Marx is to find the law of the phenomena with whose investigation he is concerned; and not only is that law of moment to him, which governs these phenomena, in so far as they have a definite form and mutual connection within a given historical period. Of still greater moment to him is the law of their variation, of their development, i.e., of their transition from one form into another, from one series of connections into a different one. This law once discovered, he investigates in detail the effects in which it manifests itself in social life. Consequently, Marx only troubles himself about one thing; to show, by rigid scientific investigation, the necessity of successive determinate orders of social conditions, and to establish, as impartially as possible, the facts that serve him for fundamental starting points. For this it is quite enough, if he proves, at the same time, both the necessity of the present order of things, and the necessity of another order into which the first must inevitably pass over; and this all the same, whether men believe or do not believe it, whether they are conscious or unconscious of it. Marx treats the social movement as a process of natural history, governed by laws not only independent of human will, consciousness and intelligence, but rather, on the contrary, determining that will, consciousness and intelligence. . . . If in the history of civilisation the conscious element plays a part so subordinate, then it is self-evident that a critical inquiry whose subject-matter is civilisation, can, less than anything else, have for its basis any form of, or any result of, consciousness. That is to say, that not the idea, but the material phenomenon alone can serve as its starting-point. Such an inquiry will confine itself to the confrontation and the comparison of a fact, not with ideas, but with another fact. For this inquiry, the one thing of moment is, that both facts be investigated as accurately as possible, and that they actually form, each with respect to the other, different momenta of an evolution; but most important of all is the rigid analysis of the series of successions, of the sequences and concatenations in which the different stages of such an evolution present themselves. But it will be said, the general laws of economic life are one and the same, no matter whether they are applied to the present or the past. This Marx directly denies. According to him, such abstract laws do not exist. On the contrary, in his opinion every historical period has laws of its own. . . . As soon as society has outlived a given period of development, and is passing over from one given stage to another, it begins to be subject also to other laws. In a word, economic life offers us a phenomenon analogous to the history of evolution in other branches of biology. The old economists misunderstood the nature of economic laws when they likened them to the laws of physics and chemistry. A more thorough analysis of phenomena shows that social organisms differ among themselves as fundamentally as plants or animals. Nay, one and the same phenomenon falls under quite different laws in consequence of the different structure of those organisms as a whole, of the variations of their individual organs, of the different conditions in which those organs function, &c. Marx, *e.g.*, denies that the law of population is the same at all times and in all places. He asserts, on the contrary, that every stage of development has its own law of population. . . . With the varying degree of development of productive power, social conditions and the laws governing them vary too. Whilst Marx sets himself the task of following and explaining from this point of view the economic system established by the sway of capital, he is only formulating, in a strictly scientific manner, the aim that every accurate investigation into economic life must have. The scientific value of such an inquiry lies in the disclosing of the special laws that regulate the origin, existence, development, and death of a given social organism and its replacement by another and higher one. And it is this value that, in point of fact, Marx's book has."

Whilst the writer pictures what he takes to be actually my method, in this striking and [as far as concerns my own application of it] generous way, what else is he picturing but the dialectic method?

Of course the method of presentation must differ in form from that of inquiry. The latter has to appropriate the material in detail, to analyse its different forms of development, to trace out their inner connection. Only after this work is done, can the actual movement be adequately described. If this is done successfully, if the life of the subject-matter is ideally reflected as in a mirror, then it may appear as if we had before us a mere a priori construction.

My dialectic method is not only different from the Hegelian, but is its direct opposite. To Hegel, the life-process of the human brain, i.e., the process of thinking, which, under the name of "the Idea," he even transforms into an independent subject, is the demiurgos of the real world, and the real world is only the external, phenomenal form of "the Idea." With me, on the contrary, the ideal is nothing else than the material world reflected by the human mind, and translated into forms of thought.

The mystifying side of Hegelian dialectic I criticised nearly thirty years ago, at a time when it was still the fashion. But just as I was working at the first volume of "Das Kapital," it was the good pleasure of the peevish, arrogant, mediocre Επίγονοι who now talk large in cultured Germany, to treat Hegel in the same way as the brave Moses Mendelssohn in Lessing's time treated Spinoza, i.e., as a "dead dog." I therefore openly avowed myself the pupil of that mighty thinker, and even here and there, in the chapter on the theory of value, coquetted with the modes of expression peculiar to him. The mystification which dialectic suffers in Hegel's hands, by no means prevents him from being the first to present its general form of working in a comprehensive and conscious manner. With him it is standing on its head. It must be turned right side up again, if you would discover the rational kernel within the mystical shell.

In its mystified form, dialectic became the fashion in Germany, because it seemed to transfigure and to glorify the existing state of things. In its rational form it is a scandal and abomination to bourgeoisdom and its doctrinaire professors, because it includes in its comprehension and affirmative recognition of the existing state of things, at the same time also, the recognition of the negation of that state, of its inevitable breaking up; because it regards every historically developed social form as in fluid movement, and therefore takes into account its transient nature not less than its momentary existence; because it lets nothing impose upon it, and is in its essence critical and revolutionary.

The contradictions inherent in the movement of capitalist society impress themselves upon the practical bourgeois most strikingly in the changes of the periodic cycle, through which modern industry runs, and whose crowning point is the universal crisis. That crisis is once again approaching, although as yet but in its preliminary stage; and by the universality of its theatre and the intensity of its action it will drum dialectics even into the heads of the mushroom-upstarts of the new, holy Prusso-German empire.

London, January 24, 1873.

CHAPTER XXXII

HISTORICAL TENDENCY OF CAPITALIST ACCUMULATION

What does the primitive accumulation of capital, *i.e.*, its historical genesis, resolve itself into? In so far as it is not immediate transformation of slaves and serfs into wage-labourers, and therefore a mere change of form, it only means the expropriation of the immediate producers, *i.e.*, the dissolution of private property based on the labour of its owner. Private property, as the antithesis to social, collective property, exists only where the means of labour and the external conditions of labour belong to private individuals. But according as these private individuals are labourers or not labourers, private property has a different character. The numberless shades, that it at first sight presents, correspond to the intermediate stages lying between these two extremes. The private property of the labourer in his means of production is the foundation of petty industry, whether agricultural, manufacturing or both; petty industry, again, is an essential condition for the development of social production and of the free individuality of the labourer himself. Of course, this petty mode of production exists also under slavery, serfdom, and other states of dependence. But it flourishes, it lets loose its whole energy, it attains its adequate classical form, only where the labourer is the private owner of his own means of labour set in action by himself: the peasant of the land which he cultivates, the artizan of the tool which he handles as a virtuoso. This mode of production pre-supposes parcelling of the soil, and scattering of the other means of production. As it excludes the concentration of these means of production, so also it excludes co-operation, division of labour within each separate process of production, the control over, and the productive application of the forces of Nature by society, and the free development of the social productive powers. It is compatible only with a system of production, and a society, moving within narrow and more or less primitive bounds. To perpetuate it would be, as Pecqueur rightly says, "to decree universal mediocrity." At a certain stage of development it brings forth the material agencies for its own dissolution. From that moment new forces and new passions spring up in the bosom of society; but the old social organization fetters them and keeps them down. It must be annihilated; it is annihilated. Its annihilation, the transformation of the individualised and scattered means of production into socially concentrated ones, of the pigmy property of the many into the huge property of the few, the expropriation of the great mass of the people from the soil, from the means of subsistence, and from the means of labour, this fearful and painful expropriation of the mass of the people forms the prelude to the history of capital. It comprises a series of forcible methods, of which we have passed in review only those that have been epoch-making as methods of the primitive accumulation of capital. The expropriation of the immediate producers was accomplished with merciless Vandalism, and under the stimulus of passions the most infamous, the most sordid, the pettiest, the most meanly odious. Self-earned private property, that is based, so to say, on the fusing together of the isolated, independent labouring-individual with the conditions of his labour, is supplanted by capitalistic private property, which rests on exploitation of the nominally free labour of others, i.e., on wages-labour.[5]

[5] "Nous sommes dans une condition tout-à-fait nouvelle de la société . . . nous tendons à séparer toute espèce de propriété d'avec toute espèce de travail." (Sismondi: Nouveaux Principes de l'Econ. Polit. t. II., p. 434.)

As soon as this process of transformation has sufficiently de-composed the old society from top to bottom, as soon as the labourers are turned into proletarians, their means of labour into capital, as soon as the capitalist mode of production stands on its own feet, then the further socialisation of labour and further transformation of the land and other means of production into socially exploited and, therefore, common means of production, as well as the further expropriation of private proprietors, takes a new form. That which is now to be expropriated is no longer the labourer working for himself, but the capitalist exploiting many labourers. This expropriation is accomplished by the action of the immanent laws of capitalistic production itself, by the centralisation of capital. One capitalist always kills many. Hand in hand with this centralisation, or this expropriation of many capitalists by few, develop, on an ever extending scale, the co-operative form of the labour-process, the conscious technical application of science, the methodical cultivation of the soil, the transformation of the instruments of labour into instruments of labour only usable in common, the economising of all means of production by their use as the means of production of combined, socialised labour, the entanglement of all peoples in the net of the world-market, and this, the international character of the capitalistic régime. Along with the constantly diminishing number of the magnates of capital, who usurp and monopolise all advantages of this process of transformation, grows the mass of misery, oppression, slavery, degradation, exploitation; but with this too grows the revolt of the working-class, a class always increasing in numbers, and disciplined, united, organised by the very mechanism of the process of capitalist production itself. The monopoly of capital becomes a fetter upon the mode of production, which has sprung up and flourished along with, and under it. Centralisation of the means of production and so-cialisation of labour at last reach a point where they become incompatible with their capitalist integument. This integument is burst asunder. The knell of capitalist private property sounds. The expropriators are expropriated.

The capitalist mode of appropriation, the result of the capitalist mode of production, produces capitalist private property. This is the first negation of individual private property, as founded on the labour of the proprietor. But capitalist production begets, with the inexorability of a law of Nature, its own negation. It is the negation of negation. This does not re-establish private property for the producer, but gives him individual property based on the acquisitions of the capitalist era: *i.e.*, on co-operation and the possession in common of the land and of the means of production.

The transformation of scattered private property, arising from individual labour, into capitalist private property is, naturally, a process, incomparably more protracted, violent, and difficult, than the transformation of capitalistic private property, already practically resting on socialised production, into socialised property. In the former case, we had the expropriation of the mass of the people by a few usurpers; in the latter, we have the expropriation of a few usurpers by the mass of the people.[6]

[6] The advance of industry, whose involuntary promoter is the bourgeoisie, replaces the isolation of the labourers, due to competition, by their revolutionary combination, due to association. The development of Modern Industry, therefore, cuts from under its feet, the very foundation on which the bourgeoisie produces and appropriates products. What the bourgeoisie therefore, produces, above all, are its own grave-diggers. Its fall and the victory of the proletariat are equally inevitable. . . . Of all the classes, that stand face to face with the bourgeoisie to-day, the proletariat alone is a really revolutionary class. The other classes perish and disappear in the face of Modern Industry, the proletariat is its special and essential product. . . . The lower middle-classes, the small manufacturers, the shop keepers, the artisan, the peasant, all these fight against the bourgeoisie, to save from extinction their existence as fractions of the middle-class . . . they are reactionary, for they try to roll back the wheel of history. "Karl Marx and Frederick Engels, Manifest der Kommunistischen Partei," London, 1847, pp. 9, 11.

SIGMUND FREUD

Freud was born in Moravia in 1856. He lived most of his life in Vienna and died in London in 1939. After receiving his medical degree, he eventually took up the practice of neurology and then of psychopathology. This in turn led to his development of psychoanalysis. Freud utilized the technique of free association to help uncover repressed experiences, and in his research he attempted to uncover his own unconscious mental processes as well as those of his patients. *The Interpretation of Dreams* appeared in 1901 and laid bare one of the routes to the unconscious. *The Psychopathology of Everyday Life* reflects Freud's conviction that normal as well as abnormal psychic life is influenced by unconscious forces which can be used to explain such everyday occurrences as the forgetting of names and slips of the tongue. He forged tools which have been widely used not only in psychology and psychopathology but also in the analysis of mythology, literature, politics, and most of the ordinary activities of human life.

3

The Psychopathology of Everyday Life

FORGETTING OF PROPER NAMES

During the year 1898 I published a short essay *On the Psychic Mechanism of Forgetfulness*.[1] I shall now repeat its contents and take it as a starting-point for further discussion. I have there undertaken a psychologic analysis of a common case of temporary forgetfulness of proper names, and from a pregnant example of my own observation I have reached the conclusion that this frequent and practically unimportant occurrence of a failure of a psychic function—of memory—admits an explanation which goes beyond the customary utilization of this phenomenon.

If an average psychologist should be asked to explain how it happens that we often fail to recall a name which we are sure we know, he would probably content himself with the answer that proper names are more apt to be forgotten than any other content of memory. He might give plausible reasons for this "forgetting preference" for proper names, but he would not assume any deep determinant for the process.

I was led to examine exhaustively the phenomenon of temporary forgetfulness through the observation of certain peculiarities, which, although not general, can, nevertheless, be seen clearly in some cases. In these there is not only *forgetfulness*, but also false *recollection*: he who strives for the escaped name brings to consciousness others—substitutive names—which, although immediately recognized as false, nevertheless obtrude

Reprinted here are Chapters I and V of *The Psychopathology of Everyday Life*, by Sigmund Freud, translated by A. A. Brill, New York: The Macmillan Company, 1914.

[1] *Monatschrift f. Psychiatrie.*

themselves with great tenacity. The process which should lead to the reproduction of the lost name is, as it were, displaced, and thus brings one to an incorrect substitute.

Now it is my assumption that the displacement is not left to psychic arbitrariness, but that it follows lawful and rational paths. In other words, I assume that the substitutive name (or names) stands in direct relation to the lost name, and I hope, if I succeed in demonstrating this connection, to throw light on the origin of the forgetting of names.

In the example which I selected for analysis in 1898 I vainly strove to recall the name of the master who made the imposing frescoes of the "Last Judgment" in the dome of *Orvieto*. Instead of the lost name—*Signorelli*—two other names of artists—*Botticelli* and *Boltraffio*—obtruded themselves, names which my judgment immediately and definitely rejected as being incorrect. When the correct name was imparted to me by an outsider I recognized it at once without any hesitation. The examination of the influence and association paths which caused the displacement from *Signorelli* to *Botticelli* and *Boltraffio* led to the following results:—

(*a*) The reason for the escape of the name *Signorelli* is neither to be sought in the strangeness in itself of this name nor in the psychologic character of the connection in which it was inserted. The forgotten name was just as familiar to me as one of the substitutive names—*Botticelli*—and somewhat more familiar than the other substitute—*Boltraffio*—of the possessor of which I could hardly say more than that he belonged to the Milanese School. The connection, too, in which the forgetting of the name took place appeared to me harmless, and led to no further explanation. I journeyed by carriage with a stranger from Ragusa, Dalmatia, to a station in Herzegovina. Our conversation drifted to travelling in Italy, and I asked my companion whether he had been in Orvieto and had seen there the famous frescoes of——

(*b*) The forgetting of the name could not be explained until after I had recalled the theme discussed immediately before this conversation. This forgetting then made itself known *as a disturbance of the newly emerging theme caused by the theme preceding it*. In brief, before I asked my travelling companion if he had been in Orvieto we had been discussing the customs of the Turks living in *Bosnia* and *Herzegovina*. I had related what I heard from a colleague who was practising medicine among them, namely, that they show full confidence in the physician and complete submission to fate. When one is compelled to inform them that there is no help for the patient, they answer: "*Sir* (Herr), what can I say? I know that if he could be saved you would save him." In these sentences alone we can find the words and names: *Bosnia, Herzegovina,* and *Herr* (sir), which may be inserted in an association series between *Signorelli, Botticelli,* and *Boltraffio.*

(*c*) I assume that the stream of thoughts concerning the customs of the Turks in Bosnia, etc., was able to disturb the next thought, because I withdrew my attention from it before it came to an end. For I recalled that I wished to relate a second anecdote which was next to the first in my memory. These Turks value the sexual pleasure above all else, and at sexual disturbances merge into an utter despair which strangely contrasts with their resignation at the peril of losing their lives. One of my colleague's patients once told him: "For you know, sir (Herr), if that ceases, life no longer has any charm."

I refrained from imparting this characteristic feature because I did not wish to touch upon such a delicate theme in conversation with a stranger. But I went still further; I also deflected my attention from the continuation of the thought which might have associated itself in me with the theme "Death and Sexuality." I was at that time under the after-effects of a message which I had received a few weeks before, during a brief sojourn in *Trafoi*. A patient on whom I had spent much effort had ended his life on account of an incurable sexual disturbance. I know positively that this sad event, and everything connected with it, did not come to my conscious recollection on that trip in Herzegovina. However, the agreement between *Trafoi* and *Boltraffio* forces me to assume that this reminiscence was at that time brought to activity despite all the intentional deviation of my attention.

(*d*) I can no longer conceive the forgetting of the name Signorelli as an accidental occurrence. I must recognize in this process the influence of a *motive*. There were motives which actuated the interruption in the communication of my thoughts (concerning the customs of the Turks, etc.), and

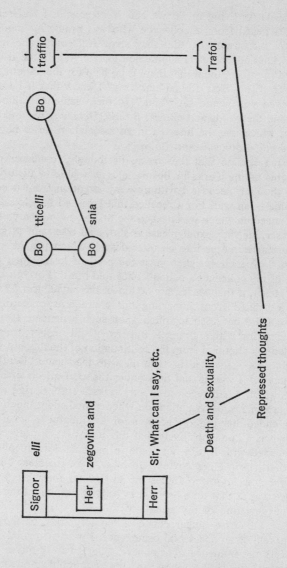

which later influenced me to exclude from my consciousness the thought connected with them, and which might have led to the message concerning the incident in Trafoi—that is, I wanted to forget something, I *repressed* something. To be sure, I wished to forget something other than the name of the master of Orvieto; but this other thought brought about an associative connection between itself and this name, so that my act of volition missed the aim, and I *forgot the one against my will*, while I *intentionally* wished to forget the other. The disinclination to recall directed itself against the one content; the inability to remember appeared in another. The case would have been obviously simpler if this disinclination and the inability to remember had concerned the same content. The substitutive names no longer seem so thoroughly justified as they were before this explanation. They remind me (after the form of a compromise) as much of what I wished to forget as of what I wished to remember, and show me that my object to forget something was neither a perfect success nor a failure.

(*e*) The nature of the association formed between the lost name and the repressed theme (death and sexuality, etc.), containing the names of Bosnia, Herzegovina, and Trafoi, is also very strange. In the scheme inserted here, which originally appeared in 1898, an attempt is made to graphically represent these associations.

The name Signorelli was thus divided into two parts. One pair of syllables (*elli*) returned unchanged in one of the substitutions, while the other had gained, through the translation of *signor* (sir, Herr), many and diverse relations to the name contained in the repressed theme, but was lost through it in the reproduction. Its substitution was formed in a way to suggest that a displacement took place along the same associations—"Herzegovina and Bosnia"—regardless of the sense and acoustic demarcation. The names were therefore treated in this process like the written pictures of a sentence which is to be transformed into a picture-puzzle (rebus). No information was given to consciousness concerning the whole process, which, instead of the name Signorelli, was thus changed to the substitutive names. At first sight no relation is apparent between the theme that contained the name Signorelli and the repressed one which immediately preceded it.

Perhaps it is not superfluous to remark that the given explanation does not contradict the conditions of memory reproduction and forgetting assumed by other psychologists, which they seek in certain relations and dispositions. Only in certain cases have we added another *motive* to the factors long recognized as causative in forgetting names, and have thus laid bare the mechanism of faulty memory. The assumed dispositions are indispensable also in our case, in order to make it possible for the repressed element to associatively gain control over the desired name and take it along into the repression. Perhaps this would not have occurred in another name having more favourable conditions of reproduction. For it is quite probable that a suppressed element continually strives to assert itself in some other way, but attains this success only where it meets with suitable conditions. At other times the suppression succeeds without disturbance of function, or, as we may justly say, without symptoms.

When we recapitulate the conditions for forgetting a name with faulty recollection we find: (1) a certain disposition to forget the same; (2) a process of suppression which has taken place shortly before; and (3) the possibility of establishing an *outer* association between the concerned name and the element previously suppressed. The last condition will probably not have to be much overrated, for the slightest claim on the association is apt in most cases to bring it about. But it is a different and farther-reaching question whether such outer association can really furnish the proper condition to enable the suppressed element to disturb the reproduction of the desired name, or whether after all a more intimate connection between the two themes is not necessarily required. On superficial consideration one may be willing to reject the latter requirement and consider the temporal meeting in perfectly dissimilar contents as sufficient. But on more thorough examination one finds more and more frequently that the two elements (the repressed and the new one) connected by an outer association, possess besides a connection in content, and this can also be demonstrated in the example *Signorelli*.

The value of the understanding gained through the analysis

of the example *Signorelli* naturally depends on whether we must explain this case as a typical or as an isolated process. I must now maintain that the forgetting of a name associated with faulty recollection uncommonly often follows the same process as was demonstrated in the case of *Signorelli*. Almost every time that I observed this phenomenon in myself I was able to explain it in the manner indicated above as being motivated by repression.

I must mention still another view-point in favour of the typical nature of our analysis. I believe that one is not justified in separating the cases of name-forgetting with faulty recollection from those in which incorrect substitutive names have not obtruded themselves. These substitutive names occur spontaneously in a number of cases; in other cases, where they do not come spontaneously, they can be brought to the surface by concentration of attention, and they then show the same relation to the repressed element and the lost name as those that come spontaneously. Two factors seem to play a part in bringing to consciousness the substitutive names: first, the effort of attention, and second, an inner determinant which adheres to the psychic material. I could find the latter in the greater or lesser facility which forms the required outer associations between the two elements. A great many of the cases of name-forgetting without faulty recollection therefore belong to the cases with substitutive name formation, the mechanism of which corresponds to the one in the example *Signorelli*. But I surely shall not venture to assert that all cases of name-forgetting belong to the same group. There is no doubt that there are cases of name-forgetting that proceed in a much simpler way. We shall represent this state of affairs carefully enough if we assert that *besides the simple forgetting of proper names there is another forgetting which is motivated by repression.*

MISTAKES IN SPEECH

Although the ordinary material of speech of our mother-tongue seems to be guarded against forgetting, its application, however, more often succumbs to another disturbance which is familiar to us as "slips of the tongue." What we observe in normal persons as slips of the tongue gives the same impression as the first step of the so-called "paraphasias" which manifest themselves under pathologic conditions.

I am in the exceptional position of being about to refer to a previous work on the subject. In the year 1895 Meringer and C. Mayer published a study on *Mistakes in Speech and Reading,* with whose view-points I do not agree. One of the authors, who is the spokesman in the text, is a philologist actuated by a linguistic interest to examine the rules governing those slips. He hoped to deduce from these rules the existence "of a definite psychic mechanism," "whereby the sounds of a word, of a sentence, and even the words themselves, would be associated and connected with one another in a quite peculiar manner" (p. 10).

The authors grouped the examples of speech-mistakes collected by them first according to purely descriptive view-points, such as interchangings (*e.g.,* the Milo of Venus instead of the Venus of Milo), as anticipations (*e.g.,* the shoes made her sorft . . . the shoes made her feet sore), as echoes and post positions, as contaminations (*e.g.,* "I will soon him home," instead of "I will soon go home and I will see him"), and substitutions (*e.g.,* "he entrusted his money to a savings crank," instead of "a savings bank").[1] Besides these principal categories there are some others of lesser importance (or of lesser significance for our purpose). In this grouping it makes no difference whether the transposition, disfigurement, fusion, etc., affects single sounds of the word or syllables, or whole words of the concerned sentence.

To explain the various forms of mistakes in speech, Meringer assumes a varied psychic value of phonetics. As soon as the innervation affects the first syllable of a word, or the first word of a sentence, the stimulating process immediately strikes the succeeding sounds, and the following words, and in so far as these innervations are synchronous they may effect some changes in one another. The stimulus of the psychically more intensive sound "rings" before or continues echoing, and thus disturbs the less important process of innervation. It is neces-

---

[1] The examples are given by the translator.

sary therefore to determine which are the most important sounds of a word. Meringer states: "If one wishes to know which sound of a word possesses the greatest intensity he should examine himself while searching for a forgotten word, for example, a name. That which first returns to consciousness invariably had the greatest intensity prior to the forgetting (p. 160). Thus the most important sounds are the initial sound of the root-syllable and the initial sound of the word itself, as well as one or another of the accentuated vowels" (p. 162).

Here I cannot help voicing a contradiction. Whether or not the initial sound of the name belongs to the most important elements of the word, it is surely not true that in the case of the forgetting of the word it first returns to consciousness; the above rule is therefore of no use. When we observe ourselves during the search for a forgotten name we are comparatively often forced to express the opinion that it begins with a certain letter. This conviction proves to be as often unfounded as founded. Indeed, I would even go so far as to assert that in the majority of cases one reproduces a false initial sound. Also in our example *Signorelli* the substitutive name lacked the initial sound, and the principal syllables were lost; on the other hand, the less important pair of syllables *elli* returned to consciousness in the substitutive name *Botticelli*.

How little substitutive names respect the initial sound of the lost names may be learned from the following case. One day I found it impossible to recall the name of the small country whose capital is Monte Carlo. The substitutive names were as follows: *Piedmont, Albania, Montevideo, Colico*. In place of Albania *Montenegro* soon appeared, and then it struck me that the syllable *Mont* (pronounced *Mon*) occurred in all but the last of the substitutive names. It thus became easy for me to find from the name of Prince Albert the forgotten name *Monaco. Colico* practically imitates the syllabic sequence and rhythm of the forgotten name.

If we admit the conjecture that a mechanism similar to that pointed out in the forgetting of names may also play a part in the phenomena of speech-blunders, we are then led to a better founded judgment of cases of speech-blunders. The speech disturbance which manifests itself as a speech-blunder may in

the first place be caused by the influence of another component
of the same speech, that is, through a fore-sound or an echo,
or through another meaning within the sentence or context
which differs from that which the speaker wishes to utter. In
the second place, however, the disturbance could be brought
about analogously to the process in the case *Signorelli,* through
influences outside this word, sentence or context, from elements
which we did not intend to express, and of whose incitement
we became conscious only through the disturbance. In both
modes of origin of the mistake in speech the common element
lies in the simultaneity of the stimulus, while the differentiating
elements lie in the arrangement within or without the same sentence or context.

The difference does not at first appear as wide as when it is
taken into consideration in certain conclusions drawn from the
symptomatology of speech-mistakes. It is clear, however, that
only in the first case is there a prospect of drawing conclusions
from the manifestations of speech-blunders concerning a
mechanism which connects together sounds and words for the
reciprocal influence of their articulation; that is, conclusions
such as the philologist hopes to gain from the study of speech-
blunders. In the case of disturbance through influence outside
of the same sentence or context, it would before all be a question of becoming acquainted with the disturbing elements, and
then the question would arise whether the mechanism of this
disturbance cannot also suggest the probable laws of the formation of speech.

We cannot maintain that Meringer and Mayer have over-
looked the possibility of speech disturbance through "complicated psychic influences," that is, through elements outside of
the same word or sentence or the same sequence of words.
Indeed, they must have observed that the theory of the psychic
variation of sounds applies, strictly speaking, only to the explanation of sound disturbances as well as to fore-sounds and
after-sounds. Where the word disturbances cannot be reduced
to sound disturbances, as, for example, in the substitutions
and contaminations of words, they, too, have without hesitation sought the cause of the mistake in speech outside of the
intended context, and proved this state of affairs by means

of fitting examples.[2] According to the author's own understanding it is some similarity between a certain word in the intended sentence and some other not intended, which allows the latter to assert itself in consciousness by causing a disfigurement, a composition, or a compromise formation (contamination).

Now, in my work on the *Interpretation of Dreams* I have shown the part played by the process of condensation in the origin of the so-called manifest contents of the dream from the latent thoughts of the dream. Any similarity of objects or of word-presentations between two elements of the unconscious material is taken as a cause for the formation of a third, which is a composite or compromise formation. This element represents both components in the dream content, and in view of this origin it is frequently endowed with numerous contradictory individual determinants. The formation of substitutions and contaminations in speech-mistakes is, therefore, the beginning of that work of condensation which we find taking a most active part in the construction of the dream.

In a small essay destined for the general reader,[3] Meringer advanced a theory of very practical significance for certain cases of interchanging of words, especially for such cases where one word is substituted by another of opposite meaning. He says: "We may still recall the manner in which the President of the Austrian House of Deputies opened the session some time ago: 'Honoured Sirs! I announce the presence of so and so many gentlemen, and therefore declare the session as "closed" '!" The general merriment first attracted his attention and he corrected his mistake. In the present case the probable explanation is that the President wished himself in a position to close this session, from which he had little good to expect, and the thought broke through at least partially—a frequent manifestation—resulting in his use of "closed" in place of "opened," that is, the opposite of the statement intended. Numerous observations have taught me, however, that we frequently interchange contrasting words; they are

[2] Those who are interested are referred to pp. 62, 73, and 97 of the author's work.
[3] *Neue Freie Presse*, August 23, 1900: "Wie man sich versprechen kann."

already associated in our speech consciousness; they lie very close together and are easily incorrectly evoked.

Still, not in all cases of contrast substitution is it so simple as in the example of the President as to appear plausible that the speech-mistake occurs merely as a contradiction which arises in the inner thought of the speaker opposing the sentence uttered. We have found the analogous mechanism in the analysis of the example *aliquis;* there the inner contradiction asserts itself in the form of forgetting a word instead of a substitution through its opposite. But in order to adjust the difference we may remark that the little word *aliquis* is incapable of a contrast similar to "closing" and "opening," and that the word "opening" cannot be subject to forgetting on account of its being a common component of speech.

Having been shown by the last examples of Meringer and Mayer that speech disturbance may be caused through the influence of fore-sounds, after-sounds, words from the same sentence that were intended for expression, as well as through the effect of words outside the sentence intended, *the stimulus of which would otherwise not have been suspected,* we shall next wish to discover whether we can definitely separate the two classes of mistakes in speech, and how we can distinguish the example of the one from a case of the other class.

But at this stage of the discussion we must also think of the assertions of Wundt, who deals with the manifestations of speech-mistakes in his recent work on the development of language.[4] Psychic influences, according to Wundt, never lack in these as well as in other phenomena related to them. "The uninhibited stream of *sound* and *word associations* stimulated by spoken sounds belongs here in the first place as a positive determinant. This is supported as a negative factor by the relaxation or suppression of the influences of the will which inhibit this stream, and by the active attention which is here a function of volition. Whether that play of association manifests itself in the fact that a coming sound is anticipated or a preceding sound reproduced, or whether a familiar practised sound becomes intercalated between others, or finally, whether it manifests itself in the fact that altogether different sounds

[4] *Völker psychologie,* vol. i., pt. i., p. 371, etc., 1900.

associatively related to the spoken sounds act upon these—all these questions designate only differences in the direction, and at most in the play of the occurring associations but not in the general nature of the same. In some cases it may be also doubtful to which form a certain disturbance may be attributed, or whether it would not be more correct to refer such disturbance to a concurrence of many motives, *following the principle of the complication of causes*[5] (cf. pp. 380-81)."

I consider these observations of Wundt as absolutely justified and very instructive. Perhaps we could emphasize with even greater firmness than Wundt that the positive factor favouring mistakes in speech (the uninhibited stream of associations, and its negative, the relaxation of the inhibiting attention) regularly attain synchronous action, so that both factors become only different determinants of the same process. With the relaxation, or, more unequivocally expressed, *through* this relaxation, of the inhibiting attention the uninhibited stream of associations becomes active.

Among the examples of the mistakes in speech collected by me I can scarcely find one in which I would be obliged to attribute the speech disturbance simply and solely to what Wundt calls "contact effect of sound." Almost invariably I discover besides this a disturbing influence of something outside of the intended speech. The disturbing element is either a single unconscious thought, which comes to light through the speech-blunder, and can only be brought to consciousness through a searching analysis, or it is a more general psychic motive, which directs itself against the entire speech.

(*Example a*) Seeing my daughter make an unpleasant face while biting into an apple, I wished to quote the following couplet:—

> "The ape he is a funny sight,
>   When in the apple he takes a bite."

But I began: "The apel . . ." This seems to be a contamination of "ape" and "apple" (compromise formation), or it may be also conceived as an anticipation of the prepared "apple." The true state of affairs, however, was this: I began the quo-

---

[5] Italics are mine.

tation once before, and made no mistake the first time. I made the mistake only during the repetition, which was necessary because my daughter, having been distracted from another side, did not listen to me. This repetition with the added impatience to disburden myself of the sentence I must include in the motivation of the speech-blunder, which represented itself as a function of condensation.

(*b*) My daughter said, "I wrote to Mrs. Schresinger." The woman's name was Schlesinger. This speech-blunder may depend on the tendency to facilitate articulation. I must state, however, that this mistake was made by my daughter a few moments after I had said *apel* instead of *ape*. Mistakes in speech are in a great measure contagious; a similar peculiarity was noticed by Meringer and Mayer in the forgetting of names. I know of no reason for this psychic contagiousness.

(*c*) "I *sut* up like a pocket-knife," said a patient in the beginning of treatment, instead of "I *shut* up." This suggests a difficulty of articulation which may serve as an excuse for the interchanging of sounds. When her attention was called to the speech-blunder, she promptly replied, "Yes, that happened because you said '*earnesht*' instead of '*earnest*.'" As a matter of fact I received her with the remark, "To-day we shall be in earnest" (because it was the last hour before her discharge from treatment), and I jokingly changed the word into *earnesht*. In the course of the hour she repeatedly made mistakes in speech, and I finally observed that it was not only because she imitated me but because she had a special reason in her unconscious to linger at the word earnest (Ernst) as a name.[6]

(*d*) A woman, speaking about a game invented by her children and called by them "the man in the box," said "the manx in the boc." I could readily understand her mistake. It was while analysing her dream, in which her husband is de-

---

[6] It turned out that she was under the influence of unconscious thoughts concerning pregnancy and prevention of conception. With the words "shut up like a pocket knife," which she uttered consciously as a complaint, she meant to describe the position of the child in the womb. The word "earnest" in my remark recalled to her the name (S. Ernst) of the well-known Vienna business firm in Kärthner Strasse, which used to advertise the sale of articles for the prevention of conception.

picted as very generous in money matters—just the reverse of reality—that she made this speech-blunder. The day before she had asked for a new set of furs, which her husband denied her, claiming that he could not afford to spend so much money. She upbraided him for his stinginess, "for putting away so much into the strong-box," and mentioned a friend whose husband has not nearly his income, and yet he presented his wife with a *mink* coat for her birthday. The mistake is now comprehensible. The word *manx* (*manks*) reduces itself to the "minks" which she longs for, and the *box* refers to her husband's stinginess.

(*e*) A similar mechanism is shown in the mistake of another patient whose memory deserted her in the midst of a long-forgotten childish reminiscence. Her memory failed to inform her on what part of the body the prying and lustful hand of another had touched her. Soon thereafter she visited one of her friends, with whom she discussed summer homes. Asked where her cottage in M. was located, she answered, "Near the *mountain loin*" instead of *"mountain lane."*

(*f*) Another patient, whom I asked at the end of her visit how her uncle was, answered: "I don't know, I only see him now *in flagranti*."

The following day she said, "I am really ashamed of myself for having given you yesterday such a stupid answer. Naturally you must have thought me a very uneducated person who always mistakes the meaning of foreign words. I wished to say *en passant*." We did not know at the time where she got the incorrectly used foreign words, but during the same session she reproduced a reminiscence as a continuation of the theme from the previous day, in which being caught *in flagranti* played the principal part. The mistake of the previous day had therefore anticipated the recollection, which at that time had not yet become conscious.

(*g*) In discussing her summer plans, a patient said, "I shall remain most of the summer in *Elberlon*." She noted her mistake, and asked me to analyse it. The associations to *Elberlon* elicited: seashore on the Jersey coast—summer resort—vacation travelling. This recalled travelling in Europe with her cousin, a topic which we had discussed the day before during the analysis of a dream. The dream dealt with her dislike for this cousin, and she admitted that it was mainly due to the fact that the latter was the favourite of the man whom they met together while travelling abroad. During the dream analysis she could not recall the name of the city in which they met this man, and I did not make any effort at the time to bring it to her consciousness, as we were engrossed in a totally different problem. When asked to focus her attention again on Elberlon and reproduce her associations, she said, "It brings to mind *Elberlawn—lawn—field*—and *Elberfield*." *Elberfeld* was the lost name of the city in Germany. Here the mistake served to bring to consciousness in a concealed manner a memory which was connected with a painful feeling.

(*h*) A woman said to me, "If you wish to buy a carpet, go to *Merchant* (Kaufmann) in *Matthew Street* (Mathäusgasse)." I repeated, "Then at Matthew's—I mean at Merchant's——" It would seem that my repeating of one name in place of the other was simply the result of distraction. The woman's remark really did distract me, as she turned my attention to something else much more vital to me than carpet. In Matthew Street stands the house in which my wife lived as a bride. The entrance to the house was in another street, and now I noticed that I had forgotten its name and could only recall it through a roundabout method. The name Matthew, which kept my attention, is thus a substitutive name for the forgotten name of the street. It is more suitable than the name Merchant, for Matthew is exclusively the name of a person, while Merchant is not. The forgotten street, too, bears the name of a person: *Radetzky*.

(*i*) A patient consulted me for the first time, and from her history it became apparent that the cause of her nervousness was largely an unhappy married life. Without any encouragement she went into details about her marital troubles. She had not lived with her husband for about six months, and she saw him last at the theatre, when she saw the play *Officer 606*. I called her attention to the mistake, and she immediately corrected herself, saying that she meant to say *Officer 666* (the name of a recent popular play). I decided to find out the reason for the mistake, and as the patient came to me for analytic treatment, I discovered that the immediate cause of the rupture between herself and husband was the disease which is treated by "606."[7]

(k) Before calling on me a patient telephoned for an appointment, and also wished to be informed about my consultation fee. He was told that the first consultation was ten dollars; after the examination was over he again asked what he was to pay, and added: "I don't like to owe money to any one, especially to doctors; I prefer to pay right away." Instead of *pay* he said *play*. His last voluntary remarks and his mistake put me on my guard, but after a few more uncalled-for remarks he set me at ease by taking money from his pocket. He counted four paper dollars and was very chagrined and surprised because he had no more money with him, and promised to send me a cheque for the balance. I was sure that his mistake betrayed him, that he was only *playing* with me, but there was nothing to be done. At the end of a few weeks I sent him a bill for the balance, and the letter was returned to me by the post-office authorities marked "Not found."

(l) Miss X. spoke very warmly of Mr. Y., which was rather strange, as before this she had always expressed her indifference, not to say her contempt, for him. On being asked about this sudden change of heart she said: "I really never had anything against him; he was always nice to me, but I never gave him the chance to cultivate my acquaintance." She said "cuptivate." This neologism was a contamination of *cultivate* and *captivate*, and foretold the coming betrothal.

(m) An illustration of the mechanisms of contamination and condensation will be found in the following *lapsus linguæ*. Speaking of Miss Z., Miss W. depicted her as a very "straitlaced" person who was not given to levities, etc. Miss X. thereupon remarked: "Yes, that is a very characteristic description, she always appealed to me as very '*straicet-brazed.*'" Here the mistake resolved itself into *straitlaced* and *brazenfaced*, which corresponded to Miss W.'s opinion of Miss Z.

(n) I shall quote a number of examples from a paper by

[7] Similar mistakes dealing with *Officer 666* were recently reported to me by other psycho-analysts.

my colleague, Dr. W. Stekel, which appeared in the Berlin *Tageblatt* of January, 1904, entitled "Unconscious Confessions."

"An unpleasant trick of my unpleasant thoughts was revealed by the following example: To begin with, I may state that in my capacity as a physician I never consider my remuneration, but always keep in view the patient's interest only: this goes without saying. I was visiting a patient who was convalescing from a serious illness. We had passed through hard days and nights. I was happy to find her improved, and I portrayed to her the pleasures of a sojourn in Abbazia, concluding with: 'If, as I hope, you will *not* soon leave your bed.' This obviously came from an unconscious selfish motive, to be able to continue treating this wealthy patient, a wish which is entirely foreign to my waking consciousness, and which I would reject with indignation."

(*o*) Another example (Dr. W. Stekel): "My wife engaged a French governess for the afternoons, and later, coming to a satisfactory agreement, wished to retain her testimonials. The governess begged to be allowed to keep them, saying, 'Je cherche encore pour les *après-midis*—pardons, pour les *avant-midis*.' She apparently intended to seek another place which would perhaps offer more profitable arrangements—an intention which she carried out."

(*p*) I was to give a lecture to a woman. Her husband, upon whose request this was done, stood behind the door listening. At the end of my sermonizing, which had made a visible impression, I said: "Good-bye, sir!" To the experienced person I thus betrayed the fact that the words were directed towards the husband; that I had spoken to oblige him.

(*q*) Dr. Stekel reports about himself that he had under treatment at the same time two patients from Triest, each of whom he always addressed incorrectly. "Good morning, Mr. Peloni!" he would say to Askoli, and to Peloni, "Good morning, Mr. Askoli!" He was at first inclined to attribute no deeper motive to this mistake, but to explain it through a number of similarities in both persons. However, he easily convinced himself that here the interchange of names bespoke a sort of boast—that is, he was acquainting each of his Italian patients with the fact that neither was the only resident of Triest who came to Vienna in search of his medical advice.

(*r*) Two women stopped in front of a drugstore, and one said to her companion, "If you will wait a few *moments* I'll soon be back," but she said *movements* instead. She was on her way to buy some castoria for her child.

(*s*) Mr. L., who is fonder of being called on than of calling, spoke to me through the telephone from a nearby summer resort. He wanted to know when I would pay him a visit. I reminded him that it was his turn to visit me, and called his attention to the fact that, as he was the happy possessor of an automobile, it would be easier for him to call on me. (We were at different summer resorts, separated by about one half-hour's railway trip.) He gladly promised to call, and asked: "How about Labour Day (September 1st), will it be convenient for you?" When I answered affirmatively, he said, "Very well, then, put me down for *Election* Day" (November). His mistake was quite plain. He likes to visit me, but it was inconvenient to travel so far. In November we would both be in the city. My analysis proved correct.

(*t*) A friend described to me a nervous patient, and wished to know whether I could benefit him. I remarked: "I believe that in time I can remove all his symptoms by psychoanalysis, because it is a durable case," wishing to say "curable"!

(*u*) I repeatedly addressed my patient as Mrs. Smith, her married daughter's name, when her real name is Mrs. James. My attention having been called to it, I soon discovered that I had another patient of the same name who refused to pay for the treatment. Mrs. Smith was also my patient and paid her bills promptly.

(*v*) A *lapsus linguæ* sometimes stands for a particular characteristic. A young woman, who is the domineering spirit in her home, said of her ailing husband that he had consulted the doctor about a wholesome diet for himself, and then added: "The doctor said that diet has nothing to do with his ailments, and that he can eat and drink what *I* want."

(*w*) I cannot omit this excellent and instructive example, although, according to my authority, it is about twenty years old. A lady once expressed herself in society—the very words show that they were uttered with fervour and under the pressure of a great many secret emotions: "Yes, a woman must be pretty if she is to please the men. A man is much better off. As long as he has *five* straight limbs, he needs no more!"

This example affords us a good insight into the intimate mechanisms of a mistake in speech by means of condensation and contamination (cf. p. 32). It is quite obvious that we have here a fusion of two similar modes of expression:—

"As long as he has his four *straight limbs*."

"As long as he has all his *five senses*."

Or the term "straight" may be the common element of the two intended expressions:—

"As long as he has his *straight* limbs."

"All five should be *straight*."

It may also be assumed that both modes of expression—viz., those of the five senses and those of the straight five—have co-operated to introduce into the sentence about the straight limbs first a number and then the mysterious five instead of the simple four. But this fusion surely would not have succeeded if it had not expressed good sense in the form resulting from the mistake; if it had not expressed a cynical truth which, naturally, could not be uttered unconcealed, coming as it did from a woman.

Finally, we shall not hesitate to call attention to the fact that the woman's saying, following its wording, could just as well be an excellent witticism as a jocose speech-blunder. It is simply a question whether she uttered these words with conscious or unconscious intention. The behaviour of the speaker in this case certainly speaks against the conscious intention, and thus excludes wit.

(*x*) Owing to similarity of material, I add here another case of speech-blunder, the interpretation of which requires less skill. A professor of anatomy strove to explain the nostril, which, as is known, is a very difficult anatomical structure. To his question whether his audience grasped his ideas he received an affirmative reply. The professor, known for his self-esteem, thereupon remarked: "I can hardly believe this, for the number of people who understand the nostril, even in a city of millions like Vienna, can be counted *on a finger*—pardon me, I meant to say *on the fingers* of a hand."

(*y*) I am indebted to Dr. Alf. Robitsek, of Vienna, for calling my attention to two speech-blunders from an old French author, which I shall reproduce in the original.

Brantôme (1527-1614), *Vies des Dames galantes,* Discours second: "Si ay-je cogneu une très belle et honneste dame de par le monde, qui, devisant avec un honneste gentilhomme de la cour des affaires de la guerre durant ces civiles, elle luy dit: 'J'ay ouy dire que le roy a faiet rompre tous les c— de ce pays là.' Elle vouloit dire le ponts. Pensez que, venant de coucher d'avec son mary, ou songeant à son amant, elle avoit encor ce nom frais en la bouche; et le gentilhomme s'en eschauffer en amours d'elle pour ce mot.

"Une autre dame que j'ai cogneue, entretenant une autre grand dame plus qu'elle, et luy louant et exaltant ses beautez, elle luy dit après: 'Non, madame, ce que je vous en dis, ce n'est point pour vous *adultérer;* voulant dire *adulater,* comme elle le rhabilla ainsi: pensez qu'elle songeoit à adultérer."

In the psychotherapeutic procedure which I employ in the solution and removal of neurotic symptoms, I am often confronted with the task of discovering from the accidental utterances and fancies of the patient the thought contents, which, though striving for concealment, nevertheless unintentionally betray themselves. In doing this the mistakes often perform the most valuable service, as I can show through most convincing and still most singular examples.

For example, patients speak of an aunt and later, without noting the mistake, call her "my mother," or designate a husband as a "brother." In this way they attract my attention to the fact that they have "identified" these persons with each other, that they have placed them in the same category, which for their emotional life signifies the recurrence of the same type. Or, a young man of twenty years presents himself during my office hours with these words: "I am the father of N. N., whom you have treated—pardon me, I mean the brother; why, he is four years older than I." I understand through this mistake that he wishes to express that, like the brother, he, too, is ill through the fault of the father; like his brother, he wishes to be cured, but that the father is the one most in need of treatment. At other times an unusual arrangement of words, or a forced expression, is sufficient to disclose in the speech of the patient the participation of a repressed thought having a different motive.

Hence, in coarse as well as in finer speech disturbances, which may, nevertheless, be subsumed as "speech-blunders," I find that it is not the contact effects of the sound, but the thoughts outside the intended speech, which determine the origin of the speech-blunder, and also suffice to explain the newly formed mistakes in speech. I do not doubt the laws whereby the sounds produce changes upon one another; but they alone do not appear to me sufficiently forcible to mar the correct execution of speech. In those cases which I have studied and investigated more closely they merely represent the preformed mechanism, which is conveniently utilized by a more remote psychic motive. The latter does not, however, form a part of the sphere of influence of these sound relations. *In a large number of substitutions caused by mistakes in talking there is an entire absence of such phonetic laws.* In this respect I am in full accord with Wundt, who likewise assumes that the conditions underlying speech-blunders are complex and go far beyond the contact effect of the sounds.

If I accept as certain "these more remote psychic influences," following Wundt's expression, there is still nothing to detain me from conceding also that in accelerated speech, with a certain amount of diverted attention, the causes of speech-blunder may be easily limited to the definite law of Meringer and Mayer. However, in a number of examples gathered by these authors a more complicated solution is quite apparent.

In some forms of speech-blunders we may assume that the disturbing factor is the result of striking against obscene words and meanings. The purposive disfigurement and distortion of words and phrases, which is so popular with vulgar persons, aims at nothing else but the employing of a harmless motive as a reminder of the obscene, and this sport is so frequent that it would not be at all remarkable if it appeared unintentionally and contrary to the will.

I trust that the readers will not depreciate the value of these interpretations, for which there is no proof, and of these examples which I have myself collected and explained by means of analysis. But if secretly I still cherish the expectation that even the apparently simple cases of speech-blunder will be traced to a disturbance caused by a half-repressed idea outside of the intended context, I am tempted to it by a noteworthy observation of Meringer. This author asserts that it is remarkable that nobody wishes to admit having made a mistake in speaking. There are many intelligent and honest people who are offended if we tell them that they made a mistake in speaking. I would not risk making this assertion as general as does Meringer, using the term "nobody." But the emotional trace which clings to the demonstration of the mistake, which manifestly belongs to the nature of shame, has its significance. It may be classed with the anger displayed at the inability to recall a forgotten name, and with the surprise at the tenaciousness of an apparently indifferent memory, and it invariably points to the participation of a motive in the formation of the disturbance.

The distorting of names amounts to an insult when done intentionally, and could have the same significance in a whole series of cases where it appears as unintentional speech-blunders. The person who, according to Mayer's report, once said "Freuder" instead of "Freud," because shortly before he pronounced the name "Breuer" (p. 38), and who at another time spoke of the "Freuer-Breudian" method (p. 28), was certainly not particularly enthusiastic over this method. Later, under the mistakes in writing, I shall report a case of name disfigurement which certainly admits of no other explanation.[8]

---

[8] It may be observed that aristocrats in particular very frequently distort the names of the physicians they consult, from which we may conclude that inwardly they slight them, in spite of the politeness with which they are wont to greet them. I shall cite here some excellent observations concerning the forgetting of names from the works of Professor E. Jones, of Toronto: *Papers on Psycho-analysis*, chap. iii. p. 49:—

"Few people can avoid feeling a twinge of resentment when they find that their name has been forgotten, particularly if it is by some one with whom they had hoped or expected it would be remembered. They instinctively realize that if they had made a greater impression on the person's mind he would certainly have remembered them again, for the name is an integral part of the personality. Similarly, few things are more flattering to most people than to find themselves addressed by name by a great personage where they could hardly have anticipated it.

As a disturbing element in these cases there is an intermingling of a criticism which must be omitted, because at the time being it does not correspond to the intention of the speaker.

Or it may be just the reverse; the substituted name, or the adoption of the strange name, signifies an appreciation of the same. The identification which is brought about by the mistake is equivalent to a recognition which for the moment must remain in the background. An experience of this kind from his schooldays is related by Dr. Ferenczi:—

"While in my first year at college I was obliged to recite a poem before the whole class. It was the first experience of the kind in my life, but I was well prepared. As soon as I began my recitation I was dismayed at being disturbed by an outburst of laughter. The professor later explained to me this strange reception. I started by giving the title 'From the Distance,' which was correct, but instead of giving the name of the real author, I mentioned—my own. The name of the poet is Alexander Petöfi. The identity of the first name with my own favoured the interchange of names, but the real reason was surely the fact that I identified myself at that time with

---

Napoleon, like most leaders of men, was a master of this art. In the midst of the disastrous campaign of France in 1814, he gave an amazing proof of his memory in this direction. When in a town near Craonne, he recollected that he had met the mayor, De Bussy, over twenty years ago in the La Fère Regiment. The delighted De Bussy at once threw himself into his service with extraordinary zeal. Conversely, there is no surer way of affronting some one than by pretending to forget his name; the insinuation is thus conveyed that the person is so unimportant in our eyes that we cannot be bothered to remember his name. This device is often exploited in literature. In Turgenev's *Smoke* (p. 255) the following passage occurs: " 'So you still find Baden entertaining, M'sieur—Litvinov.' Ratmirov always uttered Litvinov's surname with hesitation, every time, as though he had forgotten it, and could not at once recall it. In this way, as well as by the lofty flourish of his hat in saluting him, he meant to insult his pride." The same author, in his *Fathers and Children* (p. 107), writes: "The Governor invited Kirsanov and Bazarov to his ball, and within a few minutes invited them a second time, regarding them as brothers, and calling them Kisarov." Here the forgetting that he had spoken to them, the mistake in the names, and the inability to distinguish between the two young men, constitute a culmination of disparagement. Falsification of a name has the same signification as forgetting it; it is only a step towards complete amnesia."

the celebrated poet-hero. Even consciously I entertained for him a love and respect which verged on adoration. The whole ambition-complex hides itself under this faulty action."

A similar identification was reported to me concerning a young physician who timidly and reverently introduced himself to the celebrated Virchow with the following words: "I am Dr. Virchow." The surprised professor turned to him and asked, "Is your name also Virchow?" I do not know how the ambitious young man justified his speech-blunder, whether he thought of the charming excuse that he imagined himself so insignificant next to this big man that his own name slipped from him, or whether he had the courage to admit that he hoped that he, too, would some day be as great a man as Virchow, and that the professor should therefore not treat him in too disparaging a manner. One or both of these thoughts may have put this young man in an embarrassing position during the introduction.

Owing to very personal motives I must leave it undecided whether a similar interpretation may also apply in the case to be cited. At the International Congress in Amsterdam, in 1907, my theories of hysteria were the subject of a lively discussion. One of my most violent opponents, in his diatribe against me, repeatedly made mistakes in speech in such a manner that he put himself in my place and spoke in my name. He said, for example, "Breuer and I, as is well known, have demonstrated," etc., when he wished to say "Breuer and Freud." The name of this opponent does not show the slightest sound similarity to my own. From this example, as well as from other cases of interchanging names in speech-blunders, we are reminded of the fact that the speech-blunder can fully forego the facility afforded to it through similar sounds, and can achieve its purpose if only supported in content by concealed relations.

In other and more significant cases it is a self-criticism, an internal contradiction against one's own utterance, which causes the speech-blunder, and even forces a contrasting substitution for the one intended. We then observe with surprise how the wording of an assertion removes the purpose of the same, and how the error in speech lays bare the inner dishonesty. Here the *lapsus linguæ* becomes a mimicking form of expression, often, indeed, for the expression of what one does not wish to say. It is thus a means of self-betrayal.

Brill relates: "I had recently been consulted by a woman who showed many paranoid trends, and as she had no relatives who could co-operate with me, I urged her to enter a State hospital as a voluntary patient. She was quite willing to do so, but on the following day she told me that her friends with whom she leased an apartment objected to her going to a hospital, as it would interfere with their plans, and so on. I lost patience and said: 'There is no use listening to your friends who know nothing about your mental condition; you are quite *incompetent* to take care of your own affairs.' I meant to say 'competent.' Here the *lapsus linguæ* expressed my true opinion."

Favoured by chance the speech material often gives origin to examples of speech-blunders which serve to bring about an overwhelming revelation or a full comic effect, as shown by the following examples reported by Brill:—

"A wealthy but not very generous host invited his friends for an evening dance. Everything went well until about 11.30 p.m., when there was an intermission, presumably for supper. To the great disappointment of most of the guests there was no supper; instead, they were regaled with thin sandwiches and lemonade. As it was close to Election day the conversation centred on the different candidates; and as the discussion grew warmer, one of the guests, an ardent admirer of the Progressive Party candidate, remarked to the host: 'You may say what you please about Teddy, but there is one thing —he can always be relied upon; he always gives you a *square meal*,' wishing to say *square deal*. The assembled guests burst into a roar of laughter, to the great embarrassment of the speaker and the host, who fully understood each other."

"While writing a prescription for a woman who was especially weighed down by the financial burden of the treatment, I was interested to hear her say suddenly: 'Please do not give me *big bills*, because I cannot swallow them.' Of course she meant to say *pills*."

The following example illustrates a rather serious case of self-betrayal through a mistake in talking. Some accessory details justify full reproduction as first printed by Dr. A. A. Brill.[9]

"While walking one night with Dr. Frink we accidentally met a colleague, Dr. P., whom I had not seen for years, and of whose private life I knew nothing. We were naturally very pleased to meet again, and on my invitation he accompanied us to a café, where we spent about two hours in pleasant conversation. To my question as to whether he was married he gave a negative answer, and added, 'Why should a man like me marry?'

"On leaving the café, he suddenly turned to me and said: 'I should like to know what you would do in a case like this: I know a nurse who was named as co-respondent in a divorce case. The wife sued the husband for divorce and named her as co-respondent, and *he* got the divorce.' I interrupted him, saying, 'You mean *she* got the divorce.' He immediately corrected himself, saying, 'Yes, she got the divorce,' and continued to tell how the excitement of the trial had affected this nurse to such an extent that she became nervous and took to drink. He wanted me to advise him how to treat her.

"As soon as I had corrected his mistake I asked him to explain it, but, as is usually the case, he was surprised at my question. He wanted to know whether a person had no right to make mistakes in talking. I explained to him that there is a reason for every mistake, and that if he had not told me that he was unmarried, I would say that he was the hero of the divorce case in question, and that the mistake showed that he wished he had obtained the divorce instead of his wife, so as not to be obliged to pay alimony and to be permitted to marry again in New York State.

"He stoutly denied my interpretation, but his emotional agitation, followed by loud laughter, only strengthened my suspicions. To my appeal that he should tell the truth 'for science' sake,' he said, 'Unless you wish me to lie you must believe that I was never married, and hence your psychoanalytic interpretation is all wrong.' He, however, added that it was dangerous to be with a person who paid attention to such lit-

[9] *Zentralb. f. Psychoanalyse,* ii., Jahrg. 1. Cf. also Brill's *Psychoanalysis: Its Theories and Practical Application,* p. 202. Saunders, Philadelphia and London.

tle things. Then he suddenly remembered that he had another appointment and left us.

"Both Dr. Frink and I were convinced that my interpretation of his *lapsus linguæ* was correct, and I decided to corroborate or disprove it by further investigation. The next day I found a neighbour and old friend of Dr. P., who confirmed my interpretation in every particular. The divorce was granted to Dr. P.'s wife a few weeks before, and a nurse was named as co-respondent. A few weeks later I met Dr. P., and he told me that he was thoroughly convinced of the Freudian mechanisms."

The self-betrayal is just as plain in the following case reported by Otto Rank:—

A father who was devoid of all patriotic feeling and desirous of educating his children to be just as free from this superfluous sentiment, reproached his sons for participating in a patriotic demonstration, and rejected their reference to a similar behaviour of their uncle with these words: "You are not obliged to imitate him; why, he is an *idiot*." The astonished features of the children at their father's unusual tone aroused him to the fact that he had made a mistake, and he remarked apologetically, "Of course, I wished to say *patriot*."

When such a speech-blunder occurs in a serious squabble and reverses the intended meaning of one of the disputants, at once it puts him at a disadvantage with his adversary—a disadvantage which the latter seldom fails to utilize.

This clearly shows that although people are unwilling to accept the theory of my conception and are not inclined to forego the convenience that is connected with the tolerance of a faulty action, they nevertheless interpret speech-blunders and other faulty acts in a manner similar to the one presented in this book. The merriment and derision which are sure to be evoked at the decisive moment through such linguistic mistakes speak conclusively against the generally accepted convention that such a speech-blunder is a *lapsus linguæ* and psychologically of no importance. It was no less a man than the German Chancellor, Prince Bülow, who endeavoured to save the situation through such a protest when the wording of his defence of his Emperor (November, 1907) turned into the opposite through a speech-blunder.

"Concerning the present, the new epoch of Emperor Wilhelm II, I can only repeat what I said a year ago, that *it would be unfair and unjust to speak of a coterie of responsible advisers around our Emperor* (loud calls, 'Irresponsible!')—to speak of *irresponsible* advisers. Pardon the *lapsus linguæ*" (hilarity).

A nice example of speech-blunder, which aims not so much at the betrayal of the speaker as at the enlightenment of the listener outside the scene, is found in Wallenstein (*Piccolomini*, Act I, Scene 5), and shows us that the poet who here uses this means is well versed in the mechanism and intent of speech-blunders. In the preceding scene Max Piccolomini was passionately in favour of the ducal party, and was enthusiastic over the blessings of the peace which became known to him in the course of a journey while accompanying Wallenstein's daughter to the encampment. He leaves his father and the Court ambassador, Questenberg, in great consternation. The scene proceeds as follows:—

QUESTENBERG. Woe unto us! Are matters thus? Friend, should we allow him to go there with this false opinion, and not recall him at once in order to open his eyes instantly.

OCTAVIO (*rousing himself from profound meditation*). He has already opened mine, and I see more than pleases me.

QUESTENBERG. What is it, friend?

OCTAVIO. A curse on that journey!

QUESTENBERG. Why? What is it?

OCTAVIO. Come! I must immediately follow the unlucky trail, must see with my own eyes—come—— (*Wishes to lead him away.*)

QUESTENBERG. What is the matter? Where?

OCTAVIO (*urging*). To *her!*

QUESTENBERG. To——?

OCTAVIO (*corrects himself*). To the duke! Let us go, etc.

The slight speech-blunder *to her* in place of *to him* is meant to betray to us the fact that the father has seen through his son's motive for espousing the other cause, while the courtier complains that "he speaks to him altogether in riddles."

Another example wherein a poet makes use of a speech-blunder was discovered by Otto Rank in Shakespeare. I quote Rank's report from the *Zentralblatt für Psychoanalyse*, I. 3.

"A poetic speech-blunder, very delicately motivated and technically remarkably well utilized, which, like the one pointed out by Freud in Wallenstein (*Zur Psychopathologie des Alltagslebens*, 2nd Edition, p. 48), not only shows that poets knew the mechanism and sense of this error, but also presupposes an understanding of it on the part of the hearer, can be found in Shakespeare's *Merchant of Venice* (Act III, Scene 2). By the will of her father, Portia was bound to select a husband through a lottery. She escaped all her distasteful suitors by lucky chance. When she finally found in Bassanio the suitor after her own heart, she had cause to fear lest he, too, should draw the unlucky lottery. In the scene she would like to tell him that even if he chose the wrong casket, he might, nevertheless, be sure of her love. But she is hampered by her vow. In this mental conflict the poet puts these words in her mouth, which were directed to the welcome suitor:—

> "There is something tells me (but it is not love),
> I would not lose you; and you know yourself
> Hate counsels not in such a quality.
> But lest you should not understand me well
> (And yet a maiden hath no tongue but thought),
> I would detain you here some month or two,
> Before you venture for me. I could teach you
> How to choose right, but then I am forsworn;
> So will I never be; so may you miss me;
> But if you do, you'll make me wish a sin,
> That I had been forsworn. Beshrew your eyes,
> They have o'erlooked me, and divided me:
> *One half of me is yours, the other half yours—*
> *Mine own, I would say;* but if mine, then yours—
> And so all yours."

"Just the very thing which she would like to hint to him gently, because really she should keep it from him, namely, that even before the choice she is wholly his—that she loves him, the poet, with admirable psychologic sensitiveness, allows to come to the surface in the speech-blunder. It is through this artifice that he manages to allay the intolerable uncertainty of the lover as well as the like tension of the hearer concerning the outcome of the choice."

The interest merited by the confirmation of our conception of speech-blunders through the great poets justifies the citation of a third example which was reported by Dr. E. Jones.[10]

"Our great novelist, George Meredith, in his masterpiece, *The Egoist,* shows an even finer understanding of the mechanism. The plot of the novel is, shortly, as follows: Sir Willoughby Patterne, an aristocrat greatly admired by his circle, becomes engaged to a Miss Constantia Durham. She discovers in him an intense egoism, which he skilfully conceals from the world, and to escape the marriage she elopes with a Captain Oxford. Some years later Patterne becomes engaged to a Miss Clara Middleton, and most of the book is taken up with a detailed description of the conflict that arises in her mind on also discovering his egoism. External circumstances and her conception of honour hold her to her pledge, while he becomes more and more distasteful in her eyes. She partly confided in his cousin and secretary, Vernon Whitford, the man whom she ultimately marries, but from a mixture of motives he stands aloof.

"In the soliloquy Clara speaks as follows: 'If some noble gentleman could see me as I am and not disdain to aid me! Oh! to be caught out of this prison of thorns and brambles. I cannot tear my own way out. I am a coward. A beckoning of a finger would change me, I believe. I could fly bleeding and through hootings to a comrade. . . . Constantia met a soldier. Perhaps she prayed and her prayer was answered. She did ill. But, oh, how I love her for it! His name was Harry Oxford. . . . She did not waver, she cut the links, she signed herself over. Oh, brave girl, what do you think of me? But I have no Harry Whitford; I am alone. . . .' The sudden consciousness that she had put another name for Oxford struck her a buffet, drowning her in crimson.

"The fact that both men's names end in 'ford' evidently renders the confounding of them more easy, and would by many be regarded as an adequate cause for this, but the real underlying motive for it is plainly indicated by the author. In another passage the same *lapsus* occurs, and is followed by the hesitation and change of subject that one is familiar with

[10] Jones, *Papers on Psycho-analysis,* p. 60.

in psychoanalysis when a half-conscious complex is touched. Sir Willoughby patronizingly says of Whitford: 'False alarm. The resolution to do anything unaccustomed is quite beyond poor old Vernon.' Clara replies: 'But if Mr. Oxford—Whitford . . . your swans, coming sailing up the lake; how beautiful they look when they are indignant! I was going to ask you, surely men witnessing a marked admiration for some one else will naturally be discouraged?' Sir Willoughby stiffened with sudden enlightenment.

"In still another passage Clara, by another *lapsus*, betrays her secret wish that she was on a more intimate footing with Vernon Whitford. Speaking to a boy friend, she says, 'Tell Mr. Vernon—tell Mr. Whitford.'"

The conception of speech-blunders here defended can be readily verified in the smallest details. I have been able to demonstrate repeatedly that the most insignificant and most natural cases of speech-blunders have their good sense, and admit of the same interpretation as the more striking examples. A patient who, contrary to my wishes but with firm personal motives, decided upon a short trip to Budapest, justified herself by saying that she was going for only three days, but she blundered and said for only three weeks. She betrayed her secret feeling that, to spite me, she preferred spending three weeks to three days in that society which I considered unfit for her.

One evening, wishing to excuse myself for not having called for my wife at the theatre, I said: "I was at the theatre at ten minutes after ten." I was corrected: "You meant to say before ten o'clock." Naturally I wanted to say before ten. After ten would certainly be no excuse. I had been told that the theatre programme read, "Finished before ten o'clock." When I arrived at the theatre I found the foyer dark and the theatre empty. Evidently the performance was over earlier and my wife did not wait for me. When I looked at the clock it still wanted five minutes to ten. I determined to make my case more favourable at home, and say that it was ten minutes to ten. Unfortunately, the speech-blunder spoiled the intent and laid bare my dishonesty, in which I acknowledged more than there really was to confess.

This leads us to those speech disturbances which can no

longer be described as speech-blunders, for they do not injure the individual word, but affect the rhythm and execution of the entire speech, as, for example, the stammering and stuttering of embarrassment. But here, as in the former cases, it is the inner conflict that is betrayed to us through the disturbance in speech. I really do not believe that any one will make mistakes in talking in an audience with His Majesty, in a serious love declaration, or in defending one's name and honour before a jury; in short, people make no mistakes where *they are all there,* as the saying goes. Even in criticizing an author's style we are allowed and accustomed to follow the principle of explanation, which we cannot miss in the origin of a single speech-blunder. A clear and unequivocal manner of writing shows us that here the author is in harmony with himself, but where we find a forced and involved expression, aiming at more than one target, as appropriately expressed, we can thereby recognize the participation of an unfinished and complicated thought, or we can hear through it the stifled voice of the author's self-criticism.[11]

[11] "Ce qu'on conçoit bien
S'énonce clairement,
Et les mots pour le dire
Arrivent aisément."

Boileau, *Art Poétique.*

FERDINAND DE SAUSSURE

Ferdinand de Saussure (1857–1913) is generally credited with laying the foundations for much of modern linguistics. He studied at Leipzig and taught first in Paris and then at the University of Geneva. He developed a conception of language as a self-contained system which could be viewed functionally and structurally. His *Course in General Linguistics,* first published in 1916, is based primarily on the notes of his students from three courses in general linguistics which he gave at the University of Geneva between 1906 and 1911. The texts reprinted below set forth Saussure's seminal thoughts on the distinction between speech and language, signified and signifier, synchrony and diachrony, and briefly present the notion of semiology—all of which are taken up and developed by a great many thinkers in a variety of ways and in a number of different disciplines.

4

Course in General Linguistics

THE OBJECT OF LINGUISTICS

1. *Definition of Language*

What is both the integral and concrete object of linguistics?
The question is especially difficult; later we shall see why; here
I wish merely to point up the difficulty.

Other sciences work with objects that are given in advance
and that can then be considered from different viewpoints;
but not linguistics. Someone pronounces the French word *nu*
'bare': a superficial observer would be tempted to call the
word a concrete linguistic object; but a more careful examination would reveal successively three or four quite different
things, depending on whether the word is considered as a
sound, as the expression of an idea, as the equivalent of Latin
nudum, etc. Far from it being the object that antedates the
viewpoint, it would seem that it is the viewpoint that creates
the object; besides, nothing tells us in advance that one way
of considering the fact in question takes precedence over the
others or is in any way superior to them.

Moreover, regardless of the viewpoint that we adopt, the
linguistic phenomenon always has two related sides, each deriving its values from the other. For example:

1) Articulated syllables are acoustical impressions perceived by the ear, but the sounds would not exist without the

Reprinted here are pp. 7-17, 65-70, and 91-95 from *Course in General Linguistics*, by Ferdinand de Saussure, edited by Charles Bally and
Albert Sechehaye, in collaboration with Albert Riedlinger, translated
from the French by Wade Baskin, New York: Philosophical Library,
1959. Reprinted by permission of the publisher. Ellipses indicate cross
references to pages not included in this volume. [Ed.]

vocal organs; an *n,* for example, exists only by virtue of the relation between the two sides. We simply cannot reduce language to sound or detach sound from oral articulation; reciprocally, we cannot define the movements of the vocal organs without taking into account the acoustical impression. . . .

2) But suppose that sound were a simple thing: would it constitute speech? No, it is only the instrument of thought; by itself, it has no existence. At this point a new and redoubtable relationship arises: a sound, a complex acoustical-vocal unit, combines in turn with an idea to form a complex physiological-psychological unit. But that is still not the complete picture.

3) Speech has both an individual and a social side, and we cannot conceive of one without the other. Besides:

4) Speech always implies both an established system and an evolution; at every moment it is an existing institution and a product of the past. To distinguish between the system and its history, between what it is and what it was, seems very simple at first glance; actually the two things are so closely related that we can scarcely keep them apart. Would we simplify the question by studying the linguistic phenomenon in its earliest stages—if we began, for example, by studying the speech of children? No, for in dealing with speech, it is completely misleading to assume that the problem of early characteristics differs from the problem of permanent characteristics. We are left inside the vicious circle.

From whatever direction we approach the question, nowhere do we find the integral object of linguistics. Everywhere we are confronted with a dilemma: if we fix our attention on only one side of each problem, we run the risk of failing to perceive the dualities pointed out above; on the other hand, if we study speech from several viewpoints simultaneously, the object of linguistics appears to us as a confused mass of heterogeneous and unrelated things. Either procedure opens the door to several sciences—psychology, anthropology, normative grammar, philology, etc.—which are distinct from linguistics, but which might claim speech, in view of the faulty method of linguistics, as one of their objects.

As I see it there is only one solution to all the foregoing

difficulties: *from the very outset we must put both feet on the ground of language and use language as the norm of all other manifestations of speech.* Actually, among so many dualities, language alone seems to lend itself to independent definition and provide a fulcrum that satisfies the mind.

But what is language [*langue*]? It is not to be confused with human speech [*langage*], of which it is only a definite part, though certainly an essential one. It is both a social product of the faculty of speech and a collection of necessary conventions that have been adopted by a social body to permit individuals to exercise that faculty. Taken as a whole, speech is many-sided and heterogeneous; straddling several areas simultaneously—physical, physiological, and psychological—it belongs both to the individual and to society; we cannot put it into any category of human facts, for we cannot discover its unity.

Language, on the contrary, is a self-contained whole and a principle of classification. As soon as we give language first place among the facts of speech, we introduce a natural order into a mass that lends itself to no other classification.

One might object to that principle of classification on the ground that since the use of speech is based on a natural faculty whereas language is something acquired and conventional, language should not take first place but should be subordinated to the natural instinct.

That objection is easily refuted.

First, no one has proved that speech, as it manifests itself when we speak, is entirely natural, i.e. that our vocal apparatus was designed for speaking just as our legs were designed for walking. Linguists are far from agreement on this point. For instance Whitney, to whom language is one of several social institutions, thinks that we use the vocal apparatus as the instrument of language purely through luck, for the sake of convenience: men might just as well have chosen gestures and used visual symbols instead of acoustical symbols. Doubtless his thesis is too dogmatic; language is not similar in all respects to other social institutions . . . ; moreover, Whitney goes too far in saying that our choice happened to fall on the vocal organs; the choice was more or less imposed by nature. But on the essential point the American linguist is right: language is a convention, and the nature of the sign that is agreed upon does not matter. The question of the vocal apparatus obviously takes a secondary place in the problem of speech.

One definition of *articulated speech* might confirm that conclusion. In Latin, *articulus* means a member, part, or subdivision of a sequence; applied to speech, articulation designates either the subdivision of a spoken chain into syllables or the subdivision of the chain of meanings into significant units; *gegliederte Sprache* is used in the second sense in German. Using the second definition, we can say that what is natural to mankind is not oral speech but the faculty of constructing a language, i.e. a system of distinct signs corresponding to distinct ideas.

Broca discovered that the faculty of speech is localized in the third left frontal convolution; his discovery has been used to substantiate the attribution of a natural quality to speech. But we know that the same part of the brain is the center of *everything* that has to do with speech, including writing. The preceding statements, together with observations that have been made in different cases of aphasia resulting from lesion of the centers of localization, seem to indicate: (1) that the various disorders of oral speech are bound up in a hundred ways with those of written speech; and (2) that what is lost in all cases of aphasia or agraphia is less the faculty of producing a given sound or writing a given sign than the ability to evoke by means of an instrument, regardless of what it is, the signs of a regular system of speech. The obvious implication is that beyond the functioning of the various organs there exists a more general faculty which governs signs and which would be the linguistic faculty proper. And this brings us to the same conclusion as above.

To give language first place in the study of speech, we can advance a final argument: the faculty of articulating words —whether it is natural or not—is exercised only with the help of the instrument created by a collectivity and provided for its use; therefore, to say that language gives unity to speech is not fanciful.

2. *Place of Language in the Facts of Speech*

In order to separate from the whole of speech the part that

belongs to language, we must examine the individual act from which the speaking-circuit can be reconstructed. The act requires the presence of at least two persons; that is the minimum number necessary to complete the circuit. Suppose that two people, A and B, are conversing with each other:

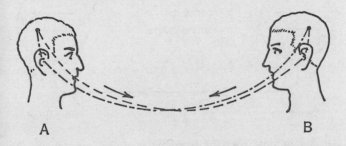

A   B

Suppose that the opening of the circuit is in A's brain, where mental facts (concepts) are associated with representations of the linguistic sounds (sound-images) that are used for their expression. A given concept unlocks a corresponding sound-image in the brain; this purely *psychological* phenomenon is followed in turn by a *physiological* process: the brain transmits an impulse corresponding to the image to the organs used in producing sounds. Then the sound waves travel from the mouth of A to the ear of B: a purely *physical* process. Next, the circuit continues in B, but the order is reversed: from the ear to the brain, the physiological transmission of the sound-image; in the brain, the psychological association of the image with the corresponding concept. If B then speaks, the new act will follow—from his brain to A's—exactly the same course as the first act and pass through the same successive phases, which I shall diagram below.

The following analysis does not purport to be complete. We might also single out the pure acoustical sensation, the identification of that sensation with the latent sound-image, the muscular image of phonation, etc. I have included only the elements thought to be essential, but the drawing brings out at a glance the distinction between the physical (sound waves), physiological (phonation and audition), and psychological parts (word-images and concepts). Indeed, we should

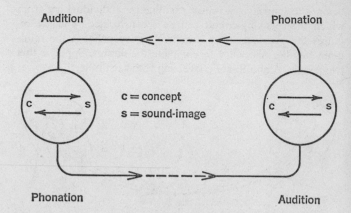

not fail to note that the word-image stands apart from the sound itself and that it is just as psychological as the concept which is associated with it.

The circuit that I have outlined can be further divided into:

a) an outer part that includes the vibrations of the sounds which travel from the mouth to the ear, and an inner part that includes everything else;

b) a psychological and a nonpsychological part, the second including the physiological productions of the vocal organs as well as the physical facts that are outside the individual;

c) an active and a passive part: everything that goes from the associative center of the speaker to the ear of the listener is active, and everything that goes from the ear of the listener to his associative center is passive;

d) finally, everything that is active in the psychological part of the circuit is executive ($c \rightarrow s$), and everything that is passive is receptive ($s \rightarrow c$).

We should also add the associative and co-ordinating faculty that we find as soon as we leave isolated signs; this faculty plays the dominant role in the organization of language as a system. . . .

But to understand clearly the role of the associative and co-ordinating faculty, we must leave the individual act, which is only the embryo of speech, and approach the social fact.

Among all the individuals that are linked together by speech, some sort of average will be set up: all will reproduce—not exactly of course, but approximately—the same signs united with the same concepts.

How does the social crystallization of language come about? Which parts of the circuit are involved? For all parts probably do not participate equally in it.

The nonpsychological part can be rejected from the outset. When we hear people speaking a language that we do not know, we perceive the sounds but remain outside the social fact because we do not understand them.

Neither is the psychological part of the circuit wholly responsible: the executive side is missing, for execution is never carried out by the collectivity. Execution is always individual, and the individual is always its master: I shall call the executive side *speaking* [*parole*].

Through the functioning of the receptive and co-ordinating faculties, impressions that are perceptibly the same for all are made on the minds of speakers. How can that social product be pictured in such a way that language will stand apart from everything else? If we could embrace the sum of word-images stored in the minds of all individuals, we could identify the social bond that constitutes language. It is a storehouse filled by the members of a given community through their active use of speaking, a grammatical system that has a potential existence in each brain, or, more specifically, in the brains of a group of individuals. For language is not complete in any speaker; it exists perfectly only within a collectivity.

In separating language from speaking we are at the same time separating: (1) what is social from what is individual; and (2) what is essential from what is accessory and more or less accidental.

Language is not a function of the speaker; it is a product that is passively assimilated by the individual. It never requires premeditation, and reflection enters in only for the purpose of classification, which we shall take up later. . . .

Speaking, on the contrary, is an individual act. It is wilful and intellectual. Within the act, we should distinguish between: (1) the combinations by which the speaker uses the language code for expressing his own thought; and (2) the psychophysical mechanism that allows him to exteriorize those combinations.

Note that I have defined things rather than words; these definitions are not endangered by certain ambiguous words that do not have identical meanings in different languages. For instance, German *Sprache* means both "language" and "speech"; *Rede* almost corresponds to "speaking" but adds the special connotation of "discourse." Latin *sermo* designates both "speech" and "speaking," while *lingua* means "language," etc. No word corresponds exactly to any of the notions specified above; that is why all definitions of words are made in vain; starting from words in defining things is a bad procedure.

To summarize, these are the characteristics of language:

1) Language is a well-defined object in the heterogeneous mass of speech facts. It can be localized in the limited segment of the speaking-circuit where an auditory image becomes associated with a concept. It is the social side of speech, outside the individual who can never create nor modify it by himself; it exists only by virtue of a sort of contract signed by the members of a community. Moreover, the individual must always serve an apprenticeship in order to learn the functioning of language; a child assimilates it only gradually. It is such a distinct thing that a man deprived of the use of speaking retains it provided that he understands the vocal signs that he hears.

2) Language, unlike speaking, is something that we can study separately. Although dead languages are no longer spoken, we can easily assimilate their linguistic organisms. We can dispense with the other elements of speech; indeed, the science of language is possible only if the other elements are excluded.

3) Whereas speech is heterogeneous, language, as defined, is homogeneous. It is a system of signs in which the only essential thing is the union of meanings and sound-images, and in which both parts of the sign are psychological.

4) Language is concrete, no less so than speaking; and this is a help in our study of it. Linguistic signs, though basically psychological, are not abstractions; associations which bear

the stamp of collective approval—and which added together constitute language—are realities that have their seat in the brain. Besides, linguistic signs are tangible; it is possible to reduce them to conventional written symbols, whereas it would be impossible to provide detailed photographs of acts of speaking [*actes de parole*]; the pronunciation of even the smallest word represents an infinite number of muscular movements that could be identified and put into graphic form only with great difficulty. In language, on the contrary, there is only the sound-image, and the latter can be translated into a fixed visual image. For if we disregard the vast number of movements necessary for the realization of sound-images in speaking, we see that each sound-image is nothing more than the sum of a limited number of elements or phonemes that can in turn be called up by a corresponding number of written symbols. . . . The very possibility of putting the things that relate to language into graphic form allows dictionaries and grammars to represent it accurately, for language is a storehouse of sound-images, and writing is the tangible form of those images.

3. *Place of Language in Human Facts: Semiology*

The foregoing characteristics of language reveal an even more important characteristic. Language, once its boundaries have been marked off within the speech data, can be classified among human phenomena, whereas speech cannot.

We have just seen that language is a social institution; but several features set it apart from other political, legal, etc. institutions. We must call in a new type of facts in order to illuminate the special nature of language.

Language is a system of signs that express ideas, and is therefore comparable to a system of writing, the alphabet of deaf-mutes, symbolic rites, polite formulas, military signals, etc. But it is the most important of all these systems.

A science that studies the life of signs within society is conceivable; it would be a part of social psychology and consequently of general psychology; I shall call it *semiology*[1] (from

---

[1] *Semiology* should not be confused with *semantics,* which studies changes in meaning, and which Saussure did not treat methodically. . . . [Ed.]

Greek *sēmeîon* 'sign'). Semiology would show what constitutes signs, what laws govern them. Since the science does not yet exist, no one can say what it would be; but it has a right to existence, a place staked out in advance. Linguistics is only a part of the general science of semiology; the laws discovered by semiology will be applicable to linguistics, and the latter will circumscribe a well-defined area within the mass of anthropological facts.

To determine the exact place of semiology is the task of the psychologist.[2] The task of the linguist is to find out what makes language a special system within the mass of semiological data. This issue will be taken up again later; here I wish merely to call attention to one thing: if I have succeeded in assigning linguistics a place among the sciences, it is because I have related it to semiology.

Why has semiology not yet been recognized as an independent science with its own object like all the other sciences? Linguists have been going around in circles: language, better than anything else, offers a basis for understanding the semiological problem; but language must, to put it correctly, be studied in itself; heretofore language has almost always been studied in connection with something else, from other viewpoints.

There is first of all the superficial notion of the general public: people see nothing more than a name-giving system in language (see p. 69), thereby prohibiting any research into its true nature.

Then there is the viewpoint of the psychologist, who studies the sign-mechanism in the individual; this is the easiest method, but it does not lead beyond individual execution and does not reach the sign, which is social.

Or even when signs are studied from a social viewpoint, only the traits that attach language to the other social institutions —those that are more or less voluntary—are emphasized; as a result, the goal is by-passed and the specific characteristics

---

[2] Cf. A. Naville, *Classification des Sciences*, (2nd. ed.), p. 104. [Ed.] The scope of semiology (or semiotics) is treated at length in Charles Morris' *Signs, Language and Behavior* (New York: Prentice-Hall, 1946). [Tr.]

of semiological systems in general and of language in particular are completely ignored. For the distinguishing characteristic of the sign—but the one that is least apparent at first sight —is that in some way it always eludes the individual or social will.

In short, the characteristic that distinguishes semiological systems from all other institutions shows up clearly only in language where it manifests itself in the things which are studied least, and the necessity or specific value of a semiological science is therefore not clearly recognized. But to me the language problem is mainly semiological, and all developments derive their significance from that important fact. If we are to discover the true nature of language we must learn what it has in common with all other semiological systems; linguistic forces that seem very important at first glance (e.g., the role of the vocal apparatus) will receive only secondary consideration if they serve only to set language apart from the other systems. This procedure will do more than to clarify the linguistic problem. By studying rites, customs, etc. as signs, I believe that we shall throw new light on the facts and point up the need for including them in a science of semiology and explaining them by its laws.

NATURE OF THE LINGUISTIC SIGN

1. *Sign, Signified, Signifier*

Some people regard language, when reduced to its elements, as a naming-process only—a list of words, each corresponding to the thing that it names. For example:

This conception is open to criticism at several points. It assumes that ready-made ideas exist before words . . . ; it does not tell us whether a name is vocal or psychological in nature (*arbor*, for instance, can be considered from either viewpoint); finally, it lets us assume that the linking of a name and a thing is a very simple operation—an assumption that is anything but true. But this rather naive approach can bring us near the truth by showing us that the linguistic unit is a double entity, one formed by the associating of two terms.

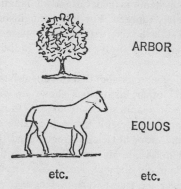

ARBOR

EQUOS

etc.   etc.

We have seen in considering the speaking-circuit (p. 63) that both terms involved in the linguistic sign are psychological and are united in the brain by an associative bond. This point must be emphasized.

The linguistic sign unites, not a thing and a name, but a concept and a sound-image.[3] The latter is not the material sound, a purely physical thing, but the psychological imprint of the sound, the impression that it makes on our senses. The sound-image is sensory, and if I happen to call it "material," it is only in that sense, and by way of opposing it to the other term of the association, the concept, which is generally more abstract.

The psychological character of our sound-images becomes apparent when we observe our own speech. Without moving our lips or tongue, we can talk to ourselves or recite mentally a selection of verse. Because we regard the words of our language as sound-images, we must avoid speaking of the "phonemes" that make up the words. This term, which sug-

---

[3] The term sound-image may seem to be too restricted inasmuch as beside the representation of the sounds of a word there is also that of its articulation, the muscular image of the phonational act. But for F. de Saussure language is essentially a depository, a thing received from without (see p. 65). The sound-image is par excellence the natural representation of the word as a fact of potential language, outside any actual use of it in speaking. The motor side is thus implied or, in any event, occupies only a subordinate role with respect to the sound-image. [Ed.]

gests vocal activity, is applicable to the spoken word only, to the realization of the inner image in discourse. We can avoid that misunderstanding by speaking of the *sounds* and *syllables* of a word provided we remember that the names refer to the sound-image.

The linguistic sign is then a two-sided psychological entity that can be represented by the drawing:

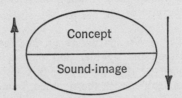

The two elements are intimately united, and each recalls the other. Whether we try to find the meaning of the Latin word *arbor* or the word that Latin uses to designate the concept "tree," it is clear that only the associations sanctioned by that language appear to us to conform to reality, and we disregard whatever others might be imagined.

Our definition of the linguistic sign poses an important question of terminology. I call the combination of a concept and a sound-image a *sign,* but in current usage the term generally designates only a sound-image, a word, for example (*arbor,* etc.). One tends to forget that *arbor* is called a sign only because it carries the concept "tree," with the result that the idea of the sensory part implies the idea of the whole.

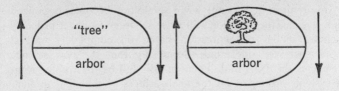

Ambiguity would disappear if the three notions involved here were designated by three names, each suggesting and opposing the others. I propose to retain the word *sign* [*signe*] to designate the whole and to replace *concept* and *sound-*

image respectively by *signified* [*signifié*] and *signifier* [*signif-iant*]; the last two terms have the advantage of indicating the opposition that separates them from each other and from the whole of which they are parts. As regards *sign,* if I am satisfied with it, this is simply because I do not know of any word to replace it, the ordinary language suggesting no other.

The linguistic sign, as defined, has two primordial characteristics. In enunciating them I am also positing the basic principles of any study of this type.

2. *Principle I: The Arbitrary Nature of the Sign*

The bond between the signifier and the signified is arbitrary. Since I mean by sign the whole that results from the associating of the signifier with the signified, I can simply say: *the linguistic sign is arbitrary.*

The idea of "sister" is not linked by any inner relationship to the succession of sounds *s-ö-r* which serves as its signifier in French; that it could be represented equally by just any other sequence is proved by differences among languages and by the very existence of different languages: the signified "ox" has as its signifier *b-ö-f* on one side of the border and *o-k-s* (*Ochs*) on the other.

No one disputes the principle of the arbitrary nature of the sign, but it is often easier to discover a truth than to assign to it its proper place. Principle I dominates all the linguistics of language; its consequences are numberless. It is true that not all of them are equally obvious at first glance; only after many detours does one discover them, and with them the primordial importance of the principle.

One remark in passing: when semiology becomes organized as a science, the question will arise whether or not it properly includes modes of expression based on completely natural signs, such as pantomime. Supposing that the new science welcomes them, its main concern will still be the whole group of systems grounded on the arbitrariness of the sign. In fact, every means of expression used in society is based, in principle, on collective behavior or—what amounts to the same thing—on convention. Polite formulas, for instance, though often imbued with a certain natural expressiveness (as in the case of a Chinese who greets his emperor by bowing down to the ground nine times), are nonetheless fixed by rule; it is this rule and not the intrinsic value of the gestures that obliges one to use them. Signs that are wholly arbitrary realize better than the others the ideal of the semiological process; that is why language, the most complex and universal of all systems of expression, is also the most characteristic; in this sense linguistics can become the master-pattern for all branches of semiology although language is only one particular semiological system.

The word *symbol* has been used to designate the linguistic sign, or more specifically, what is here called the signifier. Principle I in particular weighs against the use of this term. One characteristic of the symbol is that it is never wholly arbitrary; it is not empty, for there is the rudiment of a natural bond between the signifier and the signified. The symbol of justice, a pair of scales, could not be replaced by just any other symbol, such as a chariot.

The word *arbitrary* also calls for comment. The term should not imply that the choice of the signifier is left entirely to the speaker (we shall see below that the individual does not have the power to change a sign in any way once it has become established in the linguistic community); I mean that it is unmotivated, i.e. arbitrary in that it actually has no natural connection with the signified.

In concluding let us consider two objections that might be raised to the establishment of Principle I:

1) *Onomatopoeia* might be used to prove that the choice of the signifier is not always arbitrary. But onomatopoeic formations are never organic elements of a linguistic system. Besides, their number is much smaller than is generally supposed. Words like French *fouet* 'whip' or *glas* 'knell' may strike certain ears with suggestive sonority, but to see that they have not always had this property we need only examine their Latin forms (*fouet* is derived from *fāgus* 'beech-tree,' *glas* from *classicum* 'sound of a trumpet'). The quality of their present sounds, or rather the quality that is attributed to them, is a fortuitous result of phonetic evolution.

As for authentic onomatopoeic words (e.g. *glug-glug, tick-tock,* etc.), not only are they limited in number, but also they are chosen somewhat arbitrarily, for they are only approximate and more or less conventional imitations of certain sounds (cf. English *bow-wow* and French *ouaoua*). In addition, once these words have been introduced into the language, they are to a certain extent subjected to the same evolution—phonetic, morphological, etc.—that other words undergo (cf. *pigeon,* ultimately from Vulgar Latin *pīpiō,* derived in turn from an onomatopoeic formation): obvious proof that they lose something of their original character in order to assume that of the linguistic sign in general, which is unmotivated.

2) *Interjections,* closely related to onomatopoeia, can be attacked on the same grounds and come no closer to refuting our thesis. One is tempted to see in them spontaneous expressions of reality dictated, so to speak, by natural forces. But for most interjections we can show that there is no fixed bond between their signified and their signifier. We need only compare two languages on this point to see how much such expressions differ from one language to the next (e.g. the English equivalent of French *aïe!* is *ouch!*). We know, moreover, that many interjections were once words with specific meanings (cf. French *diable!* 'darn!' *mordieu!* 'golly!' from *mort Dieu* 'God's death,' etc.).[4]

Onomatopoeic formations and interjections are of secondary importance, and their symbolic origin is in part open to dispute.

3. *Principle II: The Linear Nature of the Signifier*

The signifier, being auditory, is unfolded solely in time from which it gets the following characteristics: (a) it represents a span, and (b) the span is measurable in a single dimension; it is a line.

While Principle II is obvious, apparently linguists have always neglected to state it, doubtless because they found it too simple; nevertheless, it is fundamental, and its consequences are incalculable. Its importance equals that of Principle I; the whole mechanism of language depends upon it. . . . In contrast to visual signifiers (nautical signals, etc.) which can offer simultaneous groupings in several dimen-

[4] Cf. English *goodness!* and *zounds!* (from *God's wounds*). [Tr.]

sions, auditory signifiers have at their command only the dimension of time. Their elements are presented in succession; they form a chain. This feature becomes readily apparent when they are represented in writing and the spatial line of graphic marks is substituted for succession in time.

Sometimes the linear nature of the signifier is not obvious. When I accent a syllable, for instance, it seems that I am concentrating more than one significant element on the same point. But this is an illusion; the syllable and its accent constitute only one phonational act. There is no duality within the act but only different oppositions to what precedes and what follows. . . .

STATIC AND EVOLUTIONARY LINGUISTICS

• • •

6. *Synchronic and Diachronic Law*

It is a popular practice to speak of laws in linguistics. But are the facts of language actually governed by laws? If so, what are they like? Since language is a social institution, one might assume *a priori* that it is governed by prescriptions analogous to those that control communities. Now every social law has two basic characteristics: it is *imperative* and it is *general;* it comes in by force and it covers all cases—within certain limits of time and place, of course.

Do the laws of language fit this definition? The first step in answering the question—in line with what has just been said— is to separate once more the synchronic and diachronic areas. The two problems must not be confused; speaking of linguistic law in general is like trying to pin down a ghost.

Here are some examples, taken from Greek, in which the two classes are intentionally jumbled:

1. Proto-Indo-European voiced aspirates became voiceless: *dhūmos* → *thūmos* 'breath of life,' *bherō* → *phérō* 'I bear,' etc.

2. The accent never falls farther back than the antepenult.

3. All words end in a vowel or in *s, n,* or *r,* to the exclusion of all other consonants.

4. Prevocalic initial *s* became *h* (sign of aspiration): *septm* (Latin *septem*) → *heptá.*

5. Final *m* changed to *n*: **jugom → zugón* (cf. Latin *jugum*).[5]

6. Final occlusives fell: **gunaik → gúnai,* **epherst → éphere,* **epheront → épheron.*

Law 1 is diachronic: *dh* became *th,* etc. Law 2 expresses a relation between the word-unit and accent, a sort of contract between two coexisting terms; it is a synchronic law. The same is true of Law 3 since it concerns the word-unit and its ending. Laws 4, 5, and 6 are diachronic: *s* became *h; –n* replaced *–m; –t, –k,* etc. disappeared without leaving a trace.

We should also notice that Law 3 is the result of 5 and 6; two diachronic facts created a synchronic fact.

After we separate the two classes of laws, we see that Laws 2 and 3 are basically different from Laws 1, 4, 5, and 6.

The synchronic law is general but not imperative. Doubtless it is imposed on individuals by the weight of collective usage . . . , but here I do not have in mind an obligation on the part of speakers. I mean that *in language* no force guarantees the maintenance of a regularity when established on some point. Being a simple expression of an existing arrangement, the synchronic law reports a state of affairs; it is like a law that states that trees in a certain orchard are arranged in the shape of a quincunx. And the arrangement that the law defines is precarious precisely because it is not imperative. Nothing is more regular than the synchronic law that governs Latin accentuation (a law comparable in every way to Law 2 above); but the accentual rule did not resist the forces of alteration and gave way to a new law, the one of French. . . . In short, if one speaks of law in synchrony, it is in the sense of an arrangement, a principle of regularity.

Diachrony, on the contrary, supposes a dynamic force

[5] According to Meillet (*Mem. de la Soc. de Ling.,* IX, pp. 365 ff.) and Gauthiot (*La fin du mot indo-européen,* pp. 158 ff.), final *–m* did not exist in Proto-Indo-European, which used only *–n;* if this theory is accepted, Law 5 can be stated in this way: Greek preserved every final *–n;* its demonstrative value is not diminished since the phonetic phenomenon that results in the preservation of a former state is the same in nature as the one that manifests a change. . . . [Ed.]

through which an effect is produced, a thing executed. But this imperativeness is not sufficient to warrant applying the concept of law to evolutionary facts; we can speak of law only when a set of facts obeys the same rule, and in spite of certain appearances to the contrary, diachronic events are always accidental and particular.

The accidental and particular character of semantic facts is immediately apparent. That French *poutre* 'mare' has acquired the meaning 'piece of wood, rafter' is due to particular causes and does not depend on other changes that might have occurred at the same time. It is only one accident among all those registered in the history of the language.

As for syntactical and morphological transformations, the issue is not so clear from the outset. At a certain time almost all old subject-case forms disappeared in French. Here a set of facts apparently obeys the same law. But such is not the case, for all the facts are but multiple manifestations of one and the same isolated fact. The particular notion of subject was affected, and its disappearance naturally caused a whole series of forms to vanish. For one who sees only the external features of language, the unique phenomenon is drowned in the multitude of its manifestations. Basically, however, there is but one phenomenon, and this historical event is just as isolated in its own order as the semantic change undergone by *poutre*. It takes on the appearance of a "law" only because it is realized within a system. The rigid arrangement of the system creates the illusion that the diachronic fact obeys the same rules as the synchronic fact.

Finally, as regards phonetic changes, exactly the same is true. Yet the popular practice is to speak of phonetic laws. Indeed, it is said that at a given time and in a given area all words having the same phonic features are affected by the same change; for example, Law 1 on page 76 (**dhūmos →* Greek *thūmos*) affects all Greek words containing a voiced aspirate (cf. **nebhos → néphos, *medhu → méthu, *anghō → ánkhō*, etc.); Law 4 (**septm → heptá*) applies to **serpō → hérpō, *sūs → hûs*, and to all words that begin with *s*. This regularity, which has at times been disputed, is apparently firmly established; obvious exceptions do not lessen the inevitability of such changes, for they can be explained either by more special phonetic laws (see the example of *trikhes: thriksi*, . . . or by the interference of facts of another class (analogy, etc.). Nothing seems to fit better the definition given above for the word law. And yet, regardless of the number of instances where a phonetic law holds, all facts embraced by it are but manifestations of a single particular fact.

The real issue is to find out whether phonetic changes affect words or only sounds, and there is no doubt about the answer: in *nephos, methu, ankhō*, etc. a certain phoneme—a voiced Proto-Indo-European aspirate—became voiceless, Proto-Greek initial *s* became *h*, etc.; each fact is isolated, independent of the other events of the same class, independent also of the words in which the change took place.[6] The phonic substance of all the words was of course modified, but this should not deceive us as to the real nature of the phenomenon.

What supports the statement that words themselves are not directly involved in phonetic transformations? The very simple observation that these transformations are basically alien to words and cannot touch their essence. The word-unit is not constituted solely by the totality of its phonemes but by characteristics other than its material quality. Suppose that one string of a piano is out of tune: a discordant note will be heard each time the one who is playing a melody strikes the corresponding key. But where is the discord? In the melody? Certainly not; the melody has not been affected; only the piano has been impaired. Exactly the same is true in phonetics. Our system of phonemes is the instrument we play in order to articulate the words of language; if one of its elements is modified, diverse consequences may ensue, but the modification itself is not concerned with the words which are, in a manner of speaking, the melodies of our repertory.

Diachronic facts are then particular; a shift in a system is

[6] Of course the examples cited above are purely schematic: linguistics is right in trying currently to relate to the same initial principle the largest possible series of phonetic changes; for instance, Meillet explains all the transformations of Greek occlusives by progressive weakening of their articulation (see *Mem. de la Soc. de Ling.*, IX, pp. 163 ff.). Naturally the conclusions on the nature of phonetic changes are in the last analysis applicable to these general facts, wherever they exist. [Ed.]

brought about by events which not only are outside the system . . . , but are isolated and form no system among themselves.

To summarize: synchronic facts, no matter what they are, evidence a certain regularity but are in no way imperative; diachronic facts, on the contrary, force themselves upon language but are in no way general.

In a word—and this is the point I have been trying to make—neither of the two classes of facts is governed by laws in the sense defined above, and if one still wishes to speak of linguistic laws, the word will embrace completely different meanings, depending on whether it designates facts of one class or the other.

JURII TYNIANOV AND
ROMAN JAKOBSON

Jurii Tynianov (1894–1943) and Roman Jakobson (see p. 84) were two prominent members of the Russian Formalist School of literary and linguistic studies. Tynianov, who worked at the Division of Literary History of the Petrograd State Institute of Art History, was interested primarily in literary studies; Jakobson, who left Moscow for Prague in 1920, concentrated primarily on linguistics. The work of Saussure strongly influenced the formalist movement, which came under attack in the Soviet Union in the 1920s from orthodox Marxists. The eight cryptic theses, translated and reprinted here, are a reformulation of the early formalist platform and present a program for the development of a structuralist approach to the study of language and literature.

5

Problems in the Study of Language and Literature

1. The immediate problems facing Russian literary and linguistic science demand a clear theoretical base. They must be decisively dissociated from the increasingly frequent practice of pasting together a new methodology with old, outmoded methods, and of surreptitiously introducing naïve psychologism and other methodological relics under cover of a new terminology.

Academic eclecticism and a scholastic "formalism" which replaces analysis with terminology and with a cataloguing of phenomena must be avoided, as must the repeated transformation of the study of literature and language, which is a systematic science, into episodic and anecdotal genres.

2. The history of literature (or art) is closely related to the other historical series. As each of the other series, it is characterized by an intricate complex of specific structural laws. Unless these laws are elucidated it is impossible scientifically to establish a correlation between the literary series and the other historical series.

3. The evolution of literature cannot be understood so long as the evolutionary problem is overshadowed by questions of episodic, unsystematic literary origins (so-called literary influences) and extra-literary origins. Both the literary and the extra-literary material which is used in literature can be brought into the realm of scientific investigation only when it is examined from a functional point of view.

4. For both linguistics and the history of literature, a sharp

Translation of "Problemy izucheniia literatury i iazyka," *Novyi Lef*, No. 12 (1928), pp. 36-37.

opposition between the synchronic (static) and the diachronic aspects was until recently a fruitful working hypothesis since it showed the systematic character of language (or literature) in each separate moment of its life. At present the achievements of the synchronic concept force us to reexamine the principles of diachrony as well. Just as the idea of a mechanical agglomeration of phenomena was replaced by the idea of system or structure in the sphere of synchronic science, it was similarly replaced in the sphere of diachronic science. The history of a system is in turn also a system. Pure synchrony is now turning out to be an illusion: each synchronic system contains its past and future as inseparable structural elements of the system (A: archaism as a stylistic fact; the linguistic and literary background is felt as a passé, old-fashioned style; B: innovating tendencies in language and literature are felt as an innovation of the system).

The opposition between synchrony and diachrony was an opposition between the notion of system and the notion of evolution. It loses its principal importance insofar as we recognize that each system is necessarily given as an evolution and that on the other hand, evolution inevitably has a systematic character.

5. The notion of a literary synchronic system does not coincide with the notion of a naïvely conceived chronological epoch since it is made up not only of works of art close in time, but also of works drawn into the system from foreign literatures and past epochs. It is not enough to catalog coexisting phenomena indiscriminately; what matters is their hierarchical significance for a given epoch.

6. The affirmation of two different notions—*parole* (speech) and *langue* (language)—and an analysis of the correlation between them (the Geneva school) were extraordinarily fruitful for the science of language. The application of these two categories (the current norm and the individual expressions) to literature and the relationship between them is a principal problem for investigation. Here too the individual expression cannot be considered apart from the existing complex of norms (the investigator who abstracts the first from the second inevitably deforms the system under consideration of ar-

tistic values and loses the possibility of ascertaining its immanent laws).

7. Analysis of the structural laws of language and literature and of their evolution inevitably leads to establishing a limited number of actually given structural types (or types of evolution of structures).

8. The uncovering of the immanent laws of the history of literature (or language) enables us to characterize each change of literary (or linguistic) systems. But it does not enable us to explain the tempo of evolution or the particular direction it takes when faced with several theoretically possible evolutionary paths. The immanent laws of literary (or linguistic) evolution give us only an indeterminate equation, which admits of the possibility of several—although a limited number—solutions, and not necessarily of only one. The question about the choice of a specific path, or at least of a dominant one, can be answered only by means of an analysis of the correlation of the literary series with the other historical series. This correlation (the system of systems) has its own structural laws which must be studied. To examine the correlation of the systems without taking into account the immanent laws of each system is methodologically a fatal step.

TRANSLATED BY R. T. DE GEORGE

ROMAN JAKOBSON

Roman Jakobson was born in Moscow in 1896. He studied at the University of Moscow where he was a research associate from 1918 until 1920 when he left Russia for Prague. He was an active and prominent member of the Russian Formalist School and of the Prague Linguistic Circle. He was a professor at Masaryk University from 1933–39, at the École Libre des Hautes Études in New York from 1942–46, and at Columbia University from 1946–49. Since 1949 he has been Samuel Cross Professor of Slavic Languages, Literatures, and General Linguistics at Harvard, and since 1957 he has also been Institute Professor at the Massachusetts Institute of Technology.

He has written widely in the field of linguistics (see his *Selected Writings,* I–IV), and is the author of such outstanding works as *Slavic Languages* (1955) and *Phonological Studies* (1962). His influence is attested to by three massive volumes of *To Honor Roman Jakobson,* the first of which contains a 475-item bibliography of his publications. The article which immediately follows relates linguistics and literary studies and constituted his "concluding statement" at a Conference on Style held in 1958 at Indiana University.

6

Linguistics and Poetics

Fortunately, scholarly and political conferences have nothing in common. The success of a political convention depends on the general agreement of the majority or totality of its participants. The use of votes and vetoes, however, is alien to scholarly discussion where disagreement generally proves to be more productive than agreement. Disagreement discloses antinomies and tensions within the field discussed and calls for novel exploration. Not political conferences but rather exploratory activities in Antarctica present an analogy to scholarly meetings: international experts in various disciplines attempt to map an unknown region and find out where the greatest obstacles for the explorer are, the insurmountable peaks and precipices. Such a mapping seems to have been the chief task of our conference, and in this respect its work has been quite successful. Have we not realized what problems are the most crucial and the most controversial? Have we not also learned how to switch our codes, what terms to expound or even to avoid in order to prevent misunderstandings with people using different departmental jargon? Such questions, I believe, for most of the members of this conference, if not for all of them, are somewhat clearer today than they were three days ago.

I have been asked for summary remarks about poetics in its relation to linguistics. Poetics deals primarily with the question, *What makes a verbal message a work of art?* Because the main subject of poetics is the *differentia specifica* of

Reprinted from *Style in Language*, edited by Thomas A. Sebeok, by permission of The M.I.T. Press, Cambridge, Massachusetts. Copyright © 1960 by The Massachusetts Institute of Technology. The numbers in parentheses refer to References, included at the end of this essay.

verbal art in relation to other arts and in relation to other kinds of verbal behavior, poetics is entitled to the leading place in literary studies.

Poetics deals with problems of verbal structure, just as the analysis of painting is concerned with pictorial structure. Since linguistics is the global science of verbal structure, poetics may be regarded as an integral part of linguistics.

Arguments against such a claim must be thoroughly discussed. It is evident that many devices studied by poetics are not confined to verbal art. We can refer to the possibility of transposing *Wuthering Heights* into a motion picture, medieval legends into frescoes and miniatures, or *L'après-midi d'un faune* into music, ballet, and graphic art. However ludicrous may appear the idea of the *Iliad* and *Odyssey* in comics, certain structural features of their plot are preserved despite the disappearance of their verbal shape. The question whether Blake's illustrations to the *Divina Commedia* are or are not adequate is a proof that different arts are comparable. The problems of baroque or any other historical style transgress the frame of a single art. When handling the surrealistic metaphor, we could hardly pass by Max Ernst's pictures or Luis Buñuel's films, *The Andalusian Dog* and *The Golden Age*. In short, many poetic features belong not only to the science of language but to the whole theory of signs, that is, to general semiotics. This statement, however, is valid not only for verbal art but also for all varieties of language since language shares many properties with some other systems of signs or even with all of them (pansemiotic features).

Likewise a second objection contains nothing that would be specific for literature: the question of relations between the word and the world concerns not only verbal art but actually all kinds of discourse. Linguistics is likely to explore all possible problems of relation between discourse and the "universe of discourse": what of this universe is verbalized by a given discourse and how is it verbalized. The truth values, however, as far as they are—to say with the logicians—"extralinguistic entities," obviously exceed the bounds of poetics and of linguistics in general.

Sometimes we hear that poetics, in contradistinction to linguistics, is concerned with evaluation. This separation of the two fields from each other is based on a current but erroneous interpretation of the contrast between the structure of poetry and other types of verbal structure: the latter are said to be opposed by their "casual," designless nature to the "noncasual," purposeful character of poetic language. In point of fact, any verbal behavior is goal-directed, but the aims are different and the conformity of the means used to the effect aimed at is a problem that evermore preoccupies inquirers into the diverse kinds of verbal communication. There is a close correspondence, much closer than critics believe, between the question of linguistic phenomena expanding in space and time and the spatial and temporal spread of literary models. Even such discontinuous expansion as the resurrection of neglected or forgotten poets—for instance, the posthumous discovery and subsequent canonization of Gerard Manley Hopkins (d. 1889), the tardy fame of Lautréamont (d. 1870) among surrealist poets, and the salient influence of the hitherto ignored Cyprian Norwid (d. 1883) on Polish modern poetry—find a parallel in the history of standard languages which are prone to revive outdated models, sometimes long forgotten, as was the case in literary Czech which toward the beginning of the nineteenth century leaned to sixteenth-century models.

Unfortunately the terminological confusion of "literary studies" with "criticism" tempts the student of literature to replace the description of the intrinsic values of a literary work by a subjective, censorious verdict. The label "literary critic" applied to an investigator of literature is as erroneous as "grammatical (or lexical) critic" would be applied to a linguist. Syntactic and morphologic research cannot be supplanted by a normative grammar, and likewise no manifesto, foisting a critic's own tastes and opinions on creative literature, may act as substitute for an objective scholarly analysis of verbal art. This statement is not to be mistaken for the quietist principle of *laissez faire;* any verbal culture involves programmatic, planning, normative endeavors. Yet why is a clear-cut discrimination made between pure and applied linguistics or between phonetics and orthoëpy but not between literary studies and criticism?

Literary studies, with poetics as their focal portion, consist like linguistics of two sets of problems: synchrony and diachrony. The synchronic description envisages not only the literary production of any given stage but also that part of the literary tradition which for the stage in question has remained vital or has been revived. Thus, for instance, Shakespeare on the one hand and Donne, Marvell, Keats, and Emily Dickinson on the other are experienced by the present English poetic world, whereas the works of James Thomson and Longfellow, for the time being, do not belong to viable artistic values. The selection of classics and their reinterpretation by a novel trend is a substantial problem of synchronic literary studies. Synchronic poetics, like synchronic linguistics, is not to be confused with statics; any stage discriminates between more conservative and more innovatory forms. Any contemporary stage is experienced in its temporal dynamics, and, on the other hand, the historical approach both in poetics and in linguistics is concerned not only with changes but also with continuous, enduring, static factors. A thoroughly comprehensive historical poetics or history of language is a superstructure to be built on a series of successive synchronic descriptions.

Insistence on keeping poetics apart from linguistics is warranted only when the field of linguistics appears to be illicitly restricted, for example, when the sentence is viewed by some linguists as the highest analyzable construction or when the scope of linguistics is confined to grammar alone or uniquely to nonsemantic questions of external form or to the inventory of denotative devices with no reference to free variations. Voegelin has clearly pointed out the two most important and related problems which face structural linguistics, namely, a revision of "the monolithic hypothesis of language" and a concern with "the interdependence of diverse structures within one language." No doubt, for any speech community, for any speaker, there exists a unity of language, but this over-all code represents a system of interconnected subcodes; each language encompasses several concurrent patterns which are each characterized by a different function.

Obviously we must agree with Sapir that, on the whole, "ideation reigns supreme in language . . ."(40), but this supremacy does not authorize linguistics to disregard the "secondary factors." The emotive elements of speech which, as Joos is prone to believe, cannot be described "with a finite number of absolute categories," are classified by him "as nonlinguistic elements of the real world." Hence, "for us they remain vague, protean, fluctuating phenomena," he concludes, "which we refuse to tolerate in our science"(19). Joos is indeed a brilliant expert in reduction experiments, and his emphatic requirement for an "expulsion" of the emotive elements "from linguistic science" is a radical experiment in reduction—*reductio ad absurdum*.

Language must be investigated in all the variety of its functions. Before discussing the poetic function we must define its place among the other functions of language. An outline of these functions demands a concise survey of the constitutive factors in any speech event, in any act of verbal communication. The ADDRESSER sends a MESSAGE to the ADDRESSEE. To be operative the message requires a CONTEXT referred to ("referent" in another, somewhat ambiguous, nomenclature), seizable by the addressee, and either verbal or capable of being verbalized; a CODE fully, or at least partially, common to the addresser and addressee (or in other words, to the encoder and decoder of the message); and, finally, a CONTACT, a physical channel and psychological connection between the addresser and the addressee, enabling both of them to enter and stay in communication. All these factors inalienably involved in verbal communication may be schematized as follows:

CONTEXT

ADDRESSER   MESSAGE   ADDRESSEE

CONTACT

CODE

Each of these six factors determines a different function of language. Although we distinguish six basic aspects of language, we could, however, hardly find verbal messages that would fulfill only one function. The diversity lies not in a monopoly of some one of these several functions but in a different hierarchical order of functions. The verbal structure of a message depends primarily on the predominant function. But even though a set (*Einstellung*) toward the referent, an orientation toward the CONTEXT—briefly the so-called REFERENTIAL, "denotative," "cognitive" function—is the leading task of numerous messages, the accessory participation of the other functions in such messages must be taken into account by the observant linguist.

The so-called EMOTIVE or "expressive" function, focused on the ADDRESSER, aims a direct expression of the speaker's attitude toward what he is speaking about. It tends to produce an impression of a certain emotion whether true or feigned; therefore, the term "emotive," launched and advocated by Marty (30) has proved to be preferable to "emotional." The purely emotive stratum in language is presented by the interjections. They differ from the means of referential language both by their sound pattern (peculiar sound sequences or even sounds elsewhere unusual) and by their syntactic role (they are not components but equivalents of sentences). "*Tut! Tut!* said McGinty": the complete utterance of Conan Doyle's character consists of two suction clicks. The emotive function, laid bare in the interjections, flavors to some extent all our utterances, on their phonic, grammatical, and lexical level. If we analyze language from the standpoint of the information it carries, we cannot restrict the notion of information to the cognitive aspect of language. A man, using expressive features to indicate his angry or ironic attitude, conveys ostensible information, and evidently this verbal behavior cannot be likened to such nonsemiotic, nutritive activities as "eating grapefruit" (despite Chatman's bold simile). The difference between [big] and the emphatic prolongation of the vowel [bi:g] is a conventional, coded linguistic feature like the difference between the short and long vowel in such Czech pairs as [vi] 'you' and [vi:] 'knows,' but in the latter pair the differential information is phonemic and in the former emotive. As long as we are interested in phonemic invariants, the English /i/ and /i:/ appear to be mere variants of one and the same phoneme, but if we are concerned with emotive units, the relation between the invariant and variants is reversed: length and shortness are invariants implemented by variable phonemes. Saporta's surmise that emotive difference is a nonlinguistic feature, "attributable to the delivery of the message and not to the message," arbitrarily reduces the informational capacity of messages.

A former actor of Stanislavskij's Moscow Theater told me how at his audition he was asked by the famous director to make forty different messages from the phrase *Segodnja večerom* 'This evening,' by diversifying its expressive tint. He made a list of some forty emotional situations, then emitted the given phrase in accordance with each of these situations, which his audience had to recognize only from the changes in the sound shape of the same two words. For our research work in the description and analysis of contemporary Standard Russian (under the auspices of the Rockefeller Foundation) this actor was asked to repeat Stanislavskij's test. He wrote down some fifty situations framing the same elliptic sentence and made of it fifty corresponding messages for a tape record. Most of the messages were correctly and circumstantially decoded by Moscovite listeners. May I add that all such emotive cues easily undergo linguistic analysis.

Orientation toward the ADDRESSEE, the CONATIVE function, finds its purest grammatical expression in the vocative and imperative, which syntactically, morphologically, and often even phonemically deviate from other nominal and verbal categories. The imperative sentences cardinally differ from declarative sentences: the latter are and the former are not liable to a truth test. When in O'Neill's play *The Fountain*, Nano, "(in a fierce tone of command)," says "Drink!"—the imperative cannot be challenged by the question "is it true or not?" which may be, however, perfectly well asked after such sentences as "one drank," "one will drink," "one would drink." In contradistinction to the imperative sentences, the declarative sentences are convertible into interrogative sentences: "did one drink?" "will one drink?" "would one drink?"

The traditional model of language as elucidated particularly by Bühler (4) was confined to these three functions—emotive, conative, and referential—and the three apexes of this model—the first person of the addresser, the second person of the addressee, and the "third person," properly—someone or something spoken of. Certain additional verbal functions can be easily inferred from this triadic model. Thus the magic, incantatory function is chiefly some kind of conversion of an absent or inanimate "third person" into an addressee of a conative message. "May this sty dry up, *tfu, tfu, tfu, tfu*" (Lithuanian spell: 28, p. 69). "Water, queen river, daybreak! Send grief beyond the blue sea, to the sea-bottom, like a grey stone never to rise from the sea-bottom, may grief never come to burden the light heart of God's servant, may grief be removed and sink away." (North Russian incantation: 39, p. 217f.). "Sun, stand thou still upon Gibeon; and thou, Moon, in the valley of Aj-a-lon. And the sun stood still, and the moon stayed . . ." (Josh. 10.12). We observe, however, three further constitutive factors of verbal communication and three corresponding functions of language.

There are messages primarily serving to establish, to prolong, or to discontinue communication, to check whether the channel works ("Hello, do you hear me?"), to attract the attention of the interlocutor or to confirm his continued attention ("Are you listening?" or in Shakespearean diction, "Lend me your ears!"—and on the other end of the wire "Um-hum!"). This set for CONTACT, or in Malinowski's terms PHATIC function (26), may be displayed by a profuse exchange of ritualized formulas, by entire dialogues with the mere purport of prolonging communication. Dorothy Parker caught eloquent examples: "'Well!' the young man said. 'Well!' she said. 'Well, here we are,' he said. 'Here we are,' she said, 'Aren't we?' 'I should say we were,' he said, 'Eeyop! Here we are.' 'Well!' she said. 'Well!' he said, 'well.'" The endeavor to start and sustain communication is typical of talking birds; thus the phatic function of language is the only one they share with human beings. It is also the first verbal function acquired by infants; they are prone to communicate before being able to send or receive informative communication.

A distinction has been made in modern logic between two levels of language, "object language" speaking of objects and "metalanguage" speaking of language. But metalanguage is not only a necessary scientific tool utilized by logicians and linguists; it plays also an important role in our everyday language. Like Molière's Jourdain who used prose without knowing it, we practice metalanguage without realizing the metalingual character of our operations. Whenever the addresser and/or the addressee need to check up whether they use the same code, speech is focused on the CODE: it performs a METALINGUAL (i.e., glossing) function. "I don't follow you—what do you mean?" asks the addressee, or in Shakespearean diction, "What is't thou say'st?" And the addresser in anticipation of such recapturing questions inquires: "Do you know what I mean?" Imagine such an exasperating dialogue: "The sophomore was plucked." "But what is *plucked?*" "*Plucked* means the same as *flunked.*" "And *flunked?*" "*To be flunked* is *to fail in an exam.*" "And what is *sophomore?*" persists the interrogator innocent of school vocabulary. "*A sophomore* is (or means) a *second-year student.*" All these equational sentences convey information merely about the lexical code of English; their function is strictly metalingual. Any process of language learning, in particular child acquisition of the mother tongue, makes wide use of such metalingual operations; and aphasia may often be defined as a loss of ability for metalingual operations.

We have brought up all the six factors involved in verbal communication except the message itself. The set (*Einstellung*) toward the MESSAGE as such, focus on the message for its own sake, is the POETIC function of language. This function cannot be productively studied out of touch with the general problems of language, and, on the other hand, the scrutiny of language requires a thorough consideration of its poetic function. Any attempt to reduce the sphere of poetic function to poetry or to confine poetry to poetic function would be a delusive oversimplification. Poetic function is not the sole function of verbal art but only its dominant, determining function, whereas in all other verbal activities it acts as a subsidiary, accessory constituent. This function, by promoting the palpability of signs, deepens the fundamental dichotomy of signs and objects. Hence, when dealing with poetic function, linguistics cannot limit itself to the field of poetry.

"Why do you always say *Joan and Margery,* yet never *Margery and Joan?* Do you prefer Joan to her twin sister?" "Not at all, it just sounds smoother." In a sequence of two coordinate names, as far as no rank problems interfere, the precedence of the shorter name suits the speaker, unaccountably for him, as a well-ordered shape of the message.

A girl used to talk about "the horrible Harry." "Why horrible?" "Because I hate him." "But why not *dreadful, terrible, frightful, disgusting?*" "I don't know why, but *horrible* fits him better." Without realizing it, she clung to the poetic device of paronomasia.

The political slogan "I like Ike" /ay layk ayk/, succinctly structured, consists of three monosyllables and counts three diphthongs /ay/, each of them symmetrically followed by one consonantal phoneme, /..l..k..k/. The make-up of the three words presents a variation: no consonantal phonemes in the first word, two around the diphthong in the second, and one final consonant in the third. A similar dominant nucleus /ay/ was noticed by Hymes in some of the sonnets of Keats. Both cola of the trisyllabic formula "I like / Ike" rhyme with each other, and the second of the two rhyming words is fully included in the first one (echo rhyme), /layk/—/ayk/, a paronomastic image of a feeling which totally envelops its object. Both cola alliterate with each other, and the first of the two alliterating words is included in the second: /ay/—/ayk/, a paronomastic image of the loving subject enveloped by the beloved object. The secondary, poetic function of this electional catch phrase reinforces its impressiveness and efficacy.

As we said, the linguistic study of the poetic function must overstep the limits of poetry, and, on the other hand, the linguistic scrutiny of poetry cannot limit itself to the poetic function. The particularities of diverse poetic genres imply a differently ranked participation of the other verbal functions along with the dominant poetic function. Epic poetry, focused on the third person, strongly involves the referential function of language; the lyric, oriented toward the first person, is intimately linked with the emotive function; poetry of the second person is imbued with the conative function and is either supplicatory or exhortative, depending on whether the first person is subordinated to the second one or the second to the first.

Now that our cursory description of the six basic functions of verbal communication is more or less complete, we may complement our scheme of the fundamental factors by a corresponding scheme of the functions:

REFERENTIAL

EMOTIVE   POETIC   CONATIVE
PHATIC

METALINGUAL

What is the empirical linguistic criterion of the poetic function? In particular, what is the indispensable feature inherent in any piece of poetry? To answer this question we must recall the two basic modes of arrangement used in verbal behavior, *selection* and *combination*. If "child" is the topic of the message, the speaker selects one among the extant, more or less similar, nouns like child, kid, youngster, tot, all of them equivalent in a certain respect, and then, to comment on this topic, he may select one of the semantically cognate verbs—sleeps, dozes, nods, naps. Both chosen words combine in the speech chain. The selection is produced on the base of equivalence, similarity and dissimilarity, synonymity and antonymity, while the combination, the build up of the sequence, is based on contiguity. *The poetic function projects the principle of equivalence from the axis of selection into the axis of combination.* Equivalence is promoted to the constitutive device of the sequence. In poetry one syllable is equalized with any other syllable of the same sequence; word stress is assumed to equal word stress, as unstress equals unstress; prosodic long is matched with long, and short with short; word boundary equals word boundary, no boundary equals no boundary; syntactic pause equals syntactic pause, no pause equals no pause. Syllables are converted into units of measure, and so are morae or stresses.

It may be objected that metalanguage also makes a sequential use of equivalent units when combining synonymic expressions into an equational sentence: $A = A$ (*"Mare is the female of the horse"*). Poetry and metalanguage, however, are in diametrical opposition to each other: in metalanguage the sequence is used to build an equation, whereas in poetry the equation is used to build a sequence.

In poetry, and to a certain extent in latent manifestations of poetic function, sequences delimited by word boundaries become commensurable whether they are sensed as isochronic or graded. "Joan and Margery" showed us the poetic principle of syllable gradation, the same principle which in the closes of Serbian folk epics has been raised to a compulsory law (cf. 29). Without its two dactylic words the combination "i*nnocent* by*stand*er" would hardly have become a hackneyed phrase. The symmetry of three disyllabic verbs with an identical initial consonant and identical final vowel added splendor to the laconic victory message of Caesar: *"Veni, vidi, vici."*

Measure of sequences is a device which, outside of poetic function, finds no application in language. Only in poetry with its regular reiteration of equivalent units is the time of the speech flow experienced, as it is—to cite another semiotic pattern—with musical time. Gerard Manley Hopkins, an outstanding searcher in the science of poetic language, defined verse as "speech wholly or partially repeating the same figure of sound" (12). Hopkins' subsequent question, "but is all verse poetry?" can be definitely answered as soon as poetic function ceases to be arbitrarily confined to the domain of poetry. Mnemonic lines cited by Hopkins (like "Thirty days hath September"), modern advertising jingles, and versified medieval laws, mentioned by Lotz, or finally Sanscrit scientific treatises in verse which in Indic tradition are strictly distinguished from true poetry (*kāvya*)—all these metrical texts make use of poetic function without, however, assigning to this function the coercing, determining role it carries in poetry. Thus verse actually exceeds the limits of poetry, but at the same time verse always implies poetic function. And apparently no human culture ignores versemaking, whereas there are many cultural patterns without "applied" verse;

and even in such cultures which possess both pure and applied verses, the latter appear to be a secondary, unquestionably derived phenomenon. The adaptation of poetic means for some heterogeneous purpose does not conceal their primary essence, just as elements of emotive language, when utilized in poetry, still maintain their emotive tinge. A filibusterer may recite *Hiawatha* because it is long, yet poeticalness still remains the primary intent of this text itself. Self-evidently, the existence of versified, musical, and pictorial commercials does not separate the questions of verse or of musical and pictorial form from the study of poetry, music, and fine arts.

To sum up, the analysis of verse is entirely within the competence of poetics, and the latter may be defined as that part of linguistics which treats the poetic function in its relationship to the other functions of language. Poetics in the wider sense of the word deals with the poetic function not only in poetry, where this function is superimposed upon the other functions of language, but also outside of poetry, when some other function is superimposed upon the poetic function.

The reiterative "figure of sound," which Hopkins saw to be the constitutive principle of verse, can be further specified. Such a figure always utilizes at least one (or more than one) binary contrast of a relatively high and relatively low prominence effected by the different sections of the phonemic sequence.

Within a syllable the more prominent, nuclear, syllabic part, constituting the peak of the syllable, is opposed to the less prominent, marginal, nonsyllabic phonemes. Any syllable contains a syllabic phoneme, and the interval between two successive syllabics is in some languages always and in others overwhelmingly carried out by marginal, nonsyllabic phonemes. In the so-called syllabic versification the number of syllabics in a metrically delimited chain (time series) is a constant, whereas the presence of a nonsyllabic phoneme or cluster between every two syllabics of a metrical chain is a constant only in languages with an indispensable occurrence of nonsyllabics between syllabics and, furthermore, in those verse systems where hiatus is prohibited. Another manifestation of a tendency toward a uniform syllabic model is the avoidance of closed syllables at the end of the line, observable, for instance, in Serbian epic songs. The Italian syllabic verse shows a tendency to treat a sequence of vowels unseparated by consonantal phonemes as one single metrical syllable (cf. 21, secs. VIII–IX).

In some patterns of versification the syllable is the only constant unit of verse measure, and a grammatical limit is the only constant line of demarcation between measured sequences, whereas in other patterns syllables in turn are dichotomized into more and less prominent, and/or two levels of grammatical limits are distinguished in their metrical function, word boundaries and syntactic pauses.

Except the varieties of the so-called vers libre that are based on conjugate intonations and pauses only, any meter uses the syllable as a unit of measure at least in certain sections of the verse. Thus in the purely accentual verse ("sprung rhythm" in Hopkins' vocabulary), the number of syllables in the upbeat (called "slack" by Hopkins) may vary, but the downbeat (ictus) constantly contains one single syllable.

In any accentual verse the contrast between higher and lower prominence is achieved by syllables under stress versus unstressed syllables. Most accentual patterns operate primarily with the contrast of syllables with and without word stress, but some varieties of accentual verse deal with syntactic, phrasal stresses, those which Wimsatt and Beardsley cite as "the major stresses of the major words" and which are opposed as prominent to syllables without such major, syntactic stress.

In the quantitative ("chronemic") verse, long and short syllables are mutually opposed as more and less prominent. This contrast is usually carried out by syllable nuclei, phonemically long and short. But in metrical patterns like Ancient Greek and Arabic, which equalize length "by position" with length "by nature," the minimal syllables consisting of a consonantal phoneme and one mora vowel are opposed to syllables with a surplus (a second mora or a closing consonant) as simpler and less prominent syllables opposed to those that are more complex and prominent.

The question still remains open whether, besides the accentual and the chronemic verse, there exists a "tonemic" type of versification in languages where differences of syllabic intonations are used to distinguish word meanings (15). In classical Chinese poetry (3), syllables with modulations (in Chinese *tsê*, 'deflected tones') are opposed to the nonmodulated syllables (*p'ing,* 'level tones'), but apparently a chronemic principle underlies this opposition, as was suspected by Polivanov (34) and keenly interpreted by Wang Li (46); in the Chinese metrical tradition the level tones prove to be opposed to the deflected tones as long tonal peaks of syllables to short ones, so that verse is based on the opposition of length and shortness.

Joseph Greenberg brought to my attention another variety of tonemic versification—the verse of Efik riddles based on the level feature. In the sample cited by Simmons (42, p. 228), the query and the response form two octosyllables with an alike distribution of *h*(igh)- and *l*(ow)-tone syllabics; in each hemistich, moreover, the last three of the four syllables present an identical tonemic pattern: *lhhl/hhhl//lhhl/hhhl//.* Whereas Chinese versification appears as a peculiar variety of the quantitative verse, the verse of the Efik riddles is linked with the usual accentual verse by an opposition of two degrees of prominence (strength or height) of the vocal tone. Thus a metrical system of versification can be based only on the opposition of syllabic peaks and slopes (syllabic verse), on the relative level of the peaks (accentual verse), and on the relative length of the syllabic peaks or entire syllables (quantitative verse).

In textbooks of literature we sometimes encounter a superstitious contraposition of syllabism as a mere mechanical count of syllables to the lively pulsation of accentual verse. If we examine, however, the binary meters of the strictly syllabic and at the same time, accentual versification, we observe two homogeneous successions of wavelike peaks and valleys. Of these two undulatory curves, the syllabic one carries nuclear phonemes in the crest and usually marginal phonemes in the bottom. As a rule the accentual curve superposed upon the syllabic curve alternates stressed and unstressed syllables in the crests and bottoms respectively.

For comparison with the English meters which we have lengthily discussed, I bring to your attention the similar Russian binary verse forms which for the last fifty years have verily undergone an exhaustive investigation (see particularly 44). The structure of the verse can be very thoroughly described and interpreted in terms of enchained probabilities. Besides the compulsory word boundary between the lines, which is an invariant throughout all Russian meters, in the classic pattern of Russian syllabic accentual verse ("syllabo-tonic" in native nomenclature) we observe the following constants: (1) the number of syllables in the line from its beginning to the last downbeat is stable; (2) this very last downbeat always carries a word stress; (3) a stressed syllable cannot fall on the upbeat if a downbeat is fulfilled by an un-stressed syllable of the same word unit (so that a word stress can coincide with an upbeat only as far as it belongs to a monosyllabic word unit).

Along with these characteristics compulsory for any line composed in a given meter, there are features that show a high probability of occurrence without being constantly present. Besides signals certain to occur ("probability one"), signals likely to occur ("probabilities less than one") enter into the notion of meter. Using Cherry's description of human communication (5), we could say that the reader of poetry obviously "may be unable to attach numerical frequencies" to the constituents of the meter, but as far as he conceives the verse shape, he unwittingly gets an inkling of their "rank order."

In the Russian binary meters all odd syllables counting back from the last downbeat—briefly, all the upbeats—are usually fulfilled by unstressed syllables, except some very low percentage of stressed monosyllables. All even syllables, again counting back from the last downbeat, show a sizable preference for syllables under word stress, but the probabilities of their occurrence are unequally distributed among the successive downbeats of the line. The higher the relative frequency of word stresses in a given downbeat, the lower the ratio shown by the preceding downbeat. Since the last downbeat is constantly stressed, the next to last gives the lowest percentage of word stresses; in the preceding downbeat their amount is again higher, without attaining the maximum, displayed by the final downbeat; one downbeat further toward the beginning of the line, the amount of the stresses sinks once more, without reaching the minimum of the next-to-last downbeat; and so on. Thus the distribution of word stresses among the downbeats within the line, the split into strong and weak downbeats, creates a *regressive undulatory curve* superposed upon the wavy alternation of downbeats and upbeats. Incidentally, there is a captivating question of the relationship between the strong downbeats and phrasal stresses.

The Russian binary meters reveal a stratified arrangement of three undulatory curves: (I) alternation of syllabic nuclei and margins; (II) division of syllabic nuclei into alternating downbeats and upbeats; and (III) alternation of strong and weak downbeats. For example, Russian masculine iambic tetrameter of the nineteenth and present centuries may be represented by Figure 1, and a similar triadic pattern appears in the corresponding English forms.

Three of five downbeats are deprived of word stress in Shelley's iambic line "Laugh with an inextinguishable laughter." Seven of sixteen downbeats are stressless in the following quatrain from Pasternak's recent iambic tetrameter *Zemlja* ("Earth"):

> I úlica za panibráta
> S okónnicej podslepovátoj,
> I béloj nóči i zakátu
> Ne razminút'sja u rekí.

Since the overwhelming majority of downbeats concur with word stresses, the listener or reader of Russian verses is prepared with a high degree of probability to meet a word stress in any even syllable of iambic lines, but at the very beginning of Pasternak's quatrain the fourth and, one foot further, the sixth syllable, both in the first and in the following line, present him with a *frustrated expectation*. The degree of such a "frustration" is higher when the stress is lacking in a strong downbeat and becomes particularly outstanding when two successive downbeats are carrying unstressed syllables. The

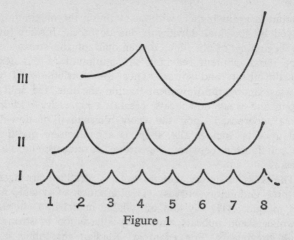

Figure 1

stresslessness of two adjacent downbeats is the less probable and the most striking when it embraces a whole hemistich as in a later line of the same poem: "Čtoby za gorodskjóu grán' ju" [stəbyzəgərackóju grán'ju]. The expectation depends on the treatment of a given downbeat in the poem and more generally in the whole extant metrical tradition. In the last downbeat but one, unstress may, however, outweigh the stress. Thus in this poem only 17 of 41 lines have a word stress on their sixth syllable. Yet in such a case the inertia of the stressed even syllables alternating with the unstressed odd syllables prompts some expectancy of stress also for the sixth syllable of the iambic tetrameter.

Quite naturally it was Edgar Allan Poe, the poet and theoretician of defeated anticipation, who metrically and psychologically appraised the human sense of gratification for the unexpected arising from expectedness, both of them unthinkable without the opposite, "as evil cannot exist without good" (33). Here we could easily apply Robert Frost's formula from "The Figure A Poem Makes": "The figure is the same as for love" (8).

The so-called shifts of word stress in polysyllabic words from the downbeat to the upbeat ("reversed feet"), which are unknown to the standard forms of Russian verse, appear quite usually in English poetry after a metrical and/or syntactic pause. A noticeable example is the rhythmical variation of the same adjective in Milton's "Infinite wrath and infinite despair." In the line "Nearer, my God, to Thee, nearer to Thee," the stressed syllable of one and the same word occurs twice in the upbeat, first at the beginning of the line and a second time at the beginning of a phrase. This license, discussed by Jespersen (18) and current in many languages, is entirely explainable by the particular import of the relation between an upbeat and the immediately preceding downbeat. Where such an immediate precedence is impeded by an inserted pause, the upbeat becomes a kind of *syllaba anceps*.

Besides the rules which underlie the compulsory features of verse, the rules governing its optional traits also pertain to meter. We are inclined to designate such phenomena as unstress in the downbeats and stress in upbeats as deviations, but it must be remembered that these are allowed oscillations, departures within the limits of the law. In British parliamentary terms, it is not an opposition to its majesty the meter but an opposition of its majesty. As to the actual infringements of metrical laws, the discussion of such violations recalls Osip Brik, perhaps the keenest of Russian formalists, who used to say that political conspirators are tried and condemned only for unsuccessful attempts at a forcible upheaval, because in the case of a successful coup it is the conspirators who assume the role of judges and prosecutors. If the violences against the meter take root, they themselves become metrical rules.

Far from being an abstract, theoretical scheme, meter—or in more explicit terms, *verse design*—underlies the structure of any single line—or, in logical terminology, any single *verse instance*. Design and instance are correlative concepts. The verse design determines the invariant features of the verse instances and sets up the limits of variations. A Serbian peasant reciter of epic poetry memorizes, performs, and, to a high extent, improvises thousands, sometimes tens of thousands of lines, and their meter is alive in his mind. Unable to abstract its rules, he nonetheless notices and repudiates even the slightest infringement of these rules. Any line of Serbian epics contains precisely ten syllables and is followed by a syntactic pause. There is furthermore a compulsory word boundary before the fifth syllable and a compulsory absence of word boundary before the fourth and tenth syllable. The verse has, moreover, significant quantitative and accentual characteristics (cf. 16, 17).

This Serbian epic break, along with many similar examples presented by comparative metrics, is a persuasive warning against the erroneous identification of a break with a syntactic pause. The obligatory word boundary must not be combined with pause and is not even meant to be perceptible by the ear. The analysis of Serbian epic songs phonographically recorded proves that there are no compulsory audible clues to the break, and yet any attempt to abolish the word boundary before the fifth syllable by a mere insignificant change in word order is immediately condemned by the narrator. The grammatical fact that the fourth and fifth syllables pertain to two different word units is sufficient for the appraisal of the break. Thus verse design goes far beyond the questions of sheer sound shape; it is a much wider linguistic phenomenon, and it yields to no isolating phonetic treatment.

I say "linguistic phenomenon" even though Chatman states that "the meter exists as a system outside the language." Yes, meter appears also in other arts dealing with time sequence. There are many linguistic problems—for instance, syntax—which likewise overstep the limit of language and are common to different semiotic systems. We may speak even about the grammar of traffic signals. There exists a signal code, where a yellow light when combined with green warns that free passage is close to being stopped and when combined with red announces the approaching cessation of the stoppage; such a yellow signal offers a close analogue to the verbal completive aspect. Poetic meter, however, has so many intrinsically linguistic particularities that it is most convenient to describe it from a purely linguistic point of view.

Let us add that no linguistic property of the verse design should be disregarded. Thus, for example, it would be an unfortunate mistake to deny the constitutive value of intonation in English meters. Not even speaking about its fundamental role in the meters of such a master of English free verse as Whitman, it is impossible to ignore the metrical significance of pausal intonation ("final juncture"), whether "cadence" or "anticadence" (20), in poems like "The Rape of The Lock" with its intentional avoidance of enjambments. Yet even a vehement accumulation of enjambments never hides their digressive, variational status; they always set off the normal coincidence of syntactic pause and pausal intonation with the metrical limit. Whatever is the reciter's way of reading, the intonational constraint of the poem remains valid. The intonational contour inherent to a poem, to a poet, to a poetic school is one of the most notable topics brought to discussion by the Russian formalists (6, 49).

The verse design is embodied in verse instances. Usually the free variation of these instances is denoted by the somewhat equivocal label "rhythm." A variation of *verse instances* within a given poem must be strictly distinguished from the variable *delivery instances*. The intention "to describe the verse line as it is actually performed" is of lesser use for the synchronic and historical analysis of poetry than it is for the study of its recitation in the present and the past. Meanwhile the truth is simple and clear: "There are many performances of the same poem—differing among themselves in many ways. A performance is an event, but the poem itself, if there *is* any poem, must be some kind of enduring object." This sage memento of Wimsatt and Beardsley belongs indeed to the essentials of modern metrics.

In Shakespeare's verses the second, stressed syllable of the word "absurd" usually falls on the downbeat, but once in the third act of *Hamlet* it falls on the upbeat: "No, let the candied tongue lick absurd pomp." The reciter may scan the word "absurd" in this line with an initial stress on the first syllable or observe the final word stress in accordance with the standard accentuation. He may also subordinate the word stress of the adjective in favor of the strong syntactic stress of the following head word, as suggested by Hill: "Nó, lèt thĕ cândĭed tóngue lîck ăbsùrd pómp" (11), as in Hopkins' conception of English antispasts—"regrét néver" (12). There is finally a possibility of emphatic modifications either through a "fluctuating accentuation" (*schwebende Betonung*) embracing both syllables or through an exclamational reinforcement of the first syllable [àb-súrd]. But whatever solution the reciter chooses, the shift of the word stress from the downbeat to the upbeat with no antecedent pause is still arresting, and the moment of frustrated expectation stays viable. Wherever the reciter put the accent, the discrepancy between the English word stress on the second syllable of "absurd" and the downbeat attached to the first syllable persists as a constitutive feature of the verse instance. The tension between the ictus and the usual word stress is inherent in this line independently of its different implementations by various actors and readers. As Gerard Manley Hopkins observes, in the preface to his poems, "two rhythms are in some manner running at once" (13). His description of such a contrapuntal run can be reinterpreted. The superinducing of an equivalence principle upon the word sequence or, in other terms, the *mounting* of the metrical form upon the usual speech form, necessarily gives the experience of a double, ambiguous shape to anyone who is familiar with the given language and with verse. Both the convergences and the divergences between the two forms, both the warranted and the frustrated expectations, supply this experience.

How the given verse-instance is implemented in the given delivery instance depends on the *delivery design* of the reciter; he may cling to a scanning style or tend toward prose-like prosody or freely oscillate between these two poles. We must be on guard against simplistic binarism which reduces two couples into one single opposition either by suppressing the cardinal distinction between verse design and verse instance (as well as between delivery design and delivery instance) or by an erroneous identification of delivery instance and delivery design with the verse instance and verse design.

> "But tell me, child, your choice; what shall I buy
> You?"—"Father, what you buy me I like best."

These two lines from "The Handsome Heart" by Hopkins contain a heavy enjambment which puts a verse boundary before the concluding monosyllable of a phrase, of a sentence, of an utterance. The recitation of these pentameters may be strictly metrical with a manifest pause between "buy" and "you" and a suppressed pause after the pronoun. Or, on the contrary, there may be displayed a prose-oriented manner without any separation of the words "buy you" and with a marked pausal intonation at the end of the question. None of these ways of recitation may, however, hide the intentional discrepancy between the metrical and syntactic division. The verse shape of a poem remains completely independent of its variable delivery, whereby I do not intend to nullify the alluring question of *Autorenleser* and *Selbstleser* launched by Sievers (41).

No doubt, verse is primarily a recurrent "figure of sound." Primarily, always, but never uniquely. Any attempts to confine such poetic conventions as meter, alliteration, or rhyme to the sound level are speculative reasonings without any empirical justification. The projection of the equational principle into the sequence has a much deeper and wider significance. Valéry's view of poetry as "hesitation between the sound and the sense" (cf. 45) is much more realistic and scientific than any bias of phonetic isolationism.

Although rhyme by definition is based on a regular recurrence of equivalent phonemes or phonemic groups, it would be an unsound oversimplification to treat rhyme merely from the standpoint of sound. Rhyme necessarily involves the semantic relationship between rhyming units ("rhyme-fellows" in Hopkins' nomenclature). In the scrutiny of a rhyme we are faced with the question of whether or not it is a homoeoteleuton, which confronts similar derivational and/or inflexional suffixes (congratulations-decorations), or whether the rhyming words belong to the same or to different grammatical categories. Thus, for example, Hopkins' fourfold rhyme is an agreement of two nouns—"kind" and "mind"—both contrasting with the adjective "blind" and with the verb "find." Is there a semantic propinquity, a sort of simile between rhyming lexical units, as in dove-love, light-bright, place-space, name-fame? Do the rhyming members carry the same syntactic function? The difference between the morphological class and the syntactic application may be pointed out in rhyme. Thus in Poe's lines, "While I nodded, nearly *napping,* suddenly there came a *tapping,* As of someone gently *rapping,*" the three rhyming words, morphologically alike, are all three syntactically different. Are totally or partly homonymic rhymes prohibited, tolerated, or favored? Such full homonyms as son-sun, I-eye, eve-eave, and on the other hand, echo rhymes like December-ember, infinite-night, swarm-warm, smiles-miles? What about compound rhymes (such as Hopkins' "enjoyment-toy meant" or "began some-ransom"), where a word unit accords with a word group?

A poet or poetic school may be oriented toward or against grammatical rhyme; rhymes must be either grammatical or antigrammatical; an agrammatical rhyme, indifferent to the relation between sound and grammatical structure, would, like any agrammatism, belong to verbal pathology. If a poet tends to avoid grammatical rhymes, for him, as Hopkins said, "There are two elements in the beauty rhyme has to the mind, the likeness or sameness of sound and the unlikeness or difference of meaning" (12). Whatever the relation between sound and meaning in different rhyme techniques, both spheres are necessarily involved. After Wimsatt's illuminating observations about the meaningfulness of rhyme (48) and the shrewd modern studies of Slavic rhyme patterns, a student in poetics can hardly maintain that rhymes signify merely in a very vague way.

Rhyme is only a particular, condensed case of a much more general, we may even say the fundamental, problem of poetry, namely *parallelism*. Here again Hopkins, in his student papers of 1865, displayed a prodigious insight into the structure of poetry:

The artificial part of poetry, perhaps we shall be right to say all artifice, reduces itself to the principle of parallelism. The structure of poetry is that of continuous parallelism, ranging from the technical so-called Parallelisms of Hebrew poetry and the antiphons of Church music up to the intricacy of Greek or Italian or English verse. But parallelism is of two kinds necessarily—where the opposition is clearly marked, and where it is transitional rather or chromatic. Only the first kind, that of marked parallelism, is concerned with the structure of verse—in rhythm, the recurrence of a certain sequence of syllables, in metre, the recurrence of a certain sequence of rhythm, in alliteration, in assonance and in rhyme. Now the force of this recurrence is to beget a recurrence or parallelism answering to it in the words or thought and, speaking roughly and rather for the tendency than the invariable result, the more marked parallelism in structure whether of elaboration or of emphasis begets more marked parallelism in the words and sense. . . . To the marked or abrupt kind of parallelism belong metaphor, simile, parable, and so on, where the effect is sought in likeness of things, and antithesis, contrast, and so on, where it is sought in unlikeness (12).

Briefly, equivalence in sound, projected into the sequence as its constitutive principle, inevitably involves semantic equivalence, and on any linguistic level any constituent of such a sequence prompts one of the two correlative experiences which Hopkins neatly defines as "comparison for likeness' sake" and "comparison for unlikeness' sake."

Folklore offers the most clear-cut and stereotyped forms of poetry, particularly suitable for structural scrutiny (as Sebeok illustrated with Cheremis samples). Those oral traditions that use grammatical parallelism to connect consecutive lines, for example, Finno-Ugric patterns of verse (see 2, 43) and to a high degree also Russian folk poetry, can be fruitfully analyzed on all linguistic levels—phonological, morphological, syntactic, and lexical: we learn what elements are conceived as equivalent and how likeness on certain levels is tempered with conspicuous difference on other ones. Such forms enable us to verify Ransom's wise suggestion that "the meter-and-meaning process is the organic act of poetry, and involves all its important characters" (37). These clear-cut traditional structures may dispel Wimsatt's doubts about the possibility of writing a grammar of the meter's interaction with the sense, as well as a grammar of the arrangement of metaphors. As soon as parallelism is promoted to canon, the interaction between meter and meaning and the arrangement of tropes cease to be "the free and individual and unpredictable parts of the poetry."

Let us translate a few typical lines from Russian wedding songs about the apparition of the bridegroom:

> A brave fellow was going to the porch,
> Vasilij was walking to the manor.

The translation is literal; the verbs, however, take the final position in both Russian clauses (Dobroj mólodec k séničkam privoráčival, // Vasílij k téremu prixážival). The lines wholly correspond to each other syntactically and morphologically. Both predicative verbs have the same prefixes and suffixes and the same vocalic alternant in the stem; they are alike in aspect, tense, number, and gender; and, moreover, they are synonymic. Both subjects, the common noun and the proper name, refer to the same person and form an appositional group. The two modifiers of place are expressed by identical prepositional constructions, and the first one stands to the second in synecdochic relation.

These verses may occur preceded by another line of similar grammatical (syntactic and morphologic) make-up: "Not a bright falcon was flying beyond the hills" or "Not a fierce horse was coming at gallop to the court." The "bright falcon" and the "fierce horse" of these variants are put in metaphorical relation with "brave fellow." This is traditional Slavic negative parallelism—the refutation of the metaphorical state in favor of the factual state. The negation *ne* may, however, be omitted: "Jasjón kokol zá gory zaljótyval" (A bright falcon was flying beyond the hills) or "Retív kon' kó dvoru priskákival" (A fierce horse was coming at a gallop to the court). In the first of the two examples the *metaphorical* relation is maintained: a brave fellow appeared at the porch, like a bright falcon from behind the hills. In the other instance, however, the semantic connection becomes ambiguous. A comparison between the appearing bridegroom and the galloping horse suggests itself, but at the same time the halt of the horse at the court actually anticipates the approach of the hero to the house. Thus before introducing the rider and the manor of his fiancée, the song evokes the contiguous, *metonymical* images of the horse and of the courtyard: possession instead of possessor, and outdoors instead of inside. The exposition of the groom may be broken up into two consecutive moments even without substituting the horse for the horseman: "A brave fellow was coming at a gallop to the court, // Vasilij was walking to the porch." Thus the "fierce horse," emerging in the preceding line at a similar metrical and syntactic place as the "brave fellow," figures simultaneously as a likeness to and as a representative possession of this fellow, properly speaking—*pars pro toto* for the horseman. The horse image is on a border line between metonymy and synecdoche. From these suggestive connotations of the "fierce horse" there ensues a metaphorical synecdoche: in the wedding songs and other varieties of Russian erotic lore, the masculine *retiv kon* becomes a latent or even patent phallic symbol.

As early as the 1880's, Potebnja, a remarkable inquirer into Slavic poetics, pointed out that in folk poetry a symbol appears to be materialized (*oveščestvlen*), converted into an accessory of the ambiance. "Still a symbol, it is put, however, in a connection with the action. Thus a simile is presented under the shape of a temporal sequence" (35). In Potebnja's examples from Slavic folklore, the willow, under which a girl passes, serves at the same time as her image; the tree and the girl are both copresent in the same verbal simulacrum of the willow. Quite similarly the horse of the love songs remains a virility symbol not only when the maid is asked by the lad to feed his steed but even when being saddled or put into the stable or attached to a tree.

In poetry not only the phonological sequence but in the same way any sequence of semantic units strives to build an equation. Similarity superimposed on contiguity imparts to poetry its thoroughgoing symbolic, multiplex, polysemantic essence which is beautifully suggested by Goethe's "Alles Vergängliche ist nur ein Gleichnis" (Anything transient is but a likeness). Said more technically, anything sequent is a simile. In poetry where similarity is superinduced upon contiguity, any metonymy is slightly metaphorical and any metaphor has a metonymical tint.

Ambiguity is an intrinsic, inalienable character of any self-focused message, briefly a corollary feature of poetry. Let us repeat with Empson: "The machinations of ambiguity are among the very roots of poetry" (7). Not only the message itself but also its addresser and addressee become ambiguous. Besides the author and the reader, there is the "I" of the lyrical hero or of the fictitious storyteller and the "you" or "thou" of the alleged addressee of dramatic monologues, supplications, and epistles. For instance the poem "Wrestling Jacob" is addressed by its title hero to the Saviour and simultaneously acts as a subjective message of the poet

Charles Wesley to his readers. Virtually any poetic message is a quasi-quoted discourse with all those peculiar, intricate problems which "speech within speech" offers to the linguist.

The supremacy of poetic function over referential function does not obliterate the reference but makes it ambiguous. The double-sensed message finds correspondence in a split addresser, in a split addressee, and besides in a split reference, as it is cogently exposed in the preambles to fairy tales of various peoples, for instance, in the usual exordium of the Majorca storytellers: "Aixo era y no era" (It was and it was not) (9). The repetitiveness effected by imparting the equivalence principle to the sequence makes reiterable not only the constituent sequences of the poetic message but the whole message as well. This capacity for reiteration whether immediate or delayed, this reification of a poetic message and its constituents, this conversion of a message into an enduring thing, indeed all this represents an inherent and effective property of poetry.

In a sequence, where similarity is superimposed on contiguity, two similar phonemic sequences near to each other are prone to assume a paronomastic function. Words similar in sound are drawn together in meaning. It is true that the first line of the final stanza in Poe's "Raven" makes wide use of repetitive alliterations, as noted by Valéry (45), but "the overwhelming effect" of this line and of the whole stanza is due primarily to the sway of poetic etymology.

And the Raven, never flitting, still is sitting, *still* is sitting
On the pallid bust of Pallas just above my chamber door;
And his eyes have all the seeming of a demon's that is dreaming,
And the lamp-light o'er him streaming throws his shadow on the
    floor;
And my soul from out that shadow that lies floating on the floor
Shall be lifted—nevermore.

The perch of the raven, "the pallid bust of Pallas," is merged through the "sonorous" paronomasia /pǽləd/—/pǽləs/ into one organic whole (similar to Shelley's molded line "Sculptured on alabaster obelisk" /sk.lp/—/l.b.st/—/b.l.sk/). Both confronted words were blended earlier in another epithet of the same bust—*placid*/plǽsId/—a poetic portmanteau, and the bond between the sitter and the seat was in turn fastened by a paronomasia: "*b*ird or *b*east upon the . . . *b*ust." The bird "is sitting // On the pallid bust of Pallas just above my chamber door," and the raven on his perch, despite the lover's imperative "take thy form from off my door," is nailed to the place by the words /žʌst əbʌv/, both of them blended in /bʌst/.

The never-ending stay of the grim guest is expressed by a chain of ingenious paronomasias, partly inversive, as we would expect from such a deliberate experimenter in anticipatory, regressive *modus operandi*, such a master in "writing backwards" as Edgar Allan Poe. In the introductory line of this concluding stanza, "raven," contiguous to the bleak refrain word "never," appears once more as an embodied mirror image of this "never": /n.v.r/—/r.v.n/. Salient paronomasias interconnect both emblems of the everlasting despair, first "the Raven, never flitting," at the beginning of the very last stanza, and second, in its very last lines the "shadow that lies floating on the floor" and "shall be lifted—nevermore": /névər flítíŋ/—/flótíŋ/ . . . /flór/ . . . /líftəd névər/. The alliterations which struck Valéry build a paronomastic string: /stí . . . /—/sít . . . /—/stí . . . /—/sít . . . /. The invariance of the group is particularly stressed by the variation in its order. The two luminous effects in the chiaroscuro—the "fiery eyes" of the black fowl and the lamplight throwing "his shadow on the floor"—are evoked to add to the gloom of the whole picture and are again bound by the "vivid effect" of paronomasias: /ɔ́lðə́ símɪŋ/ . . . /dimənz/ . . . /ɪz drímɪŋ/—/ ɔrɪm strímɪŋ/. "That shadow that lies /láyz/" pairs with the Raven's "eyes" /áyz/ in an impressively misplaced echo rhyme.

In poetry, any conspicuous similarity in sound is evaluated in respect to similarity and/or dissimilarity in meaning. But Pope's alliterative precept to poets—"the sound must seem an Echo of the sense"—has a wider application. In referential language the connection between *signans* and *signatum* is overwhelmingly based on their codified contiguity, which is often confusingly labeled "arbitrariness of the verbal sign."

The relevance of the sound-meaning nexus is a simple corollary of the superposition of similarity upon contiguity. Sound symbolism is an undeniably objective relation founded on a phenomenal connection between different sensory modes, in particular between the visual and auditory experience. If the results of research in this area have sometimes been vague or controversial, it is primarily due to an insufficient care for the methods of psychological and/or linguistic inquiry. Particularly from the linguistic point of view the picture has often been distorted by lack of attention to the phonological aspect of speech sounds or by inevitably vain operations with complex phonemic units instead of with their ultimate components. But when, on testing, for example, such phonemic oppositions as grave versus acute we ask whether /i/ or /u/ is darker, some of the subjects may respond that this question makes no sense to them, but hardly one will state that /i/ is the darkest of the two.

Poetry is not the only area where sound symbolism makes itself felt, but it is a province where the internal nexus between sound and meaning changes from latent into patent and manifests itself most palpably and intensely, as it has been noted in Hymes's stimulating paper. The superaverage accumulation of a certain class of phonemes or a contrastive assemblage of two opposite classes in the sound texture of a line, of a stanza, of a poem acts like an "undercurrent of meaning," to use Poe's picturesque expression. In two polar words phonemic relationship may be in agreement with semantic opposition, as in Russian /d,en,/ 'day' and /noč/ 'night' with the acute vowel and sharped consonants in the diurnal name and the corresponding grave vowel in the nocturnal name. A reinforcement of this contrast by surrounding the first word with acute and sharped phonemes, in contradistinction to a grave phonemic neighborhood of the second word, makes the sound into a thorough echo of the sense. But in the French *jour* 'day' and *nuit* 'night' the distribution of grave and acute vowels is inverted, so that Mallarmé's *Divagations* accuse his mother tongue of a deceiving perversity for assigning to day a dark timbre and to night a light one (27). Whorf states that when in its sound shape "a word has an acoustic similarity to its own meaning, we can notice it. . . . But, when the opposite occurs, nobody notices it." Poetic language, however, and particularly French poetry in the collision between sound and meaning detected by Mallarmé, either seeks a phonological alternation of such a discrepancy and drowns the "converse" distribution of vocalic features by surrounding *nuit* with grave and *jour* with acute phonemes, or it resorts to a semantic shift and its imagery of day and night replaces the imagery of light and dark by other synesthetic correlates of the phonemic opposition grave/acute and, for instance, puts the heavy, warm day in contrast to the airy, cool night; because "human subjects seem to associate the experiences of bright, sharp, hard, high, light (in weight), quick, high-pitched, narrow, and so on in a long series, with each other; and conversely the experiences of dark, warm, yielding, soft, blunt, low, heavy, slow, low-pitched, wide, etc., in another long series" (47, p. 267f).

However effective is the emphasis on repetition in poetry, the sound texture is still far from being confined to numerical contrivances, and a phoneme that appears only once, but in a key word, in a pertinent position, against a contrastive background, may acquire a striking significance. As painters used to say, "Un kilo de vert n'est pas plus vert qu'un demi kilo."

Any analysis of poetic sound texture must consistently take into account the phonological structure of the given language and, beside the over-all code, also the hierarchy of phonological distinctions in the given poetic convention. Thus the approximate rhymes used by Slavic peoples in oral and in some stages of written tradition admit unlike consonants in the rhyming members (e.g. Czech *boty, boky, stopy, kosy, sochy*) but, as Nitch noticed, no mutual correspondence between voiced and voiceless consonants is allowed (31), so that the quoted Czech words cannot rhyme with *body, doby, kozy, rohy*. In the songs of some American Indian peoples such as Pima-Papago and Tepecano, according to Herzog's observations—only partly communicated in print (10)—the phonemic distinction between voiced and voiceless plosives and between them and nasals is replaced by a free variation, whereas the distinction between labials, dentals, velars, and palatals is rigorously maintained. Thus in the poetry of these languages consonants lose two of the four distinctive features, voiced/ voiceless and nasal/oral, and preserve the other two, grave/ acute and compact/diffuse. The selection and hierarchic stratification of valid categories is a factor of primary importance for poetics both on the phonological and on the grammatical level.

Old Indic and Medieval Latin literary theory keenly distinguished two poles of verbal art, labeled in Sanskrit *Pāñcālī* and *Vaidarbhī* and correspondingly in Latin *ornatus difficilis* and *ornatus facilis* (see 1), the latter style evidently being much more difficult to analyze linguistically because in such literary forms verbal devices are unostentatious and language seems a nearly transparent garment. But one must say with Charles Sanders Peirce: "This clothing never can be completely stripped off, it is only changed for something more diaphanous" (32, p. 171). "Verseless composition," as Hopkins calls the prosaic variety of verbal art—where parallelisms are not so strictly marked and strictly regular as "continuous parallelism" and where there is no dominant figure of sound —present more entangled problems for poetics, as does any transitional linguistic area. In this case the transition is between strictly poetic and strictly referential language. But Propp's pioneering monograph on the structure of the fairy tale (36) shows us how a consistently syntactic approach may be of paramount help even in classifying the traditional plots and in tracing the puzzling laws that underlie their composition and selection. The new studies of Lévi-Strauss (22, 23, also, 24) display a much deeper but essentially similar approach to the same constructional problem.

It is no mere chance that metonymic structures are less explored than the field of metaphor. May I repeat my old observation that the study of poetic tropes has been directed mainly toward metaphor, and the so-called realistic literature, intimately tied with the metonymic principle, still defies interpretation, although the same linguistic methodology, which poetics uses when analyzing the metaphorical style of romantic poetry, is entirely applicable to the metonymical texture of realistic prose (14).

Textbooks believe in the occurrence of poems devoid of

imagery, but actually scarcity in lexical tropes is counter-balanced by gorgeous grammatical tropes and figures. The poetic resources concealed in the morphological and syntactic structure of language, briefly the poetry of grammar, and its literary product, the grammar of poetry, have been seldom known to critics and mostly disregarded by linguists but skillfully mastered by creative writers.

The main dramatic force of Antony's exordium to the funeral oration for Caesar is achieved by Shakespeare's playing on grammatical categories and constructions. Mark Antony lampoons Brutus's speech by changing the alleged reasons for Caesar's assassination into plain linguistic fictions. Brutus's accusation of Caesar, "as he was ambitious, I slew him," undergoes successive transformations. First Antony reduces it to a mere quotation which puts the responsibility for the statement on the speaker quoted: "The noble Brutus // Hath told you . . . ." When repeated, this reference to Brutus is put into opposition to Antony's own assertions by an adversative "but" and further degraded by a concessive "yet." The reference to the alleger's honor ceases to justify the allegation, when repeated with a substitution of the merely copulative "and" instead of the previous causal "for," and when finally put into question through the malicious insertion of a modal "sure":

> The noble Brutus
> Hath told you Cæsar was ambitious;
> For Brutus is an honourable man,
> But Brutus says he was ambitious,
> And Brutus is an honourable man.
> Yet Brutus says he was ambitious,
> And Brutus is an honourable man.
> Yet Brutus says he was ambitious,
> And, sure, he is an honourable man.

The following polyptoton—"I speak . . . Brutus spoke . . . I am to speak"—presents the repeated allegation as mere reported speech instead of reported facts. The effect lies, modal logic would say, in the oblique context of the arguments adduced which makes them into unprovable belief sentences:

> I speak not to disprove what Brutus spoke,
> But here I am to speak what I do know.

The most effective device of Antony's irony is the *modus
obliquus* of Brutus's abstracts changed into a *modus rectus*
to disclose that these reified attributes are nothing but linguistic fictions. To Brutus's saying "he was ambitious," Antony
first replies by transferring the adjective from the agent to
the action ("Did this in Caesar seem ambitious?"), then by
eliciting the abstract noun "ambition" and converting it into
a subject of a concrete passive construction "Ambition should
be made of sterner stuff" and subsequently to a predicate
noun of an interrogative sentence, "Was this ambition?"—
Brutus's appeal "hear me for my cause" is answered by the
same noun *in recto*, the hypostatized subject of an interrogative, active construction: "What cause withholds you . . . ?"
While Brutus calls "awake your senses, that you may the
better judge," the abstract substantive derived from "judge"
becomes an apostrophized agent in Antony's report: "O
judgment, thou art fled to brutish beasts . . ." Incidentally,
this apostrophe with its murderous paronomasia Brutus–
brutish is reminiscent of Caesar's parting exclamation "Et
tu, Brute!" Properties and activities are exhibited *in recto*,
whereas their carriers appear either *in obliquo* ("withholds
you," "to brutish beasts," "back to me") or as subjects of
negative actions ("men have lost," "I must pause"):

> You all did love him once, not without cause;
> What cause withholds you then to mourn for him?
> O judgment, thou art fled to brutish beasts,
> And men have lost their reason!

The last two lines of Antony's exordium display the ostensible
independence of these grammatical metonymies. The stereotyped "I mourn for so-and-so" and the figurative but still
stereotyped "so-and-so is in the coffin and my heart is with
him" or "goes out to him" give place in Antony's speech to
a daringly realized metonymy; the trope becomes a part of
poetic reality:

My heart is in the coffin there with Cæsar,
And I must pause till it come back to me.

In poetry the internal form of a name, that is, the semantic load of its constituents, regains its pertinence. The "Cocktails" may resume their obliterated kinship with plumage. Their colors are vivified in Mac Hammond's lines "The ghost of a Bronx pink lady // With orange blossoms afloat in her hair," and the etymological metaphor attains its realization: "O, Bloody Mary, // The cocktails have crowed not the cocks!" ("At an Old Fashion Bar in Manhattan"). Wallace Stevens' poem "An Ordinary Evening in New Haven" revives the head word of the city name first through a discreet allusion to heaven and then through a direct pun-like confrontation similar to Hopkins' "Heaven-Haven."

The dry eucalyptus *seeks god in the rainy cloud.*
Professor Eucalyptus of New Haven *seeks him in New Haven* . . .
The instinct *for heaven* had its counterpart:
The instinct for earth, *for New Haven,* for his room . . .

The adjective "New" of the city name is laid bare through the concatenation of opposites:

The oldest-newest day is the newest alone.
The oldest-newest night does not creak by . . .

When in 1919 the Moscow Linguistic Circle discussed how to define and delimit the range of *epitheta ornantia,* the poet Majakovskij rebuked us by saying that for him any adjective while in poetry was thereby a poetic epithet, even "great" in the *Great Bear* or "big" and "little" in such names of Moscow streets as *Bol'shaja Presnja* and *Malaja Presnja.* In other words, poeticalness is not a supplementation of discourse with rhetorical adornment but a total re-evaluation of the discourse and of all its components whatsoever.

A missionary blamed his African flock for walking undressed. "And what about yourself?" they pointed to his visage, "are not you, too, somewhere naked?" "Well, but that is my face." "Yet in us," retorted the natives, "everywhere it is face." So in poetry any verbal element is converted into a figure of poetic speech.

My attempt to vindicate the right and duty of linguistics to direct the investigation of verbal art in all its compass and extent can come to a conclusion with the same burden which summarized my report to the 1953 conference here at Indiana University: "Linguista sum; linguistici nihil a me alienum puto" (25). If the poet Ransom is right (and he is right) that "poetry is a kind of language" (38), the linguist whose field is any kind of language may and must include poetry in his study. The present conference has clearly shown that the time when both linguists and literary historians eluded questions of poetic structure is now safely behind us. Indeed, as Hollander stated, "there seems to be no reason for trying to separate the literary from the overall linguistic." If there are some critics who still doubt the competence of linguistics to embrace the field of poetics, I privately believe that the poetic incompetence of some bigoted linguists has been mistaken for an inadequacy of the linguistic science itself. All of us here, however, definitely realize that a linguist deaf to the poetic function of language and a literary scholar indifferent to linguistic problems and unconversant with linguistic methods are equally flagrant anachronisms.

REFERENCES

1. Arbusow, L., *Colores rhetorici*, Göttingen, 1948.
2. Austerlitz, R., *Ob-Ugric Metrics; Folklore Fellows Communications*, 174 (1958).
3. Bishop, J. L., "Prosodic Elements in T'ang Poetry," *Indiana University Conference on Oriental-Western Literary Relations*, Chapel Hill, 1955.
4. Bühler, K., "Die Axiomatik der Sprachwissenschaft," *Kant-Studien*, 38, pp. 19–90 (Berlin, 1933).
5. Cherry, C., *On Human Communication*, New York, 1957.
6. Èjxenbaum, B., *Melodika stixa*, Leningrad, 1922.
7. Empson, W., *Seven Types of Ambiguity*, New York, third edition, 1955.
8. Frost, R., *Collected Poems*, New York, 1939.
9. Giese, W., "Sind Märchen Lügen?" *Cahiers S. Puscariu*, 1, pp. 137ff. (1952).

10. Herzog, G., "Some Linguistic Aspects of American Indian Poetry," *Word*, 2, p. 82 (1946).

11. Hill, A. A., Review in *Language*, 29, pp. 549–61 (1953).

12. Hopkins, G. M., *The Journals and Papers*, H. House, ed., London, 1959.

13. ——, *Poems*, W. H. Gardner, ed., New York and London, third edition, 1948.

14. Jakobson, R., "The Metaphoric and Metonymic Poles," in *Fundamentals of Language*, pp. 76–82, 's-Gravenhage and New York, 1956.

15. ——, *O češskom stixe preimuščestvenno v sopostavlenii s russkim* (= Sborniki po teorii poètičeskogo jazyka, 5), Berlin and Moscow, 1923.

16. ——, "Studies in Comparative Slavic Metrics," *Oxford Slavonic Papers*, 3, pp. 21–66 (1952).

17. ——, "Über den Versbau der serbokroatischen Volksepen," *Archives néerlandaises de phonétique expérimentale*, pp. 7–9, 44–53 (1933).

18. Jespersen, O., "Cause psychologique de quelques phénomènes de métrique germanique," *Psychologie du langage*, Paris, 1933.

19. Joos, M., "Description of language design," *Journal of the Acoustical Society of America*, 22, pp. 701–08 (1950).

20. Karcevskij, S., "Sur la phonologie de la phrase," *Travaux du cercle linguistique de Prague*, 4, pp. 188–223 (1931).

21. Levi, A., "Della versificazione italiana," *Archivum Romanicum*, 14, pp. 449–526 (1930).

22. Lévi-Strauss, C., "Analyse morphologique des contes russes," *International Journal of Slavic Linguistics and Poetics*, 3 (1960).

23. ——, *La geste d' Asdival*, École Pratique des Hautes Études, Paris, 1958.

24. ——, "The Structural Study of Myth," in T. A. Sebeok, ed., *Myth: a Symposium*, pp. 50–66, Philadelphia, 1955.

25. ——, R. Jakobson, C. F. Voegelin, and T. A. Sebeok, *Results of the Conference of Anthropologists and Linguists*, Baltimore, 1953.

26. Malinowski, B., "The Problem of Meaning in Primitive Languages," in C. K. Ogden and I. A. Richards, *The Meaning of Meaning*, pp. 296–336, New York and London, ninth edition, 1953.

27. Mallarmé, S., *Divagations*, Paris, 1899.

28. Mansikka, V. T., *Litauische Zaubersprüche, Folklore Fellows Communications*, 87 (1929).

29. Maretić, T., "Metrika narodnih naših pjesama," *Rad Yugo-slavenske Akademije*, 168, 170 (Zagreb, 1907).

30. Marty, A., *Untersuchungen zur Grundlegung der allgemeinen Grammatik und Sprachphilosophie*, Vol. 1., Halle, 1908.

31. Nitsch, K., "Z historii polskich rymów," *Wybór pism polonisty-cznych*, 1, pp. 33–77 (Wrocław, 1954).

32. Peirce, C. S., *Collected papers*, Vol. 1, Cambridge, Mass., 1931.

33. Poe, E. A., "Marginalia," *The Works*, Vol. 3, New York, 1857.

34. Polivanov, E. D., "O metričeskom xaraktere kitajskogo stixo-složenija," *Doklady Rossijskoj Akademii Nauk*, serija V, 156–58 (1924).

35. Potebnja, A., *Ob" jasnenija malorusskix i srodnyx narodnyx pesen*, Warsaw, 1 (1883); 2 (1887).

36. Propp, V., *Morphology of the Folktale*, Bloomington, 1958.

37. Ransom, J. C., *The New Criticism*, Norfolk, Conn., 1941.

38. ——, *The World's Body*, New York, 1938.

39. Rybnikov, P. N., *Pesni*, Vol. 3, Moscow, 1910.

40. Sapir, E., *Language*, New York, 1921.

41. Sievers, E., *Ziele und Wege der Schallanalyse*, Heidelberg, 1924.

42. Simmons, D. C., "Specimens of Efik folklore," *Folk-Lore*, 66, pp. 417–24 (1955).

43. Steinitz, W., *Der Parallelismus in der finnisch-karelischen Volksdichtung, Folklore Fellows Communications*, 115 (1934).

44. Taranovski, K., *Ruski dvodelni ritmovi*, Belgrade, 1955.

45. Valéry, P., *The Art of Poetry*, Bollingen series 45, New York, 1958.

46. Wang Li, *Han-yü shih-lü hsüeh* (= Versification in Chinese), Shanghai, 1958.

47. Whorf, B. L., *Language, Thought, and Reality*, J. B. Carroll, ed., New York, 1956.

48. Wimsatt, W. K., Jr., *The Verbal Icon*, Lexington, 1954.

49. Žirmunskij, V., *Voprosy teorii literatury*, Leningrad, 1928.

ROMAN JAKOBSON AND
CLAUDE LÉVI-STRAUSS

Claude Lévi-Strauss (see p. 168) frankly acknowledges the influence which Jakobson's work has had on the development of his own structural approach to anthropology. In their article on Charles Baudelaire's "Les Chats," Jakobson and Lévi-Strauss join forces to present a detailed structuralist analysis of the poem. Their study has become a frequently cited model of such analysis.

7

Charles Baudelaire's "Les Chats"

It will perhaps be found surprising that a review of anthropology should publish a study devoted to a French poem of the XIXth century. Yet, the explanation is simple. A linguist and an ethnologist decided to combine their efforts in an attempt to understand the creation of a Baudelairian sonnet, because they had found themselves independently confronted by complementary problems. In poetic works, the linguist discerns structures which are strikingly analogous to those which the analysis of myths reveals to the ethnologist. For his part, the latter must recognize that the myths do not consist only in conceptual arrangements. They are also works of art which arouse in those who listen to them (and in the ethnologists themselves who read them in transcription) profound esthetic emotions. Could it be that the two problems are but one?

True, the author of this prefatory note has at times opposed the myth to the poetic work (Anthropologie structurale, p. 232), but those who reproached him for it did not notice that the very notion of contrast implied that the two forms had been first conceived as complementary terms, belonging to the same category. The comparison sketched here does not contradict the differential character which we had first stressed: namely, each poetic work, considered in isolation, contains in itself its variants which can be represented on a vertical axis, since it is formed of superimposed levels: phonological, phonetic, syntactic, prosodic, semantic, etc. On the other hand, the myth — at least in the extreme — can be interpreted at the semantic level only. The system of variants (always indis-

" 'Les Chats' de Charles Baudelaire," L'Homme, II, jan.–avril, 1962, pp. 5–21, slightly revised by Roman Jakobson. This translation has been checked and approved by Roman Jakobson and is published here with his permission.

pensable to structural analysis), might then be furnished by a plurality of versions of the same myth, that is to say by a horizontal cut practiced on a body of myths at the semantic level only. However, one must not lose sight of the fact that this distinction fulfills above all a practical requirement, that is, it allows the structural analysis of myths to forge ahead even when the actual linguistic base is lacking. Only by practicing both methods, even if it means forcing oneself to change fields briskly, will one be in a position to confirm the initial wager, that if either method can be chosen according to the circumstances, it is because, in the last analysis, they can be substituted one for the other, since they are not always able to complete each other.

1. Les amoureux fervents et les savants austères
2. Aiment également, dans leur mûre saison,
3. Les chats puissants et doux, orgueil de la maison,
4. Qui comme eux sont frileux et comme eux sédentaires.

5. Amis de la science et de la volupté,
6. Ils cherchent le silence et l'horreur des ténèbres;
7. L'Érèbe les eût pris pour ses coursiers funèbres,
8. S'ils pouvaient au servage incliner leur fierté.

9. Ils prennent en songeant les nobles attitudes
10. Des grands sphinx allongés au fond des solitudes,
11. Qui semblent s'endormir dans un rêve sans fin;

12. Leurs reins féconds sont pleins d'étincelles magiques,
13. Et des parcelles d'or, ainsi qu'un sable fin,
14. Étoilent vaguement leurs prunelles mystiques.

If one may give credence to the feuilleton, "Le Chat Trott" by Champfleury, where this sonnet of Baudelaire was published for the first time (*Le Corsaire,* the Nov. 14, 1847 issue); it had already been written in March, 1840. Contrary to the affirmations of certain exegetes, the early text of the *Corsaire* and that of the *Fleurs du Mal* (1857) coincide word for word.

In the organizations of the rhymes, the poet follows the schemes *aBBa CddC eeFgFg* (where the lines with masculine rhymes are symbolized by capital letters and the lines with feminine rhymes by small letters). This chain of rhymes is divided into three strophic units, namely two quatrains and a sestet composed of two tercets, which form a certain unit since the disposition of the rhymes within this sestet is controlled in the sonnets, as Grammont has shown, "by the same rules as in any strophe of six lines."[1]

The grouping of the rhymes in the sonnet cited is the corollary of three dissimilative rules:

1. two plain (couplet) rhymes cannot follow each other;
2. if two contiguous lines belong to different rhymes, one of them must be feminine and the other masculine;
3. at the end of contiguous stanzas, feminine lines and masculine lines alternate: [4]*sédentaires* — [8]*fierté* — [14]*mystiques*.

Following the classical pattern, the rhymes called feminine always end in a mute syllable and the masculine rhymes in a fully sounded syllable. The difference between the two classes of rhymes persists equally in the current pronunciation which suppresses the "mute *e*" of the final syllable, the last fully sounded vowel being followed by consonants in all the feminine rhymes of the sonnet (*austères-sédentaires, ténèbres-funèbres, attitudes-solitudes, magiques-mystiques*), whereas all its masculine rhymes end in a vowel (*saison-maison, volupté-fierté, fin-fin*).

The relation between the classification of rhymes and the choice of grammatical categories sets off the important role played by grammar as well as rhyme in the structure of this sonnet.

All the lines end in nominal forms, either substantive (8), or adjectival (6). All these substantives are feminine. The final noun is plural in eight lines with a feminine rhyme, which are all longer, either by a syllable in the conventional norm or by a postvocalic consonant in today's current pronunciation, whereas the shorter lines, those with a masculine rhyme, end in the six cases with a singular noun.

In the two quatrains, the masculine rhymes are formed by substantives and the feminine rhymes by adjectives, with the exception of the key word [6]*ténèbres* which rhymes with [7]*funèbres*. We will return later to the general problem of the relation between the two lines in question. As for the tercets,

---

[1] M. Grammont, *Petit traité de versification française*, Paris, 1908, p. 86.

the three lines of the first one all end with substantives, and those of the second with adjectives. Thus, the rhyme which links the two tercets, the only homonymous rhyme ([11]*sans fin*-[13]*sable fin*), opposes to a substantive of the feminine gender, an adjective of the masculine gender. Among the masculine rhymes of the sonnet, it is the only adjective and the only example of the masculine gender.

The sonnet is made up of three complex sentences delimited by a period, namely each of the two quatrains and the sestet. According to the number of independent clauses and of the finite verbal forms, the three sentences display an arithmetic progression: 1. a single finite (*aiment*); 2. two (*cherchent, eût pris*); 3. three (*prennent, sont, étoilent*). On the other hand, in their subordinate clauses the three sentences have each only one finite: 1. *qui . . . sont;* 2. *s'ils pouvaient;* 3. *qui semblent*.

This ternary division of the sonnet implies an antinomy between both two-rhyme sentences and the final, three-rhyme sentence. It is counterbalanced by a dichotomy which divides the work into two coupled stanzas, that is, into two pairs of quatrains and two pairs of tercets. This binary principle, supported in turn by the grammatical organization of the text, also implies an antinomy, this time between the first section of two different rhymes and the second section of three, as well as between the two initial subdivisions or stanzas of four lines and the two last stanzas of three lines. The composition of the whole work is based on the tension between these two kinds of arrangement, and between the symmetrical and dissymmetrical constituents.

A clear-cut syntactical parallel is observed between the pair of quatrains on the one hand, and the pair of tercets on the other. The first quatrain as well as the first tercet is made up of two clauses of which the second — relative, and introduced in each case by the same pronoun *qui* — includes the last line of the stanza. It is linked to a plural masculine substantive which serves as accessory in the principal clause ([3]*Les chats,* [10]*Des . . . sphinx*). The second quatrain (and equally the second tercet) contains two coordinate clauses of which the last, complex in turn, takes in the two final lines of the stanza (7–8 and 13–14) and includes a subordinate clause which is linked to the main clause by a conjunction. In the quatrain, this clause is conditional (*⁸S'ils pouvaient*); that of the tercet is comparative (*¹³ainsi qu'un*). The first is post-positive, whereas the second, incomplete, is an interpolated clause.

In the text of the *Corsaire* (1847), the punctuation of the sonnet corresponds to this division. The first tercet ends with a period, as does the first quatrain. In the second tercet and in the second quatrain, the last two lines are preceded by a semicolon.

The semantic aspect of the grammatical subjects reinforces this parallelism between the two quatrains on the one hand and the two tercets on the other:

I) Quatrains	II) Tercets
1. First	1. First
2. Second	2. Second

The subjects of the first quatrain and of the first tercet designate only animate beings, whereas one of the two subjects of the second quatrain, and all the grammatical subjects of the second tercet, are inanimate substantives: *⁷L'Érèbe, ¹²Leurs reins, ¹³des parcelles, ¹³un sable*. In addition to these so to speak horizontal correspondences, there is a correspondence that could be called vertical which opposes the totality of the two quatrains to the totality of the two tercets. While all the direct objects in the two tercets are inanimate substantives (*⁹les nobles attitudes, ¹⁴leurs prunelles*), the sole direct object of the first quatrain is an animate substantive (*³Les chats*). The objects of the second quatrain include, along with inanimate substantives (*⁶le silence et l'horreur*), the pronoun *les,* which refers to the cats of the preceding sentence. From the point of view of the relation between the subject and the object, the sonnet presents two correspondences which could be called diagonal. A descending diagonal unites the two exterior stanzas (the first quatrain and the last tercet) and opposes them to the ascending diagonal, which, in turn, links the two interior stanzas. In the exterior stanzas, the object partakes of the same semantic class as the subject. They are animate in the first quatrain (*amoureux, savants — chats*) and inanimate in the second tercet (*reins, parcelles — prunelles*). On the other hand, in the interior stanzas, the object belongs to a class which is opposite to that of the subject: in the first tercet, the inanimate object is opposed to the animate subject (*ils* [= chats] *— attitudes*), whereas in the second quatrain, the same relationship (*ils* [= chats] *— silence, horreur*) alternates with that of the animate object and of the inanimate subject (*Érèbe — les* [= chats]).

Thus, each of the four stanzas keeps its individuality. The animate class, which is common to the subject and to the object in the first quatrain, belongs solely to the subject in the first tercet; in the second quatrain, this class characterizes either the subject or the object, whereas in the second tercet, neither one nor the other.

The beginning and the end of the sonnet offer several striking correspondences in their grammatical structure. At the end as well as at the beginning, but in no other place, we find two subjects with only one predicate and only one direct object. Each of these subjects, as well as the object, has a modifier (*Les amoureux fervents, les savants austères — Les chats puissants et doux; des parcelles d'or, un sable fin — leurs prunelles mystiques*). The two predicates, the first and the last in the sonnet, are the only ones to be accompanied by adverbs. Each of the two are derived from adjectives and are linked to one another by a deep rhyme: [2]*Aiment également —* [14]*Étoilent vaguement.* The second predicate of the sonnet and the one before the last are the only ones that comprise a copula and a predicative adjective. In both cases, this predicative is underlined by an internal rhyme: [4]*Qui comme eux* sont fril*eux*; [12]*Leurs reins* féconds sont p*leins*. In general, the two exterior stanzas are the only ones rich in adjectives: nine in the quatrain and five in the tercet, whereas the two interior stanzas have only three adjectives in all (*funèbres, nobles, grands*).

As we have already noted, it is only at the beginning and at the end of the poem that the subjects partake of the same class as the object. Each one belongs to the animate class in the first quatrain, and to the inanimate in the second tercet. The animate beings, their functions and their activities, dominate the initial stanza. The first line contains only adjectives. Among these adjectives the two substantivized forms which serve as subjects — *Les amoureux* and *les savants* — display verbal roots: the text begins with "those who love" and with "those who know." In the last line of the work the opposite occurs: the transitive verb *Étoilent*, which serves as a predicate, is derived from a substantive. This last is related to the series of inanimate and concrete appellatives which dominate this tercet and distinguish it from the three anterior stanzas. A clear homophony is to be noted between this verb and the members of the series in question: /etēsɛlə/ — /e de parsɛlə/ — /etwalə/. Finally, the subordinate clauses, which the two stanzas have in their last line, each include an adverbial infinitive. These two complements are the only infinitives of the whole poem: [8]*S'ils pouvaient . . . incliner;* [11]*Qui semblent s'endormir.*

As we have seen, neither the dichotomous scission of the sonnet, nor the division into three stanzas, results in an equilibrium of isometric constituents. But if we divided the fourteen lines into two equal parts, the seventh verse would terminate the first half of the poem, and the eighth would mark the beginning of its second half. Thus, it is significant that just these two middle lines stand out most obviously from the rest of the poem by their grammatical make-up.

Actually, in several respects, the poem is divided into three parts: the middle pair of lines and two isometric groups, i.e., the six lines which precede and the six which follow this pair. Hence there emerges a kind of couplet inserted between two sestets.

All the personal forms of the verbs and of the pronouns, and all the subjects of the verbal clauses, are in the plural throughout the sonnet, except in the seventh verse — *L'Érèbe les eût pris pour ses coursiers funèbres* — which contains the only proper noun in the poem and the only instance where the finite verb and its subject are both singular. It is, moreover, the only line where the possessive pronoun (*ses*) refers to a singular.

The third person is the only person used in the sonnet. The

mere verbal tense is the present, except the seventh and the eighth lines where the poet envisages an imaginary action (⁷*eût pris*) emerging from an unreal premise (⁸*S'ils pouvaient*).

The sonnet manifests a pronounced tendency to provide each verb and each substantive with a modifier. Every verbal form is accompanied by a governed modifier (substantive, pronoun, infinitive) or by a predicative adjective. All the transitive verbs govern only substantives (²⁻³*Aiment . . . Les chats;* ⁶*cherchent le silence et l'horreur;* ⁹*prennent . . . les . . . attitudes;* ¹⁴*Étoilent . . . leurs prunelles*). The pronoun which serves as object in the seventh verse is the sole deviation: *les eût pris.*

Except for the adnominal adjuncts, which are never accompanied by any modifier in the sonnet, the substantives (including the substantivized adjectives) are always modified by attributes (e.g., ³*chats puissants et doux*) or by adjuncts (⁵*Amis de la science et de la volupté*). It is again in the seventh verse that we find the one exception: *L'Érèbe les eût pris.*

All five attributes in the first quatrain (¹*fervents,* ¹*austères,* ²*mûre,* ³*puissants,* ³*doux*) and all six in the two tercets (⁹*nobles,* ¹⁰*grands,* ¹²*féconds,* ¹²*magiques,* ¹³*fin,* ¹⁴*mystiques*) are qualitative epithets whereas the second quatrain has no other adjectives but the determinative attribute in the seventh line (*coursiers funèbres*).

It is also this line which inverts the order animate-inanimate underlying the relation between the subject and the object in the other lines of this quatrain, and which remains in the entire sonnet the only one to adopt the order inanimate-animate. Several striking peculiarities distinguish the seventh line only or the two last lines of the second quatrain from the rest of the sonnet. However, it must be stated that the tendency to underscore the median distich of the sonnet competes with the principle of the asymmetric trichotomy — which opposes the entire second quatrain to the first quatrain on the one hand, and to the final sestet on the other hand, and which creates in this way a kind of central strophe, distinct in several respects from the marginal strophic units. Thus, we have noted the fact that the seventh line is the only one which puts the subject and the predicate in the singular, but this observation can be enlarged. The lines of the second quatrain are the only ones where either the subject or the object is put in the singular. If, in the seventh line, the singular of the subject (*L'Érèbe*) is opposed to the plural of the object (*les*), the adjoining lines invert this relation by using the plural for the subject and the singular for the object (*6Ils cherchent le silence et l'horreur; 8S'ils pouvaient . . . incliner leur fierté*). In the other stanzas, the object and the subject are both in the plural (*1–3Les amoureux . . . et les savants . . . Aiment . . . Les chats; 9Ils prennent . . . les . . . attitudes; 13–14Et des parcelles . . . Étoilent . . . leurs prunelles*). In the second quatrain, the singular of the subject and of the object coincides with the inanimate; the plural with the animate class. The importance of grammatical numbers for Baudelaire becomes particularly noteworthy because of the role played by their opposition in the rhymes of the sonnet.

Let us add that by their structure the rhymes of the second quatrain are distinguished from all the other rhymes of the poem. Among the feminine rhymes, that of the second quatrain, *ténèbres — funèbres*, is the only one which brings together two different parts of speech. Moreover, all the rhymes of the sonnet, except those of the mentioned quatrain, comprise one or several identical phonemes which precede, immediately or at some distance, the stressed syllable which is usually furnished with a supportive consonant: *1savants austères — 4sédentaires, 2mûre saison — 3maison, 9attitudes — 10solitudes, 11un rêve sans fin — 13un sable fin, 12étincelles magiques — 14prunelles mystiques.* In the second quatrain, neither the pair *5volupté — 8fierté*, nor *6ténèbres — 7funèbres*, offer any correspondence in the syllable anterior to the rhyme itself. On the other hand, the final words of the seventh and of the eighth lines alliterate: *7funèbres — 8fierté*, and the sixth verse is linked to the fifth: *6ténèbres* repeats the last syllable of *5volupté* and an internal rhyme — *5science — 6silence* — reinforces the affinity between the two lines. Thus, the rhymes themselves exhibit a certain relaxation of the ties between the two halves of the second quatrain.

A salient role in the phonic texture of the sonnet is played by the nasal vowels. These phonemes, "as though veiled by nasality," to use Grammont's apt expression,[2] are of a high frequency in the first quatrain (9 nasals, from two to three per line) and especially in the final sestet (21 nasals, with a rising tendency in the first tercet — 9_3 — 10_4 — 11_6: "Qui semblent s'endormir dans un rêve sans fin" — and with a falling tendency in the second tercet — 12_5 — 13_3 — 14_1). On the contrary, the second quatrain has only three: one in each line except the seventh, the sole line of the sonnet without nasal vowels; and this quatrain is the only stanza whose masculine rhyme has no nasal vowel. It is in the second quatrain that the role of the phonic dominant passes from the vowels to the consonantal phonemes, the liquids in particular. The second quatrain is the only one which shows an excess of liquid phonemes, namely, 24, compared to 15 in the first quatrain, 11 in the first tercet, and 14 in the second. The total number of /r/'s is slightly lower than the number of /l/'s (31 *versus* 33), but the seventh line, which has only two /l/'s, contains five /r/'s, that is to say more than any other line of the sonnet: L'*Érèbe* les eût pris pour ses coursiers funèbres. According to Grammont, it is by opposition to /r/ that /l/ "gives the impression of a sound that is neither grating, nor scraping, nor rough, but on the contrary which runs, which flows, . . . which is limpid."[3] The abrupt character of every /r/, especially French /r/, in comparison with the *glissando* of the /l/, is brought out clearly by Miss M. Durand's acoustical analysis of the two liquids.[4] The agglomeration of the /r/'s eloquently echoes the delusive association of the cats with Erebus, followed by the antithetic ascent of the empirical felines to their miraculous transfigurations.

The first six lines of the sonnet are united by a reiterative feature: a symmetrical pair of collateral vocables, linked by the same conjunction *et*: [1]*Les amoureux fervents et les savants austères;* [3]*Les chats puissants et doux;* [4]*Qui comme eux sont frileux et comme eux sédentaires;* [5]*Amis de la science et de la volupté,* where the binarism of the modifiers forms a chiasmus with the binarism of the head words in the subsequent line —

---

[2] M. Grammont, *Traité de phonétique,* Paris, 1930, p. 384.

[3] M. Grammont, *Traité . . . ,* p. 388.

[4] M. Durand, "La spécificité du phonème. Application au cas de R/L," *Journal de Psychologie,* LVII, 1960, pp. 405–19.

[6]*le silence et l'horreur des ténèbres.* The last line puts an end to the chain of such binary constructions. This type of construction, common to almost all the lines of the initial "sestet," does not reappear. Phrases juxtaposed without any conjunction are a variation on the same scheme: [2]*Aiment également, dans leur mûre saison* (parallel circumstantial modifiers); [3]*Les chats . . . , orgueil . . .* (substantive in apposition to another).

Such pairs of collateral vocables and the rhymes (not only exterior and underlining the semantic relations, such as [1]*austères* — [4]*sédentaires,* [2]*saison* — [3]*maison,* but also and above all interior), serve to cement the lines of this introduction: [1]*amoureux* — [4]*comme eux* — [4]*frileux* — [4]*comme eux*; [1]*fervents* — [1]*savants* — [2]*également* — [2]*dans* — [3]*puissants;* [5]*science* — [6]*silence.* Thus all the adjectives which characterize the personae of the first quatrain appear to be rhyming words, with a single exception: [3]*doux.* A double etymological figure which links three lines at their beginning — [1]*Les amoureux* — [2]*Aiment* — [5]*Amis* — contributes to the unification of this "similistanza" of six lines, which starts and ends with a pair of lines, whose first hemistiches rhyme between themselves: [1]*fervents* — [2]*également;* [5]*science* — [6]*silence.*

[3]*Les chats,* direct object of the clause which encompasses the first three lines of the sonnet, becomes the implicit subject in the clauses of the three following lines ([4]*Qui comme eux sont frileux;* [6]*Ils cherchent le silence*). In this way this quasi-sestet appears to be sketchily dismembered into two quasi-tercets. The middle "distich" recapitulates the metamorphosis of the cats: from an implicit object ([7]*L'Érèbe les eût pris*), into an equally implicit grammatical subject ([8]*S'ils pouvaient*). In this respect, the eighth line coincides with the subsequent sentence ([9]*Ils prennent*).

In general, the postpositive subordinate clauses form a kind of transition between the subordinating clause and the further sentence. Thus, the implicit subject "chats" of the ninth and tenth lines changes into a reference to the metaphor "sphinx" in the relative clause of the eleventh line (*Qui semblent s'endormir dans un rêve sans fin*) and links this line to the tropes serving as grammatical subjects in the final tercet. The indefinite article, entirely alien to the first ten lines with their fourteen definite articles, is the only one allowed in the four concluding lines of the sonnet.

Thus, thanks to the ambiguous references in the two relative clauses, those of the eleventh and fourth lines, the four concluding lines allow us to glimpse at the contour of an imaginary quatrain which somehow corresponds to the initial quatrain of the sonnet. On the other hand, the final tercet has a formal structure which seems reflected in the three first lines of the sonnet.

The animate subject is never expressed by a substantive, but either by substantivized adjectives in the first line of the sonnet (*Les amoureux, les savants*) or by personal and relative pronouns in the further clauses. Human beings appear only in the first clause, where the double subject designates them by substantivized verbal adjectives.

The cats, named in the title of the sonnet, are called by their name only once in the text — in the first clause, where they serve as direct object: [1]*Les amoureux . . . et les savants . . .* [2]*Aiment . . .* [3]*Les chats.* Not only the word "chats" is avoided in the further lines of the poem, but even the initial hushing phoneme /ʃ/ recurs only in a single word: [6]/ilʃɛrʃə/. It denotes, with reduplication, the first reported action of felines. From then on the sonnet refrains from repeating this voiceless sibilant, linked to the name of the poem's heroes.

From the third line, the cats become an implicit subject, which proves to be the last animate subject of the sonnet. The substantive *chats,* in the roles of subject, object, and adnominal adjunct, is replaced by the anaphoric pronouns [6, 8, 9]*ils,* [7]*les,* [8, 12, 14]*leur(s)*; and the substantive pronouns *ils* and *les* refer only to the cats. These accessory (adverbal) forms occur solely in the two interior stanzas, i.e., in the second quatrain and in the first tercet. The corresponding autonomous form [4]*eux* is used twice in the initial quatrain and refers only to the human characters of the sonnet, whereas no substantive pronouns occur in the final tercet.

The two subjects of the initial clause of the sonnet have only one predicate and one object. Thus, [1]*Les amoureux fervents et les savants austères* end up as [2]*dans leur mûre saison* by finding their identity in an intermediary being, the animal who encompasses the antinomic traits of the two conditions, human but mutually opposite. The two human categories, sensual/intellectual, oppose each other, and the mediation is achieved by the cats. Hence, the role of subject is latently assumed by the cats, who are at one and the same time scholars and lovers.

The two quatrains objectively present the personage of the cat, whereas the two tercets carry out his transfiguration. However, the second quatrain differs fundamentally from the first and, in general, from all the other stanzas. The equivocal formulation: *ils cherchent le silence et l'horreur des ténèbres* gives rise to a misunderstanding summoned up in the seventh line of the sonnet, and denounced in the following line. The aberrant character of this quatrain, especially the perplexity of its last half and particularly of the seventh line, is thoroughly marked by the peculiar traits of its grammatical and phonic texture.

The semantic affinity between *L'Érèbe* ("dark region bordering on Hell," metonymic substitute for "the powers of darkness" and particularly for *Érèbe*, "brother of the Night") and the penchant of cats for *l'horreur des ténèbres,* corroborated by the phonic similarity between /tenɛbrə/ and /erɛbə/, came close to associating the cats, heroes of the poem, with the hair-raising job of the *coursiers funèbres.* Does the line insinuating that *L'Érèbe les eût pris pour ses coursiers* testify to a frustrated desire or to a false recognition? The meaning of this passage, which the critics have puzzled over,[5] remains purposely ambiguous.

Each of the quatrains as well as each of the tercets seeks a new identification for the cats. While the first quatrain linked the cats to two types of human condition, thanks to their pride they succeed in rejecting the new identification tried in the second quatrain, which associates them to an animal condition: that of coursers placed in mythological cadre. Throughout the whole poem, it is the one rejected equivalence. The grammatical composition of this passage, which contrasts expressly with that of the other stanzas, betrays its pe-

[5] Cf. *L'Intermédiaire des chercheurs et des curieux,* LXVII, col. 338 et 509.

culiar character: unreal conditional, lack of qualitative attributes, and an inanimate singular subject devoid of any modifier and governing an animate plural object.

Allusive oxymorons unite the stanzas. [8]*S'ils* POUVAIENT *au servage incliner leur fierté,* — but they cannot do it (ils ne "peuvent" pas), because they are truly [3]PUISSANTS. They cannot be passively taken (PRIS) to play an active role, and hence they themselves actively [9]PRENNENT a passive role, because they are obstinately *sédentaires*.

[8]*Leur fierté* predestines them to the [9]*nobles attitudes* [10]*Des grands sphinx.* The [10]*sphinx allongés* and the cats that mime them [9]*en songeant* are united by a paronomastic link between the only two participial forms in the sonnet: /ãsɔ̃ʒã/ and /alɔ̃ʒe/. The cats seem to identify with the sphinxes, who in turn [11]*semblent s'endormir,* but the illusory comparison, assimilating the sedentary cats (and implicitly all who are [4]*comme eux*), to the immobility of the supernatural beings, acquires the value of a metamorphosis. The cats and the human beings which are identified with them are reunited in the fabled monsters with human heads and bodies of beasts. Thus, the rejected identification appears to be replaced by a new identification, equally mythological.

[9]*En songeant,* the cats manage to identify themselves with the [10]*grands sphinx.* A chain of paronomasias, linked to these key words and combining nasal vowels with the continuant dentals and labials, reinforces the metamorphosis: [9]*en songeant* /ãsɔ̃../ — [10]*grands sphinx* /..ãsfɛ̃../ — [10]*fond* /fõ/ — [11]*semblent* /sã.../ — [11]*s'endormir* /sã....../ — [11]*dans un* /.ãzœ̃/ — [11]*sans fin* /sãfɛ̃/. The acute nasal /ɛ̃/ and the other phonemes of the word [10]*sphinx* /sfɛ̃ks/ recur in the last tercet: [12]*reins* /.ɛ̃/ — [12]*pleins* /..ɛ̃/ — [12]*étincelles* /..ɛ̃s.../ — [13]*ainsi* /ɛ̃s/ — [13]*qu'un sable* /kœ̃s..../ — [13]*fin* /fɛ̃/.

We read in the first quatrain: [3]*Les chats puissants et doux, orgueil de la maison.* Should we guess that the cats, proud of their home, are the incarnation of this pride, or is it the house, proud of its feline inhabitants, who is determined, like Erebus, to domesticate them? Whichever it may be, the [3]*maison* which circumscribes the cats in the first quatrain is transformed into a spacious desert, [10]*fond des solitudes.* The fear of the cold, bringing together the cats, [4]*frileux,* and the

lovers, [1]*fervents* (note the paronomasia /fɛrvã/ — frilø/)
finds a suitable climate in the austere solitudes (as austere as
the scholars) of the desert (torrid like the fervent lovers)
which surrounds the sphinxes. On the temporal level, the
[2]*mûre saison*, which rhymed with [3]*la maison* in the first
quatrain and approached it in meaning, found a clear counterpart in the first tercet: These two visibly parallel groups
([2]*dans leur mûre saison* and [11]*dans un rêve sans fin*) mutually
oppose each other, the one calling up numbered days and the
other, eternity. No constructions with *dans* or with any other
adverbial preposition occur elsewhere in the sonnet.

The miracle of the cats dominates the two tercets. The
metamorphosis unfolds up to the end of the sonnet. In the
first tercet, the image of the sphinxes stretched out in the
desert was vacillating between the creature and its simulacrum; and in the following tercet, the animate beings disappear behind particles of matter. Synecdoche replaces the cat-
sphinxes by parts of their bodies: [12]*leur reins* (the loins of
the cats), [14]*leurs prunelles* (the pupils of the cats). The implicit subject of the interior stanzas becomes once more an
accessory part of the sentence in the last tercet. The cats appear first as an implicit adjunct of the subject — [12]*Leurs reins
féconds sont pleins* — then, in the last clause of the poem, they
function as a mere implicit adjunct of the object: [14]*Étoilent
vaguement leurs prunelles*. Thus the cats appear to be linked
to the object of the transitive verb in the last clause of the
sonnet, and to the subject in the antecedent clause, second
from the end. In this way, a double correspondence is established, once with the cats, direct object in the first clause of
the sonnet, and then with the cats, subject of its second clause.

At the beginning of the sonnet, the subject and object were
both of the animate class; the two similar parts of the final
clause both belong to the inanimate class. In general, all the
substantives of the last tercet are concrete nouns of the same
class: [12]*reins, étincelles,* [13]*parcelles, or, sable,* [14]*prunelles,*
whereas in all previous stanzas, the inanimate appellatives,
except for the adnominals, were abstract nouns: [2]*saison,*
[3]*orgueil,* [6]*silence,* [6]*horreur,* [8]*servage,* [8]*fierté,* [9]*attitudes,* [11]*rêve.*
The inanimate feminine gender, common to the subject and
to the object of the final clause — [13-14]*des parcelles d'or . . .*

Étoilent . . . leurs prunelles — counterbalances the subject and the object of the initial clause, which belong to the animate masculine gender — [1-3]*Les amoureux . . . et les savants . . . Aiment . . . Les chats.* In the whole sonnet, [13]*parcelles* is the only feminine subject, and it contrasts with the masculine at the end of the same line, [13]*sable fin,* which in turn is the only example of the masculine gender in the masculine rhymes of the sonnet.

In the last tercet, the ultimate particles of matter take the place of the object and of the subject. A new identification, the last within the sonnet, associates these incandescent particles with the [13]*sable fin* and transforms them into stars.

The remarkable rhyme which links the two tercets is the one homonymous rhyme of the whole sonnet and the only one, among its masculine rhymes, which juxtaposes different parts of speech. There is a certain syntactic symmetry between the two words which rhyme, since both end subordinate clauses, the one complete and the other elliptical. The correspondence, far from being confined to the final syllable, narrowly brings together the entire lines: [11]*sāblə sādor*mir dãnzœ̃ rɛvə sã fɛ̃/ — [13]/parsɛlə dɔr ɛ̃si kœ̃ sablə fɛ̃/. It is not by chance that precisely this rhyme, uniting the two tercets, calls forth *un sable fin* by thus evoking once more the motif of the desert, which in the first tercet framed *un rêve sans fin* of the great sphinxes.

[3]*La maison,* circumscribing the cats in the first quatrain, is abolished in the first tercet with its realm of desert solitudes, true unfolded house of the cat-sphinxes. In its turn, this "non-house" yields to the cosmic innumerability of the cats (these, like all the personae of the sonnet, are treated as *pluralia tantum*). They become, so to speak, the house of the non-house, since within their pupils, they enclose the sand of the deserts and the light of the stars.

The epilogue takes up again the initial theme of lovers and scholars united in *Les chats puissants et doux.* The first line of the second tercet seems to give an answer to the initial line of the second quatrain. The cats being [5]*Amis . . . de la volupté,* [12]*Leurs reins féconds sont pleins.* One is tempted to believe that this has to do with the procreative force, but

Baudelaire's works easily invite ambiguous solutions. Is it a matter of a power peculiar to the loins, or of electric sparks in the fur of the animal? Whatever it may be, a "magic" power is attributed to them. But the second quatrain opened with two collateral adjuncts: [5]*Amis de la science et de la volupté,* and the final tercet alludes not only to the [1]*amoureux fervents* but to the [1]*savants austères* as well.

The last tercet rhymes its suffixes in order to emphasize the narrow semantic relation between the [12]*étin*CELLES, [13]*par*CELLES *d'or* and [14]*prun*ELLES of the cat-sphinxes on one hand, and on the other hand, between the sparks [12]*Mag*IQUES emanating from the animal and his pupils [14]*Myst*IQUES shining from an inner light, and opened to a hidden meaning. As if to lay bare the equivalence of the morphemes, the latter rhyme, the only one in the sonnet, is deprived of the supportive consonant, and the alliteration of the initial /m/ ties together the two adjectives. [6]*L'horreur des ténèbres* vanishes before this double luminance. This light is reflected on the phonic level by the predominance of the phonemes of light timbre (acute tonality) among nasal vowels on the final stanza (6 front *versus* 3 back vowels), whereas in the preceding stanzas, the nasal vowels of grave tonality manifest a great numeric superiority (9 *versus* 0 in the first quatrain, 2 *versus* 1 in the second, and 10 *versus* 3 in the first tercet).

With the preponderance of synecdochic tropes at the end of the sonnet, which substitute the parts for the whole of the animal and, on the other hand, the whole of the universe for the animal which is a part of it, the images seek, as if by design, to lose themselves in imprecision. The definite article gives place to the indefinite, and the adverb which accompanies the verbal metaphor — [14]*Étoilent vaguement* — wonderfully reflects the poetics of the epilogue. The conformity between the tercets and the corresponding quatrains (horizontal parallelism) is striking. The narrow limits of space ([3]*maison*) and of time ([2]*mûre saison*) in the first quatrain are opposed by the removal or the suppression of boundaries ([10]*fond des solitudes,* [11]*rêve sans fin*) in the first tercet. Similarly, in the second tercet, the magic of the light radiating from the cats triumphs over [6]*l'horreur des ténèbres,* that darkness from which the second quatrain had almost drawn misleading conclusions.

In gathering together the pieces of our analysis, let us try to show how the different levels of observations blend together, complete each other or merge, and endow the poem with the value of an absolute object.

To begin, the divisions of the text. Several can be distinguished which are perfectly clear as much from the grammatical point of view as from the semantic relations between the different parts of the poem.

As we have already pointed out, a first division corresponds to the three parts, each of which ends with a period, namely, the two quatrains and the ensemble of the two tercets. The first quatrain exhibits the supposedly actual state of affairs in the form of an objective and static picture. The second attributes to the cats a purpose which is interpreted by the powers of Erebus; and to the powers of Erebus, a purpose in regard to the cats, which is rejected by them. These two parts look at the cats from without: one in the passivity to which lovers and scholars are especially susceptible; the other in the activity perceived by the powers of Erebus. The last part of the sonnet overcomes this opposition by acknowledging a passivity actively assumed by the cats and interpreted no longer from without but from within.

A second division enables us to oppose the ensemble of the two tercets to the ensemble of the two quatrains, while showing a narrow relation between the first quatrain and the first tercet, and between the second quatrain and the second tercet. As a matter of fact:

1. The ensemble of the two quatrains is opposed to the ensemble of the two tercets since the latter eliminate the point of view of the observer (*amoureux, savants, puissance de l'Érèbe*) and place the being of the cats outside of all spatial and temporal limits.

2. The first quatrain introduced these spatio-temporal limits (*maison, saison*); the first tercet abolishes them '(*au fond des solitudes, rêve sans fin*).

3. The second quatrain defines the cats in terms of the darkness in which they place themselves, the second tercet in terms of the light they radiate (*étincelles, étoiles*).

Finally, a third division is superimposed upon the preceding one by regrouping, this time in a chiasmus, on the one hand the initial quatrain and the final tercet, and on the other hand the internal stanzas: second quatrain and first tercet. In the former couple, the independent clauses assign to the cats the role of syntactical modifiers, whereas the latter two stanzas begin by assigning to the cats the function of subject.

These phenomena of formal distribution obviously have a semantic foundation. The point of departure of the first quatrain is furnished by the proximity, within the same house, of the cats with the scholars or lovers. A double resemblance flows from this contiguity (*comme eux, comme eux*). In the final tercet again a relation of contiguity evolves to the point of resemblance; but while, in the first quatrain, the metonymical relation of the feline and human inhabitants of the house underlies their metaphorical relation, in the last tercet this situation is interiorized. The link of contiguity rests upon the synecdoche rather than upon the metonymy proper. The parts of the cat's body (loins, pupils) prepare a metaphorical evocation of the astral and cosmic cat, with a concomitant transition from precision to vagueness (*également — vaguement*). Between the interior stanzas, the analogy is based on connections of equivalence, the one turned down by the second quatrain (cats and *coursiers funèbres*), the other accepted by the first tercet (cats and *grands sphinx*). In the former case, this leads to a rejection of contiguity (between the cats and the Erebus), and in the latter case, to the settlement of the cats *au fond des solitudes*. Contrary to the former case, the transition is made from a relation of equivalence — a reinforced form of resemblance (thus a metaphorical move) 'to relations of contiguity (thus metonymical), either negative or positive.

Up to the present, the poem has appeared to consist of systems of equivalences which fit inside one another and which offer, in their totality, the aspect of a closed system. In the final remaining aspect, the poem appears to us like an open system in dynamic progression from beginning to end.

In the first part of this study, remember, we brought to light a division of the poem into two sestets, separated by a distich whose structure contrasted vigorously with the rest.

Now, during our recapitulation, we temporarily left this division aside. That is because, unlike the others, it seems to us to mark the stages of a progression, from the order of the real (first sestet) to that of the surreal (second sestet). This passage proceeds through the distich, which, for a brief instant and by the accumulation of semantic and formal devices, lures the reader into a universe doubly unreal, since it shares with the first sestet the standpoint of exteriority, while anticipating the mythological resonance of the second sestet:

verse:	1 to 6	7 and 8	9 to 14
	extrinsic		intrinsic
	empirical	mythological	
	real	unreal	surreal

By this brisk oscillation, both of tone and of theme, the distich fills a function which somewhat evokes that of a modulation in a musical composition.

The goal of this modulation is to resolve the opposition, implicit or explicit, from the beginning of the poem, between the metaphorical and metonymical procedures. The solution provided by the final sestet consists in transferring this opposition to the very heart of the metonymy while expressing it by metaphorical means. Actually, each of the two tercets puts forward an inverse image of the cats. In the first tercet, the cats originally enclosed in the house are, so to speak, extravasated from it to expand spatially and temporally in the infinite deserts and the endless dream. The movement goes from the inside toward the outside, from sequestered cats toward liberated cats. In the second tercet, the suppression of the frontiers is interiorized by the cats' attainment of cosmic proportions, since they conceal in certain parts of their bodies (*reins* and *prunelles*) the sand of the desert and the stars of the sky. In both cases, the transformation occurs through the help of metaphorical devices, but there is no thorough equilibrium between the two transformations. The first still owes something to semblance (*prennent . . . les . . . attitudes . . . qui semblent s'endormir*) and to dream (*en songeant . . . dans un rêve*), whereas in the second case, the transformation is declared and affirmed as truly achieved (*sont pleins . . . Étoilent*). In the first, the cats close their eyes to fall asleep; in the second they keep them open.

Nevertheless, these ample metaphors of the final sestet only transpose to the scale of the universe an opposition which was already implicitly formulated in the first line of the poem. The "lovers" and the "scholars" respectively assemble terms which are between them in a contracted or dilated relation. The man in love is conjoined to the woman, as the scholar is to the universe; thus two types of conjunction, the one close, the other one remote.[6] It is the same rapport that the final transfigurations evoke: dilation of the cats in time and space, constriction of time and space in the person of the cats. But, here again, as we have already noted, the symmetry is not complete between the two formulas; the last gathers together all the oppositions. The fertile loins recall the *volupté* of the lovers, as the pupils do the *science* of the scholars; *magiques* refers to the active fervor of the first ones, *mystiques* to the contemplative attitude of the others.

Two remarks to bring this to a close.

The fact that all the grammatical subjects of the sonnet (with the exception of the proper noun *L'Érèbe*) are in the plural, and that all the feminine rhymes are formed with plurals (including the substantive *solitudes*), finds a peculiar comment in a few passages from Baudelaire's *Foules* which,

[6] M. E. Benveniste, who was kind enough to read this study in manuscript, pointed out to us that between "les amoureux fervents" and "les savants austères," the "mûre saison" also plays the role of a mediating term. It is, in effect, in their advanced maturity that they reunite to identify themselves "également" with the cats. For, continues M. Benveniste, to stay "amoureux fervents" even into the "mûre saison" already signifies that one is outside of the common fold, as are the "savants austères" by their vocation. The initial situation of the sonnet is that of life out of the world (nevertheless, subterranean life is rejected), and transferred to the cats, this situation develops from chilly seclusion toward great starry solitudes where science and voluptuousness are dream without end.

In support of these remarks, for which we thank their author, one may quote another poem of *Les Fleurs du Mal:* "Le savant amour . . . fruit d'automne aux saveurs souveraines" (*L'Amour du mensonge*).

moreover, seem to throw light upon the whole of the sonnet: "Multitude, solitude: terms equal and interchangeable by the active and fertile poet. . . . The poet enjoys this incomparable privilege, that he can at will be himself and another. . . . What men call love is quite small, quite limited, and quite weak, compared to this ineffable orgy, to this holy prostitution of the soul which gives itself completely, poetry and charity, to the unforeseen which emerges, to the unknown who passes."[7]

In the poet's sonnet, the cats are initially qualified as *puissants et doux* and the final line compares their pupils to the stars. Crépet and Blin[8] refer to a verse of Sainte-Beuve: ". . . l'astre puissant et doux" (1829), and find the same epithets in a poem by Brizeux (1832) where the women are apostrophized: "Êtres deux fois doués! Êtres puissants et doux!"

That would confirm, if there were a need to, that for Baudelaire, the image of the cat is narrowly linked to that of the woman, as it is shown explicitly in two other poems entitled "Le Chat" and pertaining to the same collection. Thus the sonnet — "Viens, mon beau chat, sur mon coeur amoureux" — contains the revealing line: "Je vois ma femme en esprit. . . ." The second of these poems — "Dans ma cervelle se promene . . . Un beau chat, fort, doux . . ." squarely asks the question, "est-il fée, est-il dieu?" This motif of vacillation between male and female is subjacent in "Les Chats" where it shows through under intentional ambiguities (*Les amoureux . . . Aiment . . . Les chats puissants et doux . . . ; Leurs reins féconds . . .*). Michel Butor notes with reason that for Baudelaire "those two aspects: femininity and supervirility, far from excluding each other, are bound together."[9] All the characters in the sonnet are of masculine gender, but *les chats* and their alter ego, *les grands sphinx*, share an androgynous nature. The same ambiguity is emphasized

[7] Cf. Baudelaire, *Oeuvres*, II, Bibliothèque de la Pléiade, Paris, 1961, pp. 243 *sq.*

[8] Cf. Baudelaire, *Les Fleurs du Mal*, Édition critique établie par J. Crépet et G. Blin, Paris, 1942, p. 413.

[9] M. Butor, *Histoire extraordinaire, essai sur un rêve de Baudelaire*, Paris, 1961, p. 85.

throughout the sonnet by the paradoxical choice of feminine substantives for the so-called masculine rhymes.[10] The cats, by their mediation, permit the removal of woman from the initial assemblage formed by lovers and scholars. The poet of "Les Chats," liberated from love "bien petit, bien restreint," meets face to face and perhaps even blends with the universe delivered from the scholar's austerity.

TRANSLATED BY F. M. DE GEORGE

[10] In L. Rudrauf's study *Rime et sexe* (Tartu, 1936), a "theory of alternation of masculine and feminine rhymes in French poetry" is outlined and followed by a "controversy" with Maurice Grammont (pp. 47 sq.). According to the latter, "for the alternation established in the XVIth century based upon the presence or the absence of an unstressed *e* at the end of the word, the terms *feminine* rhymes and *masculine* rhymes were used because the unstressed *e* at the end of the word was, in the great majority of cases, the sign of the feminine: un petit chat/ une petite chatte." It could be said instead that the specific termination of the feminine, in contradistinction to the masculine, always contained "the unstressed *e*." Now, Rudrauf expresses certain doubts: "But is it uniquely the grammatical consideration which guided the poets of the XVIth century in the establishment of this rule of alternation and in the choice of epithets 'masculine' and 'feminine' to designate the two kinds of rhymes? Let us not forget that the poets of the Pléiade wrote their stanzas with an eye to song, and that song underscores, much more than does the spoken word, the alternation of a strong syllable (masculine) and of a weak syllable (feminine). More or less consciously, the musical point of view and the sexual point of view must have played a role along with grammatical analogy . . ." (p. 49).

Inasmuch as this alternation of rhymes based upon the presence or absence of an unstressed *e* at the end of the verses is no longer realized, in Grammont's view it has been replaced by an alternation of rhymes ending either with a consonant or with a stressed vowel. While ready to acknowledge that "the final syllables ending with a vowel are all masculine" (p. 46), Rudrauf is at the same time tempted to establish a scale of 24 degrees for the consonantic rhymes, "going from the most brusk and most virile end syllables to the most femininely suave" (pp. 12 sq.). The rhymes with a voiceless stop at their end form the extreme masculine pole (1°) and the rhymes with a voiced spirant are viewed as the feminine pole (24°) of Rudrauf's scale. If this attempt at classification is applied to the consonantic rhymes of "Les Chats," a gradual movement toward the masculine pole results in lessening the contrast between the two kinds of rhymes: [1]*austères* — [4]*sédentaires* (liquid: 19°); [6]*ténèbres* — [7]*funèbres* (voiced stop followed by a liquid: 15°); [9]*attitudes* — [10]*solitudes* (voiced stop: 13°); [12]*magiques* — [14]*mystiques* (voiceless stop: 1°).

ROLAND BARTHES

Roland Barthes, born in Bayonne in 1915, studied French literature and classics at the University of Paris. He taught French in Bucharest and in Alexandria before joining the Centre National de la Recherche Scientifique. He is presently Directeur d'Etudes in the VIth section of the École Pratique des Hautes Études. He is an editor of the journal *Communications*, he edits *Théâtre populaire*, and he is the author of a number of works including *Sur Racine*, *Essais critiques*, *Système de la mode*, *Critique et vérité*, *Mythologies*, *Writing Degree Zero* and *Elements of Semiology*. One of the foremost literary critics in France, he is not only a representative of French "new criticism" but has extended his structural analyses beyond the realm of literature to consider a variety of non-verbal modes of communication. The article which appears directly below is one of the clearest attempts by a French structuralist to present his view of what structuralism is.

In "To Write: An Intransitive Verb?" Barthes investigates the relation between literature and linguistics and between the writer and language. In analyzing the verb "to write," he elucidates the status of contemporary literature and writers through a study of the linguistic categories of temporality, person, and voice.

8

The Structuralist Activity

What is structuralism? Not a school, nor even a movement (at least, not yet), for most of the authors ordinarily labeled with this word are unaware of being united by any solidarity of doctrine or commitment. Nor is it a vocabulary. *Structure* is already an old word (of anatomical and grammatical provenance), today quite overworked: all the social sciences resort to it abundantly, and the word's use can distinguish no one, except to engage in polemics about the content assigned to it; *functions, forms, signs* and *significations* are scarcely more pertinent: they are, today, words of common usage, from which one asks (and obtains) whatever one wants, notably the camouflage of the old determinist schema of cause and product; we must doubtless go back to pairings like those of *significans/significatum* and *synchronic/diachronic* in order to approach what distinguishes structuralism from other modes of thought: the first because it refers to the linguistic model as originated by Saussure, and because along with economics, linguistics is, in the present state of affairs, the true science of structure, the second, more decisively, because it seems to imply a certain revision of the notion of history, insofar as the notion of the synchronic (although in Saussure this is a preeminently *operational* concept) accredits a certain immobilization of time, and insofar as that of the diachronic tends to represent the historical process as a pure succession of forms. This second pairing is all the more distinctive in that the chief resistance to structuralism today

From *Essais Critiques* by Roland Barthes. Copyright © 1964 by Editions du Seuil. English translation by Richard Howard, *Partisan Review* (Winter, 1967), vol. XXXIV, no. 1, pp. 82–88, © by Partisan Review. Reprinted by permission of the publisher and of the author.

seems to be of Marxist origin and that it focuses on the notion of history (and not of structure); whatever the case, it is
probably the serious recourse to the nomenclature of signification (and not to the word itself, which is, paradoxically, not
at all distinctive) which we must ultimately take as structuralism's *spoken sign:* watch who uses *signifier* and *signified,*
synchronic and *diachronic,* and you will know whether the
structuralist vision is constituted.

This is valid for the intellectual metalanguage, which explicitly employs methodological concepts. But since structuralism is neither a school nor a movement, there is no reason
to reduce it a priori, even in a problematical way, to the activity of philosophers; it would be better to try and find its
broadest description (if not its definition) on another level
than that of reflexive language. We can in fact presume that
there exist certain writers, painters, musicians, in whose eyes
a certain *exercise* of structure (and not only its thought)
represents a distinctive experience, and that both analysts
and creators must be placed under the common sign of what
we might call *structural man,* defined not by his ideas or his
languages, but by his imagination—in other words, by the
way in which he mentally experiences structure.

Hence the first thing to be said is that in relation to *all* its
users, structuralism is essentially an *activity,* i.e., the controlled succession of a certain number of mental operations:
we might speak of structuralist activity as we once spoke of
surrealist activity (surrealism, moreover, may well have produced the first experience of structural literature, a possibility
which must some day be explored). But before seeing what
these operations are, we must say a word about their goal.

The goal of all structuralist activity, whether reflexive or
poetic, is to reconstruct an "object" in such a way as to manifest thereby the rules of functioning (the "functions") of this
object. Structure is therefore actually a *simulacrum* of the
object, but a directed, *interested* simulacrum, since the imitated object makes something appear which remained invis-
ible, or if one prefers, unintelligible in the natural object.
Structural man takes the real, decomposes it, then recomposes
it; this appears to be little enough (which makes some say

that the structuralist enterprise is "meaningless," "uninteresting," "useless," etc.). Yet, from another point of view, this "little enough" is decisive: for between the two objects, or the two tenses, of structuralist activity, there occurs *something new,* and what is new is nothing less than the generally intelligible: the simulacrum is intellect added to object, and this addition has an anthropological value, in that it is man himself, his history, his situation, his freedom and the very resistance which nature offers to his mind.

We see, then, why we must speak of a structuralist *activity:* creation or reflection are not, here, an original "impression" of the world, but a veritable fabrication of a world which resembles the first one, not in order to copy it but to render it intelligible. Hence one might say that structuralism is essentially *an activity of imitation,* which is also why there is, strictly speaking, no *technical* difference between structuralism as an intellectual activity on the one hand and literature in particular, art in general on the other: both derive from a *mimesis,* based not on the analogy of substances (as in so-called realist art), but on the analogy of functions (what Lévi-Strauss calls *homology*). When Troubetskoy reconstructs the phonetic object as a system of variations; when Dumézil elaborates a functional mythology; when Propp constructs a folktale resulting by structuration from all the Slavic tales he has previously decomposed; when Lévi-Strauss discovers the homologic functioning of the totemic imagination, or Granger the formal rules of economic thought, or Gardin the pertinent features of prehistoric bronzes; when Richard decomposes a poem by Mallarmé into its distinctive vibrations—they are all doing nothing different from what Mondrian, Boulez or Butor are doing when they articulate a certain object—what will be called, precisely, a *composition*—by the controlled manifestation of certain units and certain associations of these units. It is of little consequence whether the initial object liable to the simulacrum-activity is given by the world in an already assembled fashion (in the case of the structural analysis made of a constituted language or society or work) or is still scattered (in the case of the structural "composition"); whether this initial object is drawn from a social reality or an imaginary reality. It is not the nature of the copied object which defines an art (though this is a tenacious prejudice in all realism), it is the fact that man adds to it in reconstructing it: technique is the very being of all creation. It is therefore to the degree that the goals of structuralist activity are indissolubly linked to a certain technique that structuralism exists in a distinctive fashion in relation to other modes of analysis or creation: we recompose the object *in order* to make certain functions appear, and it is, so to speak, the way that makes the work; this is why we must speak of the structuralist activity rather than the structuralist work.

The structuralist activity involves two typical operations: dissection and articulation. To dissect the first object, the one which is given to the simulacrum-activity, is to find in it certain mobile fragments whose differential situation engenders a certain meaning; the fragment has no meaning in itself, but it is nonetheless such that the slightest variation wrought in its configuration produces a change in the whole; a *square* by Mondrian, a *series* by Pousseur, a *versicle* of Butor's *Mobile*, the "mytheme" in Lévi-Strauss, the phoneme in the work of the phonologists, the "theme" in certain literary criticism—all these units (whatever their inner structure and their extent, quite different according to cases) have no significant existence except by their frontiers: those which separate them from other actual units of the discourse (but this is a problem of articulation) and also those which distinguish them from other virtual units, with which they form a certain class (which linguistics calls a *paradigm*); this notion of a paradigm is essential, apparently, if we are to understand the structuralist vision: the paradigm is a group, a reservoir—as limited as possible—of objects (of units) from which one summons, by an act of citation, the object or unit one wishes to endow with an actual meaning; what characterizes the paradigmatic object is that it is, vis-à-vis other objects of its class, in a certain relation of affinity and dissimilarity: two units of the same paradigm must resemble each other somewhat in order that the difference which separates them be indeed evident: *s* and *z* must have both a common feature (dentality) and a distinctive feature (presence or absence of sonority) so that we cannot, in French, attribute the same meaning to *poisson* and *poison;* Mondrian's squares must have both certain affinities by their shape as squares, and certain dissimilarities by their proportion and color; the American automobiles (in Butor's *Mobile*) must be constantly regarded in the same way, yet they must differ each time by both their make and color; the episodes of the Oedipus myth (in Lévi-Strauss's analysis) must be both identical and varied—in order that all these languages, these works may be intelligible. The dissection-operation thus produces an initial dispersed state of the simulacrum, but the units of the structure are not at all anarchic: before being distributed and fixed in the continuity of the composition, each one forms with its own virtual group or reservoir an intelligent organism, subject to a sovereign motor principle: that of the smallest difference.

Once the units are posited, structural man must discover in them or establish for them certain rules of association: this is the activity of articulation, which succeeds the summoning activity. The syntax of the arts and of discourse is, as we know, extremely varied; but what we discover in every work of structural enterprise is the submission to regular constraints whose formalism, improperly indicted, is much less important than their stability; for what is happening, at this second stage of the simulacrum-activity, is a kind of battle against chance; this is why the constraint of recurrence of the units has an almost demiurgic value: it is by the regular return of the units and of the associations of units that the work appears constructed, i.e., endowed with meaning; linguistics calls these rules of combination *forms*, and it would be advantageous to retain this rigorous sense of an overtaxed word: form, it has been said, is what keeps the contiguity of units from appearing as a pure effect of chance: the work of art is what man wrests from chance. This perhaps allows us to understand on the one hand why so-called nonfigurative works are nonetheless to the highest degree works of art, human thought being established not on the analogy of copies and models but with the regularity of assemblages; and on the other hand why these same works appear, precisely, fortuitous and thereby useless to those who discern in them no *form:* in front of an abstract painting, Khrushchev was certainly wrong to see only the traces of a donkey's tail whisked across the canvas; at least he knew in his way, though, that art is a certain conquest of chance (he simply forgot that every rule must be learned, whether one wants to apply or interpret it).

The simulacrum, thus constructed, does not render the world as it has found it, and it is here that structuralism is important. First of all, it manifests a new category of the object, which is neither the real nor the rational, but the *functional*, thereby joining a whole scientific complex which is being developed around information theory and research. Subsequently and especially, it highlights the strictly human process by which men give meaning to things. Is this new? To a certain degree, yes; of course the world has never stopped looking for the meaning of what is given it and of what it produces; what is new is a mode of thought (or a "poetics") which seeks less to assign completed meanings to the objects it discovers than to know how meaning is possible, at what cost and by what means. Ultimately, one might say that the object of structuralism is not man endowed with meanings, but man fabricating meanings, as if it could not be the *content* of meanings which exhausted the semantic goals of humanity, but only the act by which these meanings, historical and contingent variables, are produced. *Homo significans:* such would be the new man of structural inquiry.

According to Hegel, the ancient Greek was amazed by the *natural* in nature; he constantly listened to it, questioned the meaning of mountains, springs, forests, storms; without knowing what all these objects were telling him by name, he perceived in the vegetal or cosmic order a tremendous *shudder* of meaning, to which he gave the name of a god: Pan. Subsequently, nature has changed, has become social: everything that is given to man is *already* human, down to the forest and the river which we cross when we travel. But confronted with this social nature, which is quite simply culture, structural man is no different from the ancient Greek: he too listens for the natural in culture, and constantly perceives in it not so much stable, finite, "true" meanings as the shudder of an enormous machine which is humanity tirelessly undertaking to create meaning, without which it would no longer be human. And it is because this fabrication of meaning is more important, to its view, than the meanings themselves, it is because the function is extensive with the works, that structuralism constitutes itself as an activity, and refers the exercise of the work and the work itself to a single identity: a serial composition or an analysis by Lévi-Strauss are not objects except insofar as they have been *made:* their present being *is* their past act: they are *having-been-mades;* the artist, the analyst recreates the course taken by meaning, he need not designate it: his function, to return to Hegel's example, is a *manteia;* like the ancient soothsayer, he *speaks* the locus of meaning but does not name it. And it is because literature, in particular, is a mantic activity that it is both intelligible and interrogating, speaking and silent, engaged in the world by the course of meaning which it remakes with the world, but disengaged from the contingent meanings which the world elaborates: an answer to the man who consumes it yet always a question to nature, an answer which questions and a question which answers.

How then does structural man deal with the accusation of unreality which is sometimes flung at him? Are not forms in the world, are not forms responsible? Was it really his Marxism that was revolutionary in Brecht? Was it not rather the decision to link to Marxism, in the theater, the placing of a spotlight or the deliberate fraying of a costume? Structuralism does not withdraw history from the world: it seeks to link to history not only certain contents (this has been done a thousand times) but also certain forms, not only the material but also the intelligible, not only the ideological but also the esthetic. And precisely because all thought about the historically intelligible is also a participation in that intelligibility, structural man is scarcely concerned to *last;* he knows that structuralism, too, is a certain *form* of the world, which will change with the world; and just as he experiences his validity (but not his truth) in his power to speak the old languages of the world in a new way, so he knows that it will suffice that a new language rise out of history, a new language which speaks him in his turn, for his task to be done.

9

To Write: An Intransitive Verb?[1]

For centuries Western culture conceived of literature not as we do today, through a study of works, authors, and schools, but through a genuine theory of language. This theory, whose name, *rhetoric,* came to it from antiquity, reigned in the Western world from Gorgias to the Renaissance—for nearly two thousand years. Threatened as early as the sixteenth century by the advent of modern rationalism, rhetoric was completely ruined when rationalism was transformed into positivism at the end of the nineteenth century. At that point there was no longer any common ground of thought between literature and language: literature no longer regarded itself as language except in the works of a few pioneers such as Mallarmé, and linguistics claimed very few rights over literature, these being [limited to] a secondary philological discipline of uncertain status—stylistics.

As we know, this situation is changing, and it seems to me that it is in part to take cognizance of this change that we are assembled here: literature and language are in the process of finding each other again. The factors of this *rapprochement* are diverse and complex; I shall cite the most obvious. On one hand, certain writers since Mallarmé, such as Proust and Joyce, have undertaken a radical exploration of writing, making of their work a search for the total Book. On the other

[1] "Ecrire: Verbe intransitif?" The translation which follows is a composite of the communication which M. Barthes distributed in advance to the Symposium participants and the actual transcription of his address. The footnotes have been supplied by the translator. This selection is from *The Languages of Criticism and the Sciences of Man: the Structuralist Controversy,* edited by Richard Macksey and Eugenio Donato, Baltimore and London: The Johns Hopkins Press, 1970, pp. 134–45. Reprinted by permission of the publisher and of the author.

hand, linguistics itself, principally following the impetus of Roman Jakobson, has developed to include within its scope the poetic, or the order of effects linked to the message and not to its referent. Therefore, in my view, we have today a new perspective of consideration which, I would like to emphasize, is common to literature and linguistics, to the creator and the critic, whose tasks until now completely self-contained, are beginning to inter-relate, perhaps even to merge. This is at least true for certain writers whose work is becoming more and more a critique of language. It is in this perspective that I would like to place the following observations (of a prospective and not of a conclusive nature) indicating how the activity of writing can be expressed [*énoncée*] today with the help of certain linguistic categories.

This new union of literature and linguistics, of which I have just spoken, could be called, provisionally and for lack of a better name, *semio-criticism*, since it implies that writing is a system of signs. Semio-criticism is not to be identified with stylistics, even in a new form; it is much more than stylistics. It has a much broader perspective; its object is constituted not by simple accidents of form, but by the very relationships between the writer [*scripteur*, not *écrivain*] and language. This perspective does not imply a lack of interest in language but, on the contrary, a continual return to the "truths"—provisional though they may be—of linguistic anthropology. I will recall certain of these truths because they still have a power of challenge in respect to a certain current idea of literature.

One of the teachings of contemporary linguistics is that there is no archaic language, or at the very least that there is no connection between simplicity and the age of a language: ancient languages can be just as complete and as complex as recent languages; there is no progressive history of languages. Therefore, when we try to find certain fundamental categories of language in modern writing, we are not claiming to reveal a certain archaism of the "psyche"; we are not saying that the writer is returning to the origin of language, but that language is the origin for him.

A second principle, particularly important in regard to literature, is that language cannot be considered as a simple instrument, whether utilitarian or decorative, of thought. Man does not exist prior to language, either as a species or as an individual. We never find a state where man is separated from language, which he then creates in order to "express" what is taking place within him: it is language which teaches the definition of man, not the reverse.

Moreover, from a methodological point of view, linguistics accustoms us to a new type of objectivity. The objectivity that has been required in the human sciences up until now is an objectivity of the given, a total acceptance of the given. Linguistics suggests, on the one hand, that we distinguish levels of analysis and that we describe the distinctive elements of each of these levels; in short, that we establish the distinctness of the fact and not the fact itself. On the other hand, linguistics asks us to recognize that unlike physical and biological facts, cultural facts are always double, that they refer us to something else. As Benveniste remarked, the discovery of the "duplicity" of language gives Saussure's reflection all its value.[2]

These few preliminaries are contained in one final proposition which justifies all semio-critical research. We see culture more and more as a general system of symbols, governed by the same operations. There is unity in this symbolic field: culture, in all its aspects, is a language. Therefore it is possible today to anticipate the creation of a single, unified science of culture, which will depend on diverse disciplines, all devoted to analyzing, on different levels of description, culture as language. Of course semio-criticism will be only a part of this science, or rather of this discourse on culture. I feel authorized by this unity of the human symbolic field to work on a postulate, which I shall call a postulate of *homology:* the structure of the sentence, the object of linguistics, is found again, homologically, in the structure of works. Discourse is not simply an adding together of sentences: it is, itself, one

[2] Emile Benveniste, *Problèmes de la linguistique générale* (Paris, 1966), p. 40. "Qu'est-ce donc que cet objet, que Saussure érige sur une table rase de toutes les notions reçues? Nous touchons ici à ce qu'il y a de primordial dans la doctrine saussurienne, à un principe qui présume une intuition totale du langage, totale à la fois parce qu'elle embrasse la totalité de son objet. Ce principe est que *le langage,* sous quelque point de vue qu'on l'étudie, *est toujours un objet double,* formé de deux parties dont l'une ne vaut que par l'autre."

great sentence. In terms of this hypothesis I would like to confront certain categories of language with the situation of the writer in relation to his writing.

The first of these categories is *temporality*. I think we can all agree that there is a linguistic temporality. This specific time of language is equally different from physical time and from what Benveniste calls "chronicle time" [*temps chronique*], that is, calendar time.[3] Linguistic time finds quite different expression and *découpages* in various languages. For example, since we are going to be interested in the analysis of myths, many languages have a particular past tense of the verb to indicate the past time of myth. One thing is sure: linguistic time always has its primary center [*centre générateur*] in the present of the statement [*énonciation*]. This leads us to ask whether there is, homological to linguistic time, a specific time of discourse. On this point we may take Benveniste's explanation that many languages, especially in the Indo-European group, have a double system of time. The first temporal system is that of the discourse itself, which is adapted to the temporality of the speaker [*énonciateur*] and for which the *énonciation* is always the point of origin [*moment générateur*]. The second is the system of history or of narrative, which is adapted to the recounting of past events without any intervention by the speaker and which is consequently deprived of present and future (except periphrastically). The specific tense of this second system is the aorist or its equivalent, such as our *passé simple* or the preterit. This tense (the aorist) is precisely the only one missing from the temporal system of discourse. Naturally the existence of this a-personal system does not contradict the essentially logocentric nature of linguistic time that I have just affirmed. The second system simply lacks the characteristics of the first.

Understood thus as the opposition of two radically different systems, temporality does not have the morphological mark of verbs for its only sign; it is marked by all the signs, often very indirect, which refer either to the a-personal tense of the event or to the personal tense of the locutor. The opposi-

[3] Cf. Benveniste, "Les Relations de temps dans le verbe français," *ibid.*, pp. 237–50.

tion in its fullness permits us first to account for some pure, or we might say classic, cases: a popular story and the history of France retold in our manuals are purely aoristic narratives; on the contrary, Camus' *L'Etranger,* written in the compound past, is not only a perfect form of autobiography (that of the narrator, and not of the author) but, what is more valuable, it permits us to understand better the apparently anomalous cases.[4] Being a historian, Michelet made all historical time pivot around a point of discourse with which he identified himself—the Revolution. His history is a narrative without the aorist, even if the simple past abounds in it; inversely, the preterit can very well serve to signify not the objective *récit,* but the depersonalization of the discourse—a phenomenon which is the object of the most lively research in today's literature.

What I would like to add to this linguistic analysis, which comes from Benveniste, is that the distinction between the temporal system of discourse and the temporal system of history is not at all the same distinction as is traditionally made between objective discourse and subjective discourse. For the relationship between the speaker [*énonciateur*] and the referent on the one hand and that between the speaker and his utterance [*énonciation*] on the other hand are not to be confused, and it is only the second relationship which determines the temporal system of discourse.

It seems to me that these facts of language were not readily perceptible so long as literature pretended to be a transparent expression of either objective calendar time or of psychological subjectivity, that is to say, as long as literature maintained a totalitarian ideology of the referent, or more commonly speaking, as long as literature was realistic. Today, however, the literature of which I speak is discovering fundamental subtleties relative to temporality. In reading certain writers who are engaged in this type of exploration we sense that what is recounted in the aorist doesn't seem at all immersed in the past, in what has taken place, but simply in the impersonal [*la non-personne*], which is neither history, nor discursive information [*la science*], and even less the *one*

[4] Cf. Jean-Paul Sartre, "Explication de *L'Etranger*," *Situations* I (Paris, 1947), pp. 99–121.

of anonymous writing. (The *one* is dominated by the indefinite and not by the absence of person. I would even say that the pronoun *one* is marked in relation to person, while, paradoxically, *he* is not.) At the other extreme of the experience of discourse, the present-day writer can no longer content himself with expressing his own present, according to a lyrical plan, for example. He must learn to distinguish between the present of the speaker, which is grounded on a psychological fullness, and the present of what is spoken [*la locution*] which is mobile and in which the event and the writing become absolutely coincidental. Thus literature, at least in some of its pursuits, seems to me to be following the same path as linguistics when, along with Gustave Guillaume (a linguist not presently in fashion but who may become so again), it concerns itself with operative time and the time proper to the utterance [*énonciation*] itself.[5]

A second grammatical category which is equally important in linguistics and in literature is that of *person*. Taking linguists and especially Benveniste as my basis once more, I would like to recall that person (in the grammatical sense of the term) certainly seems to be a universal of language, linked to the anthropology of language. Every language, as Benveniste has shown, organizes person into two broad pairs of opposites: a correlation of personality which opposes person (*I* or *thou*) to non-person, which is *il* (*he* or *it*), the sign of absence; and, within this first opposing pair, a correlation of subjectivity (once again in the grammatical sense) which opposes two persons, the *I* and the *non-I* (the *thou*). For our purposes we must, along with Benveniste, make three observations. First, the polarity of persons, a fundamental condition of language, is nevertheless peculiar and enigmatic, for this polarity involves neither equality nor symmetry: *I* always has a position of transcendence with respect to *thou*, *I* being in-

[5] Gustave Guillaume, *L'Architectonique du temps dans les langues classiques* (Copenhagen, 1945). The work of Guillaume (who died in 1960) toward a "psycho-systématique" has been continued in the contributions of Roch Valin (*Petite introduction à la psychomécanique du langage* [Québec, 1954]). For a statement by Guillaume about his relation to the tradition of Saussure, see *La langue est-elle ou n'est-elle pas un système? Cahiers de linguistique structurale de l'Université de Québec*, I (1952), p. 4.

terior to the *énoncé* and *thou* remaining exterior to it; however, *I* and *thou* are reversible—*I* can always become *thou* and vice versa. This is not true of the non-person (*he* or *it*) which can never reverse itself into person or vice versa. The second observation is that the linguistic *I* can and must be defined in a strictly a-psychological way: *I* is nothing other than "la personne qui énonce la présente instance de discours contenant l'instance linguistique *je*" (Benveniste ["the person who utters the present instance of discourse containing the linguistic instance *I*"]).[6] The last remark is that the *he* or the non-person never reflects the instance of discourse; *he* is situated outside of it. We must give its full weight to Benveniste's recommendation not to represent the *he* as a more or less diminished or removed person: *he* is absolutely non-person, marked by the absence of what specifically constitutes, linguistically, the *I* and the *thou*.

The linguistic explanation provides several suggestions for an analysis of literary discourse. First, whatever varied and clever forms person may take in passing from the level of the sentence to that of discourse, the discourse of the literary work is rigorously submitted to a double system of person and non-person. This fact may be obscured because classical discourse (in a broad sense) to which we are habituated is a mixed discourse which alternates—very quickly, sometimes within the same sentence—personal and a-personal *énonciation,* through a complex play of pronouns and descriptive verbs. In this type of classical or bourgeois story the mixture of person and non-person produces a sort of ambiguous consciousness which succeeds in keeping the personal quality of what is stated while, however, continuously breaking the participation of the *énonciateur* in the *énoncé.*

Many novelistic utterances, written with *he* (in the third person), are nevertheless discourses of the *person* each time that the contents of the statement depend on its subject. If in a novel we read *"the tinkling of the ice against the glass seemed to give Bond a sudden inspiration,"* it is certain that the subject of the statement cannot be Bond himself—not because the sentence is written in the third person, since Bond

---

[6] Benveniste, *Problèmes,* p. 252.

could very well express himself through a *he,* but because of the verb *seem,* which becomes a mark of the absence of person. Nevertheless, in spite of the diversity and often even the ruse of the narrative signs of the person, there is never but one sole and great opposition in the discourse, that of the person and the non-person; every narrative or fragment of a narrative is obliged to join one or the other of these extremes. How can we determine this division? In "re-writing" the discourse. If we can translate the *he* into *I* without changing anything else in the utterance, the discourse is in fact personal. In the sentence which we have cited, this transformation is impossible; we cannot say *"the tinkling of the ice seemed to give me a sudden inspiration."* The sentence is impersonal. Starting from there, we catch a glimpse of how the discourse of the traditional novel is made; on the one hand it alternates the personal and the impersonal very rapidly, often even in the course of the same sentence, so as to produce, if we can speak thus, a proprietary consciousness which retains the mastery of what it states without participating in it; and on the other hand, in this type of novel, or rather, according to our perspective, in this type of discourse, when the narrator is explicitly an *I* (which has happened many times), there is confusion between the subject of the discourse and the subject of the reported action, as if—and this is a common belief— he who is speaking today were the same as he who acted yesterday. It is as if there were a continuity of the referent and the utterance through the person, as if the declaring were only a docile servant of the referent.

Now if we return to the linguistic definition of the first person (the one who says "I" in the present instance of discourse), we may better understand the effort of certain contemporary writers (in France I think of Philippe Sollers's latest novel *Drame*) when they try to distinguish, at the level of the story, psychological person and the author of the writing. When a narrator recounts what has happened to him, the *I* who recounts is no longer the same *I* as the one that is recounted. In other words—and it seems to me that this is seen more and more clearly—the *I* of discourse can no longer be a place where a previously stored-up person is innocently restored. Absolute recourse to the instance of discourse to determine person is termed *nyn-egocentrism* by Damourette and Pichon (*nyn* from the Greek *nun*, "now").[7] Robbe-Grillet's novel *Dans le labyrinthe* begins with an admirable declaration of nyn-egocentrism: "Je suis seul ici maintenant." [I am alone here now.][8] This recourse, imperfectly as it may still be practiced, seems to be a weapon against the general "bad faith" of discourse which would make literary form simply the expression of an interiority constituted previous to and outside of language.

To end this discussion of person, I would like to recall that in the process of communication the course of the *I* is not homogenous. For example, when I use [*libère*] the sign *I*, I refer to myself inasmuch as I am talking: here there is an act which is always new, even if it is repeated, an act whose sense is always new. However, arriving at its destination, this sign is received by my interlocutor as a stable sign, product of a complete code whose contents are recurrent. In other words, the *I* of the one who writes *I* is not the same as the *I* which is read by *thou*. This fundamental dissymmetry of language, linguistically explained by Jespersen and then by Jakobson under the name of "shifter" [*embrayeur*] or an overlapping of message and code, seems to be finally beginning to trouble literature in showing it that intersubjectivity, or rather interlocution, cannot be accomplished simply by wishing, but only by a deep, patient, and often circuitous descent into the labyrinths of meaning.[9]

There remains one last grammatical notion which can, in

---

[7] J. Damourette and E. Pichon, *Des mots à la pensée: Essai de grammaire de la langue française* (Paris, 1911–36), V, #1604 and VII, #2958. "Le langage est naturellement centré sur le moi-ici-maintenant, c'est-à-dire sur la personne qui parle s'envisageant au moment même où elle parle; c'est ce qu'on peut appeler le *nynégocentrisme* naturel du langage" [#1604].

[8] *Dans le labyrinthe* (Paris: Editions de Minuit, 1959). For essays by Roland Barthes bearing on the fictional method and theory of Robbe-Grillet, see *Essais critiques* (Paris, 1964), pp. 29–40, 63–70, 198–205.

[9] Cf. Jakobson, *Shifters, Verbal Categories, and the Russian Verb* (Cambridge [Mass.], 1957). [Translated into French by Nicolas Ruwet in *Essais de linguistique générale* (Paris, 1963), pp. 176–96.] For the origin of the term "shifter," see Otto Jespersen, *Language, its Nature, Development and Origin* (London, 1922), p. 123, and *ibid.*, *The Philosophy of Grammar* (London, 1923), pp. 83–84.

my opinion, further elucidate the activity of writing at its center, since it concerns the verb *to write* itself. It would be interesting to know at what point the verb *to write* began to be used in an apparently intransitive manner, the writer being no longer one who writes *something,* but one who writes, absolutely. (How often now we hear in conversations, at least in more or less intellectual circles: "What is he doing?" — "He's writing.") This passage from the verb *to write,* transitive, to the verb *to write,* apparently intransitive, is certainly the sign of an important change in mentality. But is it really a question of intransitivity? No writer, whatever age he belongs to, can fail to realize that he always writes *something:* one might even say that it was paradoxically at the moment when the verb *to write* appeared to become intransitive that its object, the book or the text, took on a particular importance. It is not, therefore, in spite of the appearances, on the side of intransitivity that we must look for the definition of the modern verb *to write.* Another linguistic notion will perhaps give us the key: that of *diathesis,* or, as it is called in classical grammars, *voice* (active, passive, middle). Diathesis designates the way in which the subject of the verb is affected by the action [*procès*]; this is obvious for the passive (if I say "I am beaten," it is quite obvious that I am profoundly affected by the action of the verb *to beat*). And yet linguists tell us that, at least in Indo-European, the diathetical opposition is actually not between the active and the passive, but between the active and the middle. According to the classic example, given by Meillet and Benveniste, the verb *to sacrifice* (ritually) is active if the priest sacrifices the victim in my place for me, and it is middle voice if, taking the knife from the priest's hands, I make the sacrifice for myself.[10] In the case of the active, the action is accomplished outside the subject, because, although the priest makes the sacrifice, he is not affected by it. In the case of the middle voice, on the contrary, the subject affects

[10] Benveniste, "Actif et moyen dans le verbe," *Problèmes,* pp. 168–75. Cf. the distinction initiated by Pānini (fl. 350 B.C.): *parasmaipada,* "word for another," i.e., active, and *āmanepada,* "word for self," i.e., middle. Thus *yajati* ("he sacrifices" [for another, *qua* priest]) vs. *yajate* ("he sacrifices" [for himself, *qua* offering]). Cf. Berthold Delbrück, *Vergleichende Syntax der Indogermanischen Sprachen* (Strassburg, 1893).

himself in acting; he always remains inside the action, even if an object is involved. The middle voice does not, therefore, exclude transitivity. Thus defined, the middle voice corresponds exactly to the state of the verb *to write:* today to write is to make oneself the center of the action of speech [*parole*]; it is to effect writing in being affected oneself; it is to leave the writer [*scripteur*] inside the writing, not as a psychological subject (the Indo-European priest could very well overflow with subjectivity in actively sacrificing for his client), but as the agent of the action.

I think the diathetical analysis of the modern verb *to write,* which I have just tried to show a verb of middle voice, can be carried even further. You know that in French—for I am obliged to refer to strictly French examples—certain verbs have an active meaning in the simple form, for example, *aller, arriver, rentrer, sortir* [to go, to arrive, to return, to go out], but, curiously, these active verbs take the passive auxiliary, the verb *être* [to be] in the forms of the *passé composé.* Instead of saying *j'ai allé,* we say *je suis allé, je suis sorti, je suis arrivé, je suis rentré,* etc. To explain this bifurcation peculiar to the middle voice, Guillaume distinguishes between two *passés composés.* The first, which he calls *diriment,* "separated," is a *passé composé* with the auxiliary *avoir* [to have]; this tense supposes an interruption of the action due to the initiative of the speaker. Take for example the verb *marcher* [to walk], an entirely commonplace active verb: *"je marche; je m'arrête de marcher; j'ai marché* [I walk; I stop walking (by my own initiative); I have walked]—this is the *passé composé diriment.* The other *passé composé* that he calls *intégrant* is constructed with the verb *être* [to be]; it designates a sort of semantic entity which cannot be delivered by the simple initiative of the subject. *"Je suis sorti"* or *"il est mort"* ["I went out" or "he died"] (for I can't say "I am dead") never refer to an interruption that would be at all like the *diriment* of the going out or the dying. I believe that this is an important opposition, for we see very well that the verb *to write* was traditionally an active verb and that its past tense is still today formally a *diriment* past: *"j'écris un livre; je le termine; je l'ai écrit."* [I write a book; I end it; I have written it.] But in our literature, it seems to me, the verb is changing status, if not form, and the verb *to write* is becoming a middle verb with an *intégrant* past. This is true inasmuch as the modern verb *to write* is becoming a sort of indivisible semantic entity. So that if language followed literature—which, for once perhaps, has the lead—I would say that we should no longer say today *"j'ai écrit"* but, rather, *"je suis écrit,"* just as we say *"je suis né, il est mort, elle est éclose."* There is no passive idea in these expressions, in spite of the verb *to be,* for it is impossible to transform *"je suis écrit"* (without forcing things, and supposing that I dare to use this expression at all) into *"on m'a écrit"* ["I have been written" or "somebody wrote me"]. It is my opinion that in the middle verb *to write* the distance between the writer and the language diminishes asymptotically. We could even say that it is subjective writings, like romantic writing, which are active, because in them the agent is not interior but *anterior* to the process of writing. The one who writes here does not write for himself, but, as if by proxy, for a person who is exterior and antecedent (even if they both have the same name). In the modern verb of middle voice *to write,* however, the subject is immediately contemporary with the writing, being effected and affected by it. The case of the Proustian narrator is exemplary: he exists only in writing.

These remarks suggest that the central problem of modern writing exactly coincides with what we could call the problematic of the verb in linguistics; just as temporality, person, and diathesis define the positional field of the subject, so modern literature is trying, through various experiments, to establish a new status in writing for the agent of writing. The meaning or the goal of this effort is to substitute the instance of discourse for the instance of reality (or of the referent), which has been, and still is, a mythical "alibi" dominating the idea of literature. The field of the writer is nothing but writing itself, not as the pure "form" conceived by an aesthetic of art for art's sake, but, much more radically, as the only area [*espace*] for the one who writes.

It seems to me to be necessary to remind those who might be tempted to accuse this kind of inquiry of solipsism, formalism, or, inversely, of scientism, that in returning to the fundamental categories of language, such as person, tense, and voice, we place ourselves at the very heart of a problematic of *inter*locution. For these categories are precisely those in which we may examine the relationships between the *je* and that which is deprived of the mark of *je*. Inasmuch as person, tense, and voice imply these remarkable linguistic beings— the "shifters"—they oblige us to conceive language and discourse no longer in terms of an instrumental and reified nomenclature but in the very exercise of language [*parole*]. The pronoun, for example, which is without doubt the most staggering of the "shifters," belongs structurally to speech [*parole*]. That is its scandal, if you like, and it is on this scandal that we must work today, in linguistics and literature. We are all trying, with different methods, styles, perhaps even prejudices, to get to the core of this linguistic pact [*pacte de parole*] which unites the writer and the other, so that—and this is a contradiction which will never be sufficiently pondered— each moment of discourse is both absolutely new and absolutely understood. I think that, with a certain amount of temerity, we could even give a historical dimension to this research. We know that the medieval *septenium,* in its grandiose classification of the universe, prescribed two great areas of exploration: on the one hand, the secrets of nature (the *quadrivium*) and, on the other, the secrets of language [*parole*] (the *trivium: grammatica, rhetorica, dialectica*). From the end of the Middle Ages to the present day, this opposition was lost, language being considered only as an instrument in the service of either reason or the heart. Today, however, something of this ancient opposition lives again: once again the exploration of language, conducted by linguistics, psychoanalysis, and literature, corresponds to the exploration of the cosmos. For literature is itself a science, or at least knowledge, no longer of the "human heart" but of human language [*parole*]. Its investigation is not, however, addressed to the secondary forms and figures that were the object of rhetoric, but to the fundamental categories of language. Just as in Western culture grammar was not born until long after rhetoric, so it is only after having made its way for centuries through *le beau littéraire* that literature can begin to ponder the fundamental problems of language, without which it would not exist.

CLAUDE LÉVI-STRAUSS

Claude Lévi-Strauss was born in 1908 in Brussels. He studied at the University of Paris, where he received an Agrégé en Philosophie and a Docteur ès Lettres. From 1935–39 he was a professor at the University of São Paulo, and headed several anthropological expeditions in central Brazil. In his book *Tristes Tropiques* he reports the results of some of his Brazilian experiences. From 1942–45 he was a professor at the New School for Social Research in New York. In 1950 he became Directeur d'Études at the École Pratique des Hautes Études, and since 1959 he holds the Chair of Social Anthropology at the Collège de France. He is a prolific author and many of his works have been translated into English, including *Structural Anthropology*, which is a collection of essays written between 1944 and 1957, *The Raw and the Cooked*, which is the first volume of his series "Introduction to a Science of Mythology," and *The Savage Mind*. In the article immediately following he explains, in greater detail than anywhere else, structuralist method as applied to the study of myth.

In "Four Winnebago Myths," Lévi-Strauss employs the method he described in "The Structural Study of Myth." Using only four myths he illustrates the technique which he develops and utilizes in an impressive and extended way in the volumes which make up his "Introduction to a Science of Mythology."

"History and Dialectic," reprinted as the third following selection, is the last chapter of *The Savage Mind*. The thesis of the book is that primitive ways of thinking, though less abstract, are not necessarily inferior to the present modes of thought of Western society. In his final chapter Lévi-Strauss develops this theme in opposition to some of the views of Jean-Paul Sartre, and presents his own approach to history.

10

The Structural Study of Myth

"It would seem that mythological worlds have been built up only to be shattered again, and that new worlds were built from the fragments."

> Franz Boas, in Introduction to James Teit *Traditions of the Thompson River Indians of British Columbia*, Memoirs of the American Folklore Society, VI (1898), 18.

1.0. Despite some recent attempts to renew them, it would seem that during the past twenty years anthropology has more and more turned away from studies in the field of religion. At the same time, and precisely because professional anthropologists' interest has withdrawn from primitive religion, all kinds of amateurs who claim to belong to other disciplines have seized this opportunity to move in, thereby turning into their private playground what we had left as a wasteland. Thus, the prospects for the scientific study of religion have been undermined in two ways.

1.1. The explanation for that situation lies to some extent in the fact that the anthropological study of religion was started by men like Tylor, Frazer, and Durkheim who were psychologically oriented, although not in a position to keep up with the progress of psychological research and theory.

From *Journal of American Folklore* (Oct.–Dec. 1955), vol. LXXVIII, no. 270, pp. 428–44. Reprinted by permission of the publisher.

Therefore, their interpretation soon became vitiated by the outmoded psychological approach which they used as their backing. Although they were undoubtedly right in giving their attention to intellectual processes, the way they handled them remained so coarse as to discredit them altogether. This is much to be regretted since, as Hocart so profoundly noticed in his introduction to a posthumous book recently published,[1] psychological interpretations were withdrawn from the intellectual field only to be introduced again in the field of affectivity, thus adding to "the inherent defects of the psychological school . . . the mistake of deriving clear-cut ideas . . . from vague emotions." Instead of trying to enlarge the framework of our logic to include processes which, whatever their apparent differences, belong to the same kind of intellectual operations, a naive attempt was made to reduce them to inarticulate emotional drives which resulted only in withering our studies.

1.2. Of all the chapters of religious anthropology probably none has tarried to the same extent as studies in the field of mythology. From a theoretical point of view the situation remains very much the same as it was fifty years ago, namely, a picture of chaos. Myths are still widely interpreted in conflicting ways: collective dreams, the outcome of a kind of esthetic play, the foundation of ritual. . . . Mythological figures are considered as personified abstractions, divinized heroes or decayed gods. Whatever the hypothesis, the choice amounts to reducing mythology either to an idle play or to a coarse kind of speculation.

1.3. In order to understand what a myth really is, are we compelled to choose between platitude and sophism? Some claim that human societies merely express, through their mythology, fundamental feelings common to the whole of mankind, such as love, hate, revenge; or that they try to provide some kind of explanations for phenomena which they cannot understand otherwise: astronomical, meteorological, and the like. But why should these societies do it in such

---

[1] A. M. Hocart, *Social Origins* (London, 1954), p. 7.

elaborate and devious ways, since all of them are also acquainted with positive explanations? On the other hand, psychoanalysts and many anthropologists have shifted the problems to be explained away from the natural or cosmological towards the sociological and psychological fields. But then the interpretation becomes too easy: if a given mythology confers prominence to a certain character, let us say an evil grandmother, it will be claimed that in such a society grandmothers are actually evil and that mythology reflects the social structure and the social relations; but should the actual data be conflicting, it would be readily claimed that the purpose of mythology is to provide an outlet for repressed feelings. Whatever the situation may be, a clever dialectic will always find a way to pretend that a meaning has been unravelled.

2.0. Mythology confronts the student with a situation which at first sight could be looked upon as contradictory. On the one hand, it would seem that in the course of a myth anything is likely to happen. There is no logic, no continuity. Any characteristic can be attributed to any subject; every conceivable relation can be met. With myth, everything becomes possible. But on the other hand, this apparent arbitrariness is belied by the astounding similarity between myths collected in widely different regions. Therefore the problem: if the content of a myth is contingent, how are we going to explain that throughout the world myths do resemble one another so much?

2.1. It is precisely this awareness of a basic antinomy pertaining to the nature of myth that may lead us towards its solution. For the contradiction which we face is very similar to that which in earlier times brought considerable worry to the first philosophers concerned with linguistic problems; linguistics could only begin to evolve as a science after this contradiction had been overcome. Ancient philosophers were reasoning about language the way we are about mythology. On the one hand, they did notice that in a given language certain sequences of sounds were associated with definite meanings, and they earnestly aimed at discovering a reason for the linkage between those sounds and that meaning. Their attempt, however, was thwarted from the very beginning by the fact that the same sounds were equally present in other languages though the meaning they conveyed was entirely different. The contradiction was surmounted only by the discovery that it is the combination of sounds, not the sounds in themselves, which provides the significant data.

2.2. Now, it is easy to see that some of the more recent interpretations of mythological thought originated from the same kind of misconception under which those early linguists were laboring. Let us consider, for instance, Jung's idea that a given mythological pattern—the so-called archetype—possesses a certain signification. This is comparable to the long supported error that a sound may possess a certain affinity with a meaning: for instance, the "liquid" semi-vowels with water, the open vowels with things that are big, large, loud, or heavy, etc., a kind of theory which still has its supporters.[2] Whatever emendations the original formulation may now call for, everybody will agree that the Saussurean principle of the arbitrary character of the linguistic signs was a prerequisite for the acceding of linguistics to the scientific level.

2.3. To invite the mythologist to compare his precarious situation with that of the linguist in the prescientific stage is not enough. As a matter of fact we may thus be led only from one difficulty to another. There is a very good reason why myth cannot simply be treated as language if its specific problems are to be solved; myth *is* language: to be known, myth has to be told; it is a part of human speech. In order to preserve its specificity we should thus put ourselves in a position to show that it is both the same thing as language, and also something different from it. Here, too, the past experience of linguists may help us. For language itself can be analyzed into things which are at the same time similar and different. This is precisely what is expressed in Saussure's distinction between *langue* and *parole,* one being the structural side of language, the other the statistical aspect of it, *langue* belong-

[2] See, for instance, Sir R. A. Paget, "The Origin of Language. . . ," *Journal of World History,* I, No. 2 (UNESCO, 1953).

ing to a revertible time, whereas *parole* is non-revertible. If those two levels already exist in language, then a third one can conceivably be isolated.

2.4. We have just distinguished *langue* and *parole* by the different time referents which they use. Keeping this in mind, we may notice that myth uses a third referent which combines the properties of the first two. On the one hand, a myth always refers to events alleged to have taken place in time: before the world was created, or during its first stages—anyway, long ago. But what gives the myth an operative value is that the specific pattern described is everlasting; it explains the present and the past as well as the future. This can be made clear through a comparison between myth and what appears to have largely replaced it in modern societies, namely, politics. When the historian refers to the French Revolution it is always as a sequence of past happenings, a non-revertible series of events the remote consequences of which may still be felt at present. But to the French politician, as well as to his followers, the French Revolution is both a sequence belonging to the past—as to the historian—and an everlasting pattern which can be detected in the present French social structure and which provides a clue for its interpretation, a lead from which to infer the future developments. See, for instance, Michelet who was a politically-minded historian. He describes the French Revolution thus: "This day . . . everything was possible. . . . Future became present . . . that is, no more time, a glimpse of eternity." It is that double structure, altogether historical and anhistorical, which explains that myth, while pertaining to the realm of the *parole* and calling for an explanation as such, as well as to that of the *langue* in which it is expressed, can also be an absolute object on a third level which, though it remains linguistic by nature, is nevertheless distinct from the other two.

2.5. A remark can be introduced at this point which will help to show the singularity of myth among other linguistic phenomena. Myth is the part of language where the formula *traduttore, traditore* reaches its lowest truth-value. From that point of view it should be put in the whole gamut of linguistic expressions at the end opposite to that of poetry, in spite of all the claims which have been made to prove the contrary. Poetry is a kind of speech which cannot be translated except at the cost of serious distortions; whereas the mythical value of the myth remains preserved, even through the worst translation. Whatever our ignorance of the language and the culture of the people where it originated, a myth is still felt as a myth by any reader throughout the world. Its substance does not lie in its style, its original music, or its syntax, but in the *story* which it tells. It is language, functioning on an especially high level where meaning succeeds practically at "taking off" from the linguistic ground on which it keeps on rolling.

2.6. To sum up the discussion at this point, we have so far made the following claims: 1. If there is a meaning to be found in mythology, this cannot reside in the isolated elements which enter into the composition of a myth, but only in the way those elements are combined. 2. Although myth belongs to the same category as language, being, as a matter of fact, only part of it, language in myth unveils specific properties. 3. Those properties are only to be found *above* the ordinary linguistic level; that is, they exhibit more complex features beside those which are to be found in any kind of linguistic expression.

3.0. If the above three points are granted, at least as a working hypothesis, two consequences will follow: 1. Myth, like the rest of language, is made up of constituent units. 2. These constituent units presuppose the constituent units present in language when analyzed on other levels, namely, phonemes, morphemes, and semantemes, but they, nevertheless, differ from the latter in the same way as they themselves differ from morphemes, and these from phonemes; they belong to a higher order, a more complex one. For this reason, we will call them *gross constituent units*.

3.1. How shall we proceed in order to identify and isolate these gross constituent units? We know that they cannot be found among phonemes, morphemes, or semantemes, but only on a higher level; otherwise myth would become confused with any other kind of speech. Therefore, we should look for them on the sentence level. The only method we can suggest at this stage is to proceed tentatively, by trial and error, using as a check the principles which serve as a basis for any kind of structural analysis: economy of explanation; unity of solution; and ability to reconstruct the whole from a fragment, as well as further stages from previous ones.

3.2. The technique which has been applied so far by this writer consists in analyzing each myth individually, breaking down its story into the shortest possible sentences, and writing each such sentence on an index card bearing a number corresponding to the unfolding of the story.

3.3. Practically each card will thus show that a certain function is, at a given time, predicated to a given subject. Or, to put it otherwise, each gross constituent unit will consist in a relation.

3.4. However, the above definition remains highly unsatisfactory for two different reasons. In the first place, it is well known to structural linguists that constituent units on all levels are made up of relations and the true difference between our gross units and the others stays unexplained; moreover, we still find ourselves in the realm of a non-revertible time since the numbers of the cards correspond to the unfolding of the informant's speech. Thus, the specific character of mythological time, which as we have seen is both revertible and non-revertible, synchronic and diachronic, remains unaccounted for. Therefrom comes a new hypothesis which constitutes the very core of our argument: the true constituent units of a myth are not the isolated relations but *bundles of such relations* and it is only as bundles that these relations can be put to use and combined so as to produce a meaning. Relations pertaining to the same bundle may appear diachronically at remote intervals, but when we have succeeded in grouping them together, we have reorganized our myth according to a time referent of a new nature corresponding to the prerequisite of the initial hypothesis, namely, a two-dimensional time referent which is simultaneously diachronic and synchronic and which accordingly integrates the characteristics of the *langue* on one hand, and those of the *parole* on the other. To put it in even more linguistic terms, it is as though a phoneme were always made up of all its variants.

4.0. Two comparisons may help to explain what we have in mind.

4.1. Let us first suppose that archaeologists of the future coming from another planet would one day, when all human life had disappeared from the earth, excavate one of our libraries. Even if they were at first ignorant of our writing, they might succeed in deciphering it—an undertaking which would require, at some early stage, the discovery that the alphabet, as we are in the habit of printing it, should be read from left to right and from top to bottom. However, they would soon find out that a whole category of books did not fit the usual pattern: these would be the orchestra scores on the shelves of the music division. But after trying, without success, to decipher staffs one after the other, from the upper down to the lower, they would probably notice that the same patterns of notes recurred at intervals, either in full or in part, or that some patterns were strongly reminiscent of earlier ones. Hence the hypothesis: what if patterns showing affinity, instead of being considered in succession, were to be treated as one complex pattern and read globally? By getting at what we call *harmony*, they would then find out that an orchestra score, in order to become meaningful, has to be read diachronically along one axis—that is, page after page, and from left to right—and also synchronically along the other axis, all the notes which are written vertically making up one gross constituent unit, i.e. one bundle of relations.

4.2. The other comparison is somewhat different. Let us take an observer ignorant of our playing cards, sitting for a long time with a fortune-teller. He would know something of the visitors: sex, age, look, social situation, etc. in the same way as we know something of the different cultures whose myths we try to study. He would also listen to the séances and keep them recorded so as to be able to go over them and make comparisons—as we do when we listen to myth telling and record it. Mathematicians to whom I have put the problem agree that if the man is bright and if the material available to him is sufficient, he may be able to reconstruct the nature of the deck of cards being used, that is: fifty-two or thirty-two cards according to case, made up of four homologous series consisting of the same units (the individual cards) with only one varying feature, the suit.

4.3. The time has come to give a concrete example of the method we propose. We will use the Oedipus myth which has the advantage of being well-known to everybody and for which no preliminary explanation is therefore needed. By doing so, I am well aware that the Oedipus myth has only reached us under late forms and through literary transfigurations concerned more with esthetic and moral preoccupations than with religious or ritual ones, whatever these may have been. But as will be shown later, this apparently unsatisfactory situation will strengthen our demonstration rather than weaken it.

4.4. The myth will be treated as would be an orchestra score perversely presented as a unilinear series and where our task is to re-establish the correct disposition. As if, for instance, we were confronted with a sequence of the type: 1,2,4,7,8,2,3,4,6,8,1,4,5,7,8,1,2,5,7,3,4,5,6,8 . . . , the assignment being to put all the 1's together, all the 2's, the 3's, etc.; the result is a chart:

1	2		4			7	8
	2	3	4		6		8
1			4	5		7	8
1	2			5		7	
		3	4	5			
					6		8

4.5. We will attempt to perform the same kind of operation on the Oedipus myth, trying out several dispositions until we find one which is in harmony with the principles enumerated under 3.1. Let us suppose, for the sake of argument, that the best arrangement is the following (although it might certainly be improved by the help of a specialist in Greek mythology):

Kadmos seeks his sister Europa ravished by Zeus			
		Kadmos kills the dragon	
	The Spartoi kill each other		
			Labdacos (Laios' father) = *lame* (?)
	Oedipus kills his father Laios		
			Laios (Oedipus' father) = *left-sided* (?)
		Oedipus kills the Sphinx	
Oedipus marries his mother Jocasta			
	Eteocles kills his brother Polynices		Oedipus = *swollen-foot* (?)
Antigone buries her brother Polynices despite prohibition			

4.6. Thus, we find ourselves confronted with four vertical columns each of which include several relations belonging to the same bundle. Were we to *tell* the myth, we would disregard the columns and read the rows from left to right and from top to bottom. But if we want to *understand* the myth, then we will have to disregard one half of the diachronic dimension (top to bottom) and read from left to right, column after column, each one being considered as a unit.

4.7. All the relations belonging to the same column exhibit one common feature which it is our task to unravel. For instance, all the events grouped in the first column on the left have something to do with blood relations which are over-emphasized, i.e. are subject to a more intimate treatment than they should be. Let us say, then, that the first column has as its common feature the *overrating of blood relations*. It is obvious that the second column expresses the same thing, but inverted: *underrating of blood relations*. The third column refers to monsters being slain. As to the fourth, a word of clarification is needed. The remarkable connotation of the surnames in Oedipus' father-line has often been noticed. However, linguists usually disregard it, since to them the only way to define the meaning of a term is to investigate all the contexts in which it appears, and personal names, precisely because they are used as such, are not accompanied by any context. With the method we propose to follow the objection disappears since the myth itself provides its own context. The meaningful fact is no longer to be looked for in the eventual sense of each name, but in the fact that all the names have a common feature: i.e. that they may eventually mean something and that all these hypothetical meanings (which may well remain hypothetical) exhibit a common feature, namely they refer to *difficulties to walk and to behave straight*.

4.8. What is then the relationship between the two columns on the right? Column three refers to monsters. The dragon is a chthonian being which has to be killed in order that mankind be born from the earth; the Sphinx is a monster unwilling to permit men to live. The last unit reproduces the first one which has to do with the *autochthonous origin* of mankind. Since the monsters are overcome by men, we may thus say that the common feature of the third column is *the denial of the autochthonous origin of man*.

4.9. This immediately helps us to understand the meaning of the fourth column. In mythology it is a universal character of men born from the earth that at the moment they emerge from the depth, they either cannot walk or do it clumsily. This is the case of the chthonian beings in the mythology of the Pueblo: Masauwu, who leads the emergence, and the chthonian Shumaikoli are lame ("bleeding-foot," "sore-foot"). The same happens to the Koskimo of the Kwakiutl after they have been swallowed by the chthonian monster, Tsiakish: when they returned to the surface of the earth "they limped forward or tripped sideways." Then the common feature of the fourth column is: *the persistence of the autochthonous origin of man.* It follows that column four is to column three as column one is to column two. The inability to connect two kinds of relationships is overcome (or rather replaced) by the positive statement that contradictory relationships are identical inasmuch as they are both self-contradictory in a similar way. Although this is still a provisional formulation of the structure of mythical thought, it is sufficient at this stage.

4.10. Turning back to the Oedipus myth, we may now see what it means. The myth has to do with the inability, for a culture which holds the belief that mankind is autochthonous (see, for instance, Pausanias, VIII, xxix, 4: vegetals provide a *model* for humans), to find a satisfactory transition between this theory and the knowledge that human beings are actually born from the union of man and woman. Although the problem obviously cannot be solved, the Oedipus myth provides a kind of logical tool which, to phrase it coarsely, replaces the original problem: born from one or born from two? born from different or born from same? By a correlation of this type, the overrating of blood relations is to the underrating of blood relations as the attempt to escape autochthony is to the impossibility to succeed in it. Although experience contradicts theory, social life verifies the cosmology by its similarity of structure. Hence cosmology is true.

4.11.0. Two remarks should be made at this stage.

4.11.1. In order to interpret the myth, we were able to leave aside a point which has until now worried the specialists, namely, that in the earlier (Homeric) versions of the Oedipus myth, some basic elements are lacking, such as Jocasta killing herself and Oedipus piercing his own eyes. These events do not alter the substance of the myth although they can easily be integrated, the first one as a new case of autodestruction (column three) while the second is another case of crippledness (column four). At the same time there is something significant in these additions since the shift from foot to head is to be correlated with the shift from: autochthonous origin negated to: self-destruction.

4.11.2. Thus, our method eliminates a problem which has been so far one of the main obstacles to the progress of mythological studies, namely, the quest for the *true* version, or the *earlier* one. On the contrary, we define the myth as consisting of all its versions; to put it otherwise: a myth remains the same as long as it is felt as such. A striking example is offered by the fact that our interpretation may take into account, and is certainly applicable to, the Freudian use of the Oedipus myth. Although the Freudian problem has ceased to be that of autochthony *versus* bisexual reproduction, it is still the problem of understanding how *one* can be born from *two:* how is it that we do not have only one procreator, but a mother plus a father? Therefore, not only Sophocles, but Freud himself, should be included among the recorded versions of the Oedipus myth on a par with earlier or seemingly more "authentic" versions.

5.0. An important consequence follows. If a myth is made up of all its variants, structural analysis should take all of them into account. Thus, after analyzing all the known variants of the Theban version, we should treat the others in the same way: first, the tales about Labdacos' collateral line including Agavé, Pentheus, and Jocasta herself; the Theban variant about Lycos with Amphion and Zetos as the city founders; more remote variants concerning Dionysos (Oedipus' matrilateral cousin), and Athenian legends where Cecrops takes the place of Kadmos, etc. For each of them a similar chart should be drawn, and then compared and reorganized according to the findings: Cecrops killing the serpent with the parallel episode of Kadmos; abandonment of Dionysos with abandonment of Oedipus; "Swollen Foot" with Dionysos *loxias*, i.e. walking obliquely; Europa's quest with Antiope's; the foundation of Thebes by the Spartoi or by the brothers Amphion and Zetos; Zeus kidnapping Europa and Antiope and the same with Semele; the Theban Oedipus and the Argian Perseus, etc. We will then have several two-dimensional charts, each dealing with a variant, to be organized in a three-dimensional order

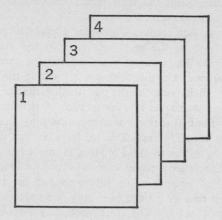

so that three different readings become possible: left to right, top to bottom, front to back. All of these charts cannot be expected to be identical; but experience shows that any difference to be observed may be correlated with other differences, so that a logical treatment of the whole will allow simplifications, the final outcome being the structural law of the myth.

5.1. One may object at this point that the task is impossible to perform since we can only work with known versions. Is it not possible that a new version might alter the picture? This is true enough if only one or two versions are available, but the objection becomes theoretical as soon as a reasonably large number has been recorded (a number which experience will progressively tell, at least as an approximation). Let us make this point clear by a comparison. If the furniture of a room and the way it is arranged in the room were known to us only through its reflection in two mirrors placed on opposite walls, we would theoretically dispose of an almost infinite number of mirror-images which would provide us with a complete knowledge. However, should the two mirrors be obliquely set, the number of mirror-images would become very small; nevertheless, four or five such images would very likely give us, if not complete information, at least a sufficient coverage so that we would feel sure that no large piece of furniture is missing in our description.

5.2. On the other hand, it cannot be too strongly emphasized that all available variants should be taken into account. If Freudian comments on the Oedipus complex are a part of the Oedipus myth, then questions such as whether Cushing's version of the Zuni origin myth should be retained or discarded become irrelevant. There is no one true version of which all the others are but copies or distortions. Every version belongs to the myth.

5.3. Finally it can be understood why works on general mythology have given discouraging results. This comes from two reasons. First, comparative mythologists have picked up preferred versions instead of using them all. Second, we have seen that the structural analysis of *one* variant of *one* myth belonging to *one* tribe (in some cases, even *one* village) already requires two dimensions. When we use several variants of the same myth for the same tribe or village, the frame of reference becomes three-dimensional and as soon as we try to enlarge the comparison, the number of dimensions required increases to such an extent that it appears quite impossible to handle them intuitively. The confusions and platitudes which are the outcome of comparative mythology can be explained by the fact that multi-dimensional frames of reference cannot be ignored, or naively replaced by two- or three-dimensional ones. Indeed, progress in comparative mythology depends largely on the cooperation of mathematicians who would undertake to express in symbols multi-dimensional relations which cannot be handled otherwise.

6.0. In order to check this theory,[3] an attempt was made in 1953-54 towards an exhaustive analysis of all the known versions of the Zuni origin and emergence myth: Cushing, 1883 and 1896; Stevenson, 1904; Parsons, 1923; Bunzel, 1932; Benedict, 1934. Furthermore, a preliminary attempt was made at a comparison of the results with similar myths in other Pueblo tribes, Western and Eastern. Finally, a test was undertaken with Plains mythology. In all cases, it was found that the theory was sound, and light was thrown, not only on North

[3] Thanks are due to an unsolicited, but deeply appreciated, grant from the Ford Foundation.

American mythology, but also on a previously unnoticed kind of logical operation, or one known only so far in a wholly different context. The bulk of material which needs to be handled almost at the beginning of the work makes it impossible to enter into details, and we will have to limit ourselves here to a few illustrations.

6.1. An over-simplified chart of the Zuni emergence myth would read as follows:

INCREASE			DEATH
mechanical growth of vegetals (used as ladders)	emergence led by Beloved Twins	sibling incest	gods kill children
food value of wild plants	migration led by the two Newekwe		magical contest with people of the dew (collecting wild food *versus* cultivation)
		sibling sacrificed (to gain victory)	
food value of cultivated plants		sibling adopted (in exchange for corn)	
periodical character of agricultural work			war against Kyanakwe (gardeners *versus* hunters)
hunting	war led by two war-gods		
			salvation of the tribe (center of the world found)

warfare	siblings sacri- ficed (to avoid flood)
DEATH	PERMANENCY

6.2. As may be seen from a global inspection of the chart, the basic problem consists in discovering a mediation between life and death. For the Pueblo, the problem is especially difficult since they understand the origin of human life on the model of vegetal life (emergence from the earth). They share that belief with the ancient Greeks, and it is not without reason that we chose the Oedipus myth as our first example. But in the American case, the highest form of vegetal life is to be found in agriculture which is periodical in nature, i.e. which consists in an alternation between life and death. If this is disregarded, the contradiction surges at another place: agriculture provides food, therefore life; but hunting provides food and is similar to warfare which means death. Hence there are three different ways of handling the problem. In the Cushing version, the difficulty revolves around an opposition between activities yielding an immediate result (collecting wild food) and activities yielding a delayed result —death has to become integrated so that agriculture can exist. Parsons' version goes from hunting to agriculture, while Stevenson's version operates the other way around. It can be shown that all the differences between these versions can be rigorously correlated with these basic structures. For instance:

	CUSHING	PARSONS	STEVENSON
Gods Kyanakwe	⎱ allied, use fiber ⎰ strings on their ⎱ bows (garden- ⎰ ers)	Kyanakwe alone, use fiber string	Gods ⎱ allied, use Men ⎰ fiber string

	VICTORIOUS OVER	VICTORIOUS OVER	VICTORIOUS OVER
Men	alone, use sinew (hunters) (until men shift to fiber)	Gods ⎱ allied, use Men ⎰ sinew string	Kyanakwe alone, use sinew string

Since fiber strings (vegetal) are always superior to sinew strings (animal) and since (to a lesser extent) the gods' alliance is preferable to their antagonism, it follows that in Cushing's version, men begin to be doubly underprivileged (hostile gods, sinew string); in Stevenson, doubly privileged (friendly gods, fiber string); while Parsons' version confronts us with an intermediary situation (friendly gods, but sinew strings since men begin by being hunters). Hence:

	CUSHING	PARSONS	STEVENSON
gods/men	—	+	+
fiber/sinew	—	—	+

6.3. Bunzel's version is from a structural point of view of the same type as Cushing's. However, it differs from both Cushing's and Stevenson's inasmuch as the latter two explain the emergence as a result of man's need to evade his pitiful condition, while Bunzel's version makes it the consequence of a call from the higher powers—hence the inverted sequences of the means resorted to for the emergence: in both Cushing and Stevenson, they go from plants to animals; in Bunzel, from mammals to insects and from insects to plants.

6.4. Among the Western Pueblo the logical approach always remains the same: the starting point and the point of arrival are the simplest ones and ambiguity is met with halfway:

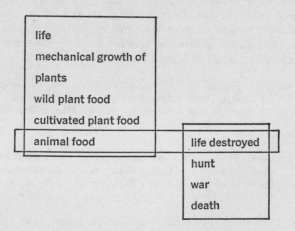

The fact that contradiction appears in the middle of the dialectical process has as its result the production of a double series of dioscuric pairs the purpose of which is to operate a mediation between conflicting terms:

1. 3 divine messengers	2 ceremonial clowns		2 war-gods
2. homogeneous pair: dioscurs (2 brothers)	siblings (brother and sister)	couple (husband and wife)	heterogeneous pair: grandmother/grandchild

which consists in combinatory variants of the same function; (hence the war attribute of the clowns which has given rise to so many queries).

6.5. Some Central and Eastern Pueblos proceed the other way around. They begin by stating the identity of hunting and cultivation (first corn obtained by Game-Father sowing deer-dewclaws), and they try to derive both life and death from that central notion. Then, instead of extreme terms being simple and intermediary ones duplicated as among the Western groups, the extreme terms become duplicated (i.e., the two sisters of the Eastern Pueblo) while a simple mediating term comes to the foreground (for instance, the Poshaiyanne of the Zia), but endowed with equivocal attributes. Hence the attributes of this "messiah" can be deduced from the place it occupies in the time sequence: good when at the beginning (Zuni, Cushing), equivocal in the middle (Central Pueblo), bad at the end (Zia), except in Bunzel where the sequence is reversed as has been shown.

6.6. By using systematically this kind of structural analysis it becomes possible to organize all the known variants of a myth as a series forming a kind of permutation group, the two variants placed at the far-ends being in a symmetrical, though inverted, relationship to each other.

7.0. Our method not only has the advantage of bringing some kind of order to what was previously chaos; it also enables us to perceive some basic logical processes which are at the root of mythical thought. Three main processes should be distinguished.

7.1.0. The trickster of American mythology has remained
so far a problematic figure. Why is it that throughout North
America his part is assigned practically everywhere to either
coyote or raven? If we keep in mind that mythical thought
always works from the awareness of oppositions towards their
progressive mediation, the reason for those choices becomes
clearer. We need only to assume that two opposite terms with
no intermediary always tend to be replaced by two equivalent
terms which allow a third one as a mediator; then one of the
polar terms and the mediator becomes replaced by a new
triad and so on. Thus we have:

INITIAL PAIR	FIRST TRIAD	SECOND TRIAD
Life		
	Agriculture	
		Herbivorous animals
		Carrion-eating animals (raven; coyote)
	Hunt	
		Prey animals
	War	
Death		

With the unformulated argument: carrion-eating animals are
like prey animals (they eat animal food), but they are also
like food-plant producers (they do not kill what they eat).
Or, to put it otherwise, Pueblo style: ravens are to gardens as
prey animals are to herbivorous ones. But it is also clear that
herbivorous animals may be called first to act as mediators
on the assumption that they are like collectors and gatherers
(vegetal-food eaters) while they can be used as animal food
though not themselves hunters. Thus we may have mediators
of the first order, of the second order, and so on, where each
term gives birth to the next by a double process of opposition
and correlation.

7.1.1. This kind of process can be followed in the mythology
of the Plains where we may order the data according to the
sequence:

Unsuccessful mediator between earth and sky
(Star husband's wife)

Heterogeneous pair of mediators
(grandmother/grandchild)

Semi-homogeneous pair of mediators
(Lodge-Boy and Thrown-away)

While among the Pueblo we have:

Successful mediator between earth and sky
(Poshaiyanki)

Semi-homogeneous pair of mediators
(Uyuyewi and Matsailema)

Homogeneous pair of mediators
(the Ahaiyuta)

7.1.2. On the other hand, correlations may appear on a transversal axis; (this is true even on the linguistic level; see the manifold connotation of the root *pose* in Tewa according to Parsons: coyote, mist, scalp, etc.). Coyote is intermediary between herbivorous and carnivorous in the same way as mist between sky and earth; scalp between war and hunt (scalp is war-crop); corn smut between wild plants and cultivated plants; garments between "nature" and "culture"; refuse between village and outside; ashes between roof and hearth (chimney). This string of mediators, if one may call them so, not only throws light on whole pieces of North American mythology—why the Dew-God may be at the same time the Game-Master and the giver of raiments and be personified as an "Ash-Boy"; or why the scalps are mist producing; or why the Game-Mother is associated with corn smut; etc.—but it also probably corresponds to a universal way of organizing daily experience. See, for instance, the French for vegetal smut; *nielle*, from Latin *nebula;* the luck-bringing power attributed to refuse (old shoe) and ashes (kissing chimney-sweepers); and compare the American Ash-Boy cycle with the Indo-European Cinderella: both phallic figures (mediator between male and female); master of the dew and of the game; owners of fine raiments; and social bridges (low class marrying into high class); though impossible to interpret through recent diffusion as has been sometimes contended since Ash-Boy and Cinderella are symmetrical but inverted in every detail (while the borrowed Cinderella tale in America—Zuni Turkey-Girl—is parallel to the prototype):

	EUROPE	AMERICA
Sex	female	male
Family Status	double family	no family
Appearance	pretty girl	ugly boy
Sentimental status	nobody likes her	in hopeless love with girl
Transformation	luxuriously clothed with supernatural help	stripped of ugliness with supernatural help
etc.		

7.2.0. Thus, the mediating function of the trickster explains that since its position is halfway between two polar terms he must retain something of that duality, namely an ambiguous and equivocal character. But the trickster figure is not the only conceivable form of mediation; some myths seem to devote themselves to the task of exhausting all the possible solutions to the problem of bridging the gap between *two* and *one*. For instance, a comparison between all the variants of the Zuni emergence myth provides us with a series of mediating devices, each of which creates the next one by a process of opposition and correlation:

$$\text{messiah} > \text{dioscurs} > \text{trickster} > \begin{array}{c}\text{bisexual}\\\text{being}\end{array} > \begin{array}{c}\text{sibling}\\\text{pair}\end{array} > \begin{array}{c}\text{married}\\\text{couple}\end{array} > \begin{array}{c}\text{grandmother-}\\\text{grandchild}\end{array}$$

$$> \begin{array}{c}\text{4 terms}\\\text{group}\end{array} > \text{triad}$$

In Cushing's version, this dialectic is accompanied by a change from the space dimension (mediating between sky and earth) to the time dimension (mediating between summer and winter, i.e., between birth and death). But while the shift is being made from space to time, the final solution (triad) re-introduces space, since a triad consists in a dioscur pair *plus* a messiah simultaneously present; and while the point of departure was ostensibly formulated in terms of a space referent (sky and earth) this was nevertheless implicitly conceived in terms of a time referent (first the messiah calls; *then* the dioscurs descend). Therefore the logic of myth confronts us with a double, reciprocal exchange of functions to which we shall return shortly (7.3.).

7.2.1. Not only can we account for the ambiguous character of the trickster, but we may also understand another property of mythical figures the world over, namely, that the same god may be endowed with contradictory attributes; for instance, he may be *good* and *bad* at the same time. If we compare the variants of the Hopi myth of the origin of Shalako, we may order them so that the following structure becomes apparent:

$$(\text{Masauwu: } x) \cong (\text{Muyingwu: Masauwu}) \cong (\text{Shalako: Muyingwu})$$
$$\cong (y: \text{Masauwu})$$

where x and y represent arbitrary values corresponding to the fact that in the two "extreme" variants the god Masauwu, while appearing alone instead of associated with another god, as in variant two, or being absent, as in three, still retains intrinsically a relative value. In variant one, Masauwu (alone) is depicted as helpful to mankind (though not as helpful as he could be), and in version four, harmful to mankind (though not as harmful as he could be); whereas in two, Muyingwu is relatively more helpful than Masauwu, and in three, Shalako more helpful than Muyingwu. We find an identical series when ordering the Keresan variants:

$$(\text{Poshaiyanki: } x) \cong (\text{Lea: Poshaiyanki}) \cong (\text{Poshaiyanki: Tiamoni})$$
$$\cong (y: \text{Poshaiyanki})$$

7.2.2. This logical framework is particularly interesting since sociologists are already acquainted with it on two other levels: first, with the problem of the pecking order among hens; and second, it also corresponds to what this writer has

called *general exchange* in the field of kinship. By recognizing
it also on the level of mythical thought, we may find ourselves
in a better position to appraise its basic importance in sociological studies and to give it a more inclusive theoretical interpretation.

7.3.0. Finally, when we have succeeded in organizing a
whole series of variants in a kind of permutation group, we
are in a position to formulate the law of that group. Although
it is not possible at the present stage to come closer than an
approximate formulation which will certainly need to be made
more accurate in the future, it seems that every myth (considered as the collection of all its variants) corresponds to a
formula of the following type:

$$f_x(a) : f_y(b) \cong f_x(b) : f_{a-1}(y)$$

where, two terms being given as well as two functions of these
terms, it is stated that a relation of equivalence still exists
between two situations when terms and relations are inverted,
under two conditions: 1. that one term be replaced by its contrary; 2. that an inversion be made between the *function* and
the *term* value of two elements.

7.3.1. This formula becomes highly significant when we recall that Freud considered that *two traumas* (and not one as
it is so commonly said) are necessary in order to give birth
to this individual myth in which a neurosis consists. By trying to apply the formula to the analysis of those traumatisms
(and assuming that they correspond to conditions 1. and 2.
respectively) we should not only be able to improve it, but
would find ourselves in the much desired position of developing side by side the sociological and the psychological aspects
of the theory; we may also take it to the laboratory and subject it to experimental verification.

8.0. At this point it seems unfortunate that, with the limited
means at the disposal of French anthropological research, no
further advance can be made. It should be emphasized that
the task of analyzing mythological literature, which is extremely bulky, and of breaking it down into its constituent
units, requires team work and secretarial help. A variant of
average length needs several hundred cards to be properly

analyzed. To discover a suitable pattern of rows and columns for those cards, special devices are needed, consisting of vertical boards about two meters long and one and one-half meters high, where cards can be pigeon-holed and moved at will; in order to build up three-dimensional models enabling one to compare the variants, several such boards are necessary, and this in turn requires a spacious workshop, a kind of commodity particularly unavailable in Western Europe nowadays. Furthermore, as soon as the frame of reference becomes multi-dimensional (which occurs at an early stage, as has been shown in 5.3.) the board-system has to be replaced by perforated cards which in turn require I.B.M. equipment, etc. Since there is little hope that such facilities will become available in France in the near future, it is much desired that some American group, better equipped than we are here in Paris, will be induced by this paper to start a project of its own in structural mythology.

8.1.0. Three final remarks may serve as conclusion.

8.1.1. First, the question has often been raised why myths, and more generally oral literature, are so much addicted to duplication, triplication or quadruplication of the same sequence. If our hypotheses are accepted, the answer is obvious: repetition has as its function to make the structure of the myth apparent. For we have seen that the synchro-diachronical structure of the myth permits us to organize it into diachronical sequences (the rows in our tables) which should be read synchronically (the columns). Thus, a myth exhibits a "slated" structure which seeps to the surface, if one may say so, through the repetition process.

8.1.2. However, the slates are not absolutely identical to each other. And since the purpose of myth is to provide a logical model capable of overcoming a contradiction (an impossible achievement if, as it happens, the contradiction is real), a theoretically infinite number of slates will be generated, each one slightly different from the others. Thus, myth grows spiral-wise until the intellectual impulse which has originated it is exhausted. Its growth is a continuous process whereas its structure remains discontinuous. If this is the case we should consider that it closely corresponds, in the realm of the spoken word, to the kind of being a crystal is in the realm of physical matter. This analogy may help us understand better the relationship of myth on one hand to both *langue* and *parole* on the other.

8.1.3. Prevalent attempts to explain alleged differences between the so-called "primitive" mind and scientific thought have resorted to qualitative differences between the working processes of the mind in both cases while assuming that the objects to which they were applying themselves remained very much the same. If our interpretation is correct, we are led toward a completely different view, namely, that the kind of logic which is used by mythical thought is as rigorous as that of modern science, and that the difference lies not in the quality of the intellectual process, but in the nature of the things to which it is applied. This is well in agreement with the situation known to prevail in the field of technology: what makes a steel ax superior to a stone one is not that the first one is better made than the second. They are equally well made, but steel is a different thing than stone. In the same way we may be able to show that the same logical processes are put to use in myth as in science, and that man has always been thinking equally well; the improvement lies, not in an alleged progress of man's conscience, but in the discovery of new things to which it may apply its unchangeable abilities.

11

Four Winnebago Myths

A STRUCTURAL SKETCH

Among the many talents which make him one of the great anthropologists of our time, Paul Radin has one which gives a singular flavor to his work. He has the authentic esthetic touch, rather uncommon in our profession. This is what we call in French *flair:* the gift of singling out those facts, observations, and documents which possess an especially rich meaning, sometimes undisclosed at first, but likely to become evident as one ponders the implications woven into the material. A crop harvested by Paul Radin, even if he does not choose to mill it himself, is always capable of providing lasting nourishment for many generations of students.

This is the reason why I intend to pay my tribute to the work of Paul Radin by giving some thought to four myths which he has published under the title *The Culture of the Winnebago: As Described by Themselves.*[1] Although Radin himself pointed out in the Preface: "In publishing these texts I have only one object in view, to put at the disposal of students, authentic material for the study of Winnebago culture," and although the four myths were each obtained from different informants, it seems that, on a structural level, there was

From *Culture in History: Essays in Honor of Paul Radin,* edited by Stanley Diamond, published for Brandeis University by Columbia University Press, New York, 1960, pp. 351-62. Reprinted by permission of the publisher.

[1] Paul Radin, *The Culture of the Winnebago: As Described by Themselves,* Special Publication of the Bollingen Foundation (also published as Memoir 2 of the *International Journal of American Linguistics,* 1949, pp. iv, 1-119).

good reason for making them the subject of a single publication. A deep unity underlies all four, notwithstanding the fact that one myth, as Radin has shown in his introduction and notes, appears to differ widely in content, style, and structure from the other three. My purpose will be to analyze the structural relationships between the four myths and to suggest that they can be grouped together not only because they are part of a collection of ethnographic and linguistic data referring to one tribe, which Radin too modestly claimed as his sole purpose, but because they are of the same genre, i.e., their meanings logically complement each other.

The title of the first myth is "The Two Friends Who Became Reincarnated: The Origin of the Four Nights' Wake." This is the story of two friends, one of them a chief's son, who decide to sacrifice their lives for the welfare of the community. After undergoing a series of ordeals in the underworld, they reach the lodge of Earthmaker, who permits them to become reincarnated and to resume their previous lives among their relatives and friends.

As explained by Radin in his commentary,[2] there is a native theory underlying the myth: every individual is entitled to a specific quota of years of life and experience. If a person dies before his time, his relatives can ask the spirits to distribute among them what he has failed to utilize. But there is more in this theory than meets the eye. The unspent life-span given up by the hero, when he lets himself be killed by the enemies, will be added to the capital of life, set up in trust for the group. Nevertheless, his act of dedication is not entirely without personal profit: by becoming a hero an individual makes a choice, he exchanges a full life-span for a shortened one, but while the full life-span is unique, granted once and for all, the shortened one appears as a kind of lease taken on eternity. That is, by giving up one full life, an indefinite succession of half-lives is gained. But since all the unlived halves will increase the life expectancy of the ordinary people, everybody gains in the process: the ordinary people whose average life expectancy will slowly but substantially increase generation after generation, and the warriors with shortened but

[2] *Ibid.,* p. 41, para. 32.

indefinitely renewable lives, provided their minds remain set on self-dedication.

It is not clear, however, that Radin pays full justice to the narrator when he treats as a "secondary interpretation" the fact that the expedition is undertaken by the heroes to show their appreciation of the favors of their fellow villagers.[3] My contention is that this motive of the heroes deserves primary emphasis, and it is supported by the fact that there are two war parties. The first one is undertaken by the warriors while the heroes are still in their adolescent years, so they are neither included in, nor even informed of it; they hear about the party only as a rumor,[4] and they decide to join it uninvited. We must conclude then that the heroes have no responsibility for the very venture wherein they distinguish themselves, since it has been instigated and led by others. Moreover, they are not responsible for the second war party, during which they are killed, since this latter foray has been initiated by the enemy in revenge for the first.

The basic idea is clear: the two friends have developed into successful social beings;[5] accordingly, they feel obliged to repay their fellow tribesmen who have treated them so well.[6] As the story goes, they set out to expose themselves in the wilderness; later they die in an ambush prepared by the enemy in revenge for the former defeat. The obvious conclusion is that the heroes have willingly died for the sake of their people. And because they died without responsibility of their own, but instead that of others, those will inherit the unspent parts of their lives, while the heroes themselves will be permitted to return to earth and the same process will be repeated all over again. This interpretation is in agreement with information given elsewhere by Radin: i.e., in order to pass the test of the Old Woman who rids the soul of all the recollections belonging to its earthly life, each soul must be solicitous not of its own welfare but of the welfare of the living members of the group.

[3] *Ibid.*, p. 37, para. 2.
[4] *Ibid.*, paras. 11-14.
[5] *Ibid.*, paras. 66-70.
[6] *Ibid.*, para. 72.

Now at the root of this myth we find—as the phonologist would say—a double opposition. First there is the opposition between *ordinary life* and *heroic life,* the former realizing a full life-span, not renewable, the latter gambling with life for the benefit of the group. The second opposition is between two kinds of death, one "straight" and final, although it provides a type of unearthly immortality in the villages of the dead; the other "undulating," and swinging between life and death. Indeed one is tempted to see the reflection of this double fate in the Winnebago symbol of the ladder of the afterworld as it appears in the Medicine Rite. One side is "like a frog's leg, twisted and dappled with light-and-life. The other [is] like a red cedar, blackened from frequent usage and very smooth and shiny."[7]

To sum up the meaning of the myth so far: if one wants a full life one gets a full death; if one renounces life and seeks death, then one increases the full life of his fellow-tribesmen, and, moreover, secures for oneself a state composed of an indefinite series of half-lives and half-deaths. Thus we have a triangular system:

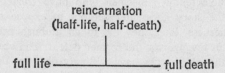

The second myth, entitled "The Man Who Brought His Wife Back from Spiritland," is a variation on the same theme, although there is a significant difference involved. Here too, we find a hero—the husband—ready to sacrifice his unspent life-span; not, as in the first myth, for the benefit of the group, but rather for the benefit of only one individual, his beloved wife. Indeed, the hero is not aware at first that by seeking death he will secure a new lease on life for both his dead wife and himself. Had he been so aware, and this holds equally for the protagonists in the first myth, the essential

---

[7] *Ibid.,* p. 71, paras. 91-93; see also Paul Radin, *The Road of Life and Death,* Bollingen Series, Vol. V (New York, 1945), especially the author's illuminating comments on pp. 63-65.

element of sacrifice would have been missing. In both cases the result is similar: an altruistic loss of life means life regained, not only for the self-appointed victim, but also for the one or more persons to whom the sacrifice was consecrated.

The third myth, "The Journey of the Ghost to Spiritland, as Told in the Medicine Rite," belongs, as the title suggests, to a religious society. It explains how the members of the Medicine Rite, after death, undergo (as do the protagonists of the other myths) several tests in Spiritland, which they overcome, thus gaining the right to become reincarnated.

At first sight this situation seems to differ from the others, since nobody sacrificed his life. However, the members of the Medicine Rite actually spend their lives in symbolic sacrifice. As Radin has shown, in *The Road of Life and Death* and elsewhere, the Medicine Rite follows the familiar pattern of letting oneself be "killed" and then "revived." Thus the only departure consists in the fact that whereas in the first and second myths the heroes are willing to die once and, so they anticipate, permanently, the heroes of the third myth (the members of the Rite) repeatedly, though symbolically, have trained themselves to self-sacrifice. They have, so to speak, mithridatized themselves against a full death by renouncing a full ordinary life which is replaced, in ritual practice, by a lifelong succession of half-lives and half-deaths. Therefore we are entitled to assume that, in this case too, the myth is made up of the same elements, although Ego—and not another person, nor the group as a whole—is conceived as the primary beneficiary.

Let us now consider the fourth myth, "How an Orphan Restored the Chief's Daughter to Life," a tale which has given Radin some concern. This myth, he says, is not only different from the other three, its plot appears unusual relative to the rest of Winnebago mythology. After recalling that in his book *Method and Theory of Ethnology*[8] he suggested that this myth was a version, altered almost beyond recognition, of a type which he then called village-origin myths, he

[8] Paul Radin, *Method and Theory of Ethnology* (New York, 1933), pp. 238-45.

proceeds to explain in *The Culture of the Winnebago*[9] why
he can no longer support this earlier interpretation.

It is worthwhile to follow closely Radin's new line of reasoning. He begins by recapitulating the plot—such a simple
plot, he says, that there is practically no need for doing so:
"The daughter of a tribal chief falls in love with an orphan,
dies of a broken heart and is then restored to life by the
orphan who must submit to and overcome certain tests, not in
Spiritland but here, on earth, in the very lodge in which the
young woman died."[10]

If this plot is "simplicity itself," where do the moot points
lie? Radin lists three which he says every modern Winnebago
would question: (1) the plot seems to refer to a highly stratified society; (2) in order to understand the plot one should
assume that in that society women occupied a high position
and that, possibly, descent was reckoned in the matrilineal
line; (3) the tests which in Winnebago mythology take place,
as a rule, in the land of ghosts occur, in this instance, on
earth.

After dismissing two possible explanations—that we are
dealing here with a borrowed European tale or that the myth
was invented by some Winnebago radical—Radin concludes
that the myth must belong to "a very old stratum of Winnebago history." He also suggests that two distinct types of literary tradition, divine tales on the one hand and human tales
on the other, have merged while certain primitive elements
have been reinterpreted to make them fit together.[11]

I am certainly not going to challenge this very elegant reconstruction backed by an incomparable knowledge of Winnebago culture, language, and history. The kind of analysis
I intend to offer is no alternative to Radin's own analysis. It
lies on a different level, logical rather than historical. It takes
as its context the three myths already discussed, not Winnebago culture, old or recent. My purpose is to explicate the
structural relationship—if any—which prevails between this
myth and the other three.

First, there is a theoretical problem which should be noted

[9] Radin, *The Culture of the Winnebago*, pp. 74 ff.
[10] *Ibid.*, p. 74.
[11] *Ibid.*, pp. 74-77.

briefly. Since the publication of Boas's *Tsimshian Mythology,* anthropologists have often simply assumed that a full correlation exists between the myths of a given society and its culture. This, I feel, is going further than Boas intended. In the work just referred to, he did not suppose that myths automatically reflect the culture, as some of his followers seem always to anticipate. Rather, he tried to find out how much of the culture actually did pass into the myths, if any, and he convincingly showed that *some* of it does. It does not follow that whenever a social pattern is alluded to in a myth this pattern must correspond to something real which should be attributed to the past if, under direct scrutiny, the present fails to offer an equivalent.

There must be, and there is, a correspondence between the unconscious meaning of a myth—the problem it tries to solve—and the conscious content it makes use of to reach that end, i.e., the plot. However, this correspondence should not always be conceived as a kind of mirror-image, it can also appear as a *transformation.* If the problem is presented in "straight" terms, that is, in the way the social life of the group expresses and tries to solve it, the overt content of the myth, the plot, can borrow its elements from social life itself. But should the problem be formulated, and its solution sought for, "upside down," that is *ab absurdo,* then the overt content will become modified accordingly to form an inverted image of the social pattern actually present to the consciousness of the natives.

If this hypothesis is true, it follows that Radin's assumption that the pattern of social life referred to in the fourth myth must belong to a past stage of Winnebago history, is not inescapable.

We may be confronted with the pattern of a nonexistent society, contrary to the Winnebago traditional pattern, only because the structure of that particular myth is itself inverted, in relation to those myths which use as overt content the traditional pattern. To put it simply, if a certain correspondence is assumed between A and B, then if A is replaced by $-A$, B must be replaced by $-B$, without implying that, since B corresponds to an external object, there should exist another external object $-B$, which must exist somewhere: either in another society (borrowed element) or in a past stage of the same society (survival).

Obviously, the problem remains: why do we have three myths of the *A* type and one of the —*A* type? This could be the case because —*A* is older than *A*, but it can also be because —*A* is one of the transformations of *A* which is already known to us under three different guises: A_1, A_2, A_3, since we have seen that the three myths of the assumed *A* type are not identical.

We have already established that the group of myths under consideration is based upon a fundamental opposition: on the one hand, the lives of ordinary people unfolding towards a natural death, followed by immortality in one of the spirit villages; and, on the other hand, heroic life, self-abridged, the gain being a supplementary life quota for the others as well as for oneself. The former alternative is not envisaged in this group of myths which, as we have seen, is mostly concerned with the latter. There is, however, a secondary difference which permits us to classify the first three myths according to the particular end assigned to the self-sacrifice in each. In the first myth the group is intended to be the immediate beneficiary, in the second it is another individual (the wife), and in the third it is oneself.

When we turn to the fourth myth, we may agree with Radin that it exhibits "unusual" features in relation to the other three. However, the difference seems to be of a logical more than of a sociological or historical nature. It consists in a new opposition introduced within the first pair of opposites (between "ordinary" life and "extraordinary" life). Now there are two ways in which an "extraordinary" phenomenon may be construed as such; it may consist either in a *surplus* or in a *lack*. While the heroes of the first three myths are all overgifted, through social success, emotions or wisdom, the heroes of the fourth myth are, if one may say so, "below standard," at least in one respect.

The chief's daughter occupies a high social position; so high, in fact, that she is cut off from the rest of the group and is therefore paralyzed when it comes to expressing her feelings. Her exalted position makes her a defective human being, lacking an essential attribute of life. The boy is also defective, but socially, that is, he is an orphan and very poor. May we say, then, that the myth reflects a stratified society? This would compel us to overlook the remarkable symmetry which prevails between our two heroes, for it would be wrong to say simply that one is high and the other low: as a matter of fact, each of them is high in one respect and low in the other, and this pair of symmetrical structures, wherein the two terms are inverted relative to each other, belongs to the realm of ideological constructs rather than of sociological systems. We have just seen that the girl is "socially" above and "naturally" below. The boy is undoubtedly very low in the social scale; however, he is a miraculous hunter, i.e. he entertains privileged relations with the natural world, the world of animals. This is emphasized over and over again in the myth.[12]

Therefore may we not claim that the myth actually confronts us with a polar system consisting in two individuals, one male, the other female, and both exceptional insofar as each of them is overgifted in one way (+) and undergifted in the other (−).

	Nature	Culture
Boy	+	−
Girl	−	+

The plot consists in carrying this disequilibrium to its logical extreme; the girl dies a *natural* death, the boy stays alone, i.e. he also dies, but in a *social* way. Whereas during their ordinary lives the girl was overtly above, the boy overtly below, now that they have become segregated (either from the living or from society) their positions are inverted: the girl is below (in her grave), the boy above (in his lodge). This, I think, is clearly implied in a detail stated by the narrator which seems to have puzzled Radin: "On top of the grave they then piled loose dirt, placing everything in such a way

[12] *Ibid.*, see paras. 10-14, 17-18, 59-60, 77-90.

that nothing could seep through."[13] Radin comments: "I do not understand why piling the dirt loosely would prevent seepage. There must be something else involved that has not been mentioned."[14] May I suggest that this detail be correlated with a similar detail about the building of the young man's lodge: ". . . the bottom was piled high with dirt so that, in this fashion, they could keep the lodge warm."[15] There is implied here, I think, not a reference to recent or past custom but rather a clumsy attempt to emphasize that, relative to the earth's surface, i.e. dirt, the boy is now above and the girl below.

This new equilibrium, however, will be no more lasting than the first. *She who was unable to live cannot die;* her ghost lingers "on earth." Finally she induces the young man to fight the ghosts and take her back among the living. With a wonderful symmetry, the boy will meet, a few years later, with a similar, although inverted, fate; "Although I am not yet old, he says to the girl (now his wife,) I have been here (lasted) on earth as long as I can. . . ."[16] *He who overcame death, proves unable to live.* This recurring antithesis could develop indefinitely, and such a possibility is noted in the text, (with an only son surviving his father, he too an orphan, he too a sharpshooter) but a different solution is finally reached. The heroes, equally unable to die or to live, will assume an intermediate identity, that of twilight creatures living under the earth but also able to come up on it; they will be neither men nor gods, but wolves, that is, ambivalent spirits combining good and evil features. So ends the myth.

If the above analysis is correct, two consequences follow: first, our myth makes up a consistent whole wherein the details balance and fit each other nicely; secondly, the three problems raised by Radin can be analyzed in terms of the myth itself; and no hypothetical past stage of Winnebago society need be invoked.

Let us, then, try to solve these three problems, following the pattern of our analysis.

[13] *Ibid.*, p. 87, para. 52.
[14] *Ibid.*, p. 100, n. 40.
[15] *Ibid.*, p. 87, para. 74.
[16] *Ibid.*, p. 94, para. 341.

1. The society of the myth appears stratified, only because the two heroes are conceived as a pair of opposites, but they are such both from the point of view of nature *and* of culture. Thus, the so-called stratified society should be interpreted not as a sociological vestige but as a projection of a logical structure wherein everything is given both in opposition and correlation.

2. The same answer can be given to the question of the assumed exalted position of the women. If I am right, our myths state three propositions, the first by implication, the second expressly stated in myths 1, 2 and 3, the third expressly stated in myth 4.

These propositions are as follow:

a. Ordinary people live (their full lives) and die (their full deaths).
b. Positive extraordinary people die (earlier) and live (more).
c. Negative extraordinary people are able neither to live nor to die.

Obviously proposition c offers an inverted demonstration of the truth of a and b. Hence, it must use a plot starting with protagonists (here, man and woman) in inverted positions. This leads us to state that a plot and its component parts should neither be interpreted by themselves nor relative to something outside the realm of the myth proper, but as *substitutions* given in, and understandable only with reference to *the group made up of all the myths of the same series.*

3. We may now revert to the third problem raised by Radin about myth 4, that is, the contest with the ghosts takes place on earth instead of, as was usually the case, in Spiritland. To this query I shall suggest an answer along the same lines as the others.

It is precisely because our two heroes suffer from a state of *under-life* (in respect either to culture or nature) that, in the narrative, the ghosts become a kind of *super-dead*. It will be recalled that the whole myth develops and is resolved on an intermediary level, where humans become underground animals and ghosts linger on earth. It tells about people who are, from the start, half-alive and half-dead while, in the preceding myths, the opposition between life and death is strongly emphasized at the beginning, and overcome only at the end. Thus, the integral meaning of the four myths is that, in order to be overcome the opposition between life and death should be first acknowledged, or else the ambiguous state will persist indefinitely.

I hope to have shown that the four myths under consideration all belong to the same *group* (understood as in *group theory*) and that Radin was even more right than he supposed in publishing them together. In the first place, the four myths deal with extraordinary, in opposition to ordinary, fate. The fact that ordinary fate is not illustrated here and thus is reckoned as an "empty" category, does not imply, of course, that it is not illustrated elsewhere. In the second place, we find an opposition between two types of extraordinary fate, positive and negative. This new dichotomy which permits us to segregate myth 4 from myths 1, 2 and 3 corresponds, on a logical level, to the discrimination that Radin makes on psychological, sociological, and historical grounds. Finally, myths 1, 2 and 3 have been classified according to the purpose of the sacrifice which is the theme of each.

Thus the four myths can be organized in a dichotomous structure of correlations and oppositions. But we can go even further and try to order them on a common scale. This is suggested by the curious variations which can be observed in each myth with respect to the kind of test the hero is put to by the ghosts.

In myth 3 there is no test at all, so far as the ghosts are concerned. The tests consist in overcoming material obstacles while the ghosts themselves figure as indifferent fellow travelers. In myth 1 they cease to be indifferent without yet becoming hostile. On the contrary, the tests result from their overfriendliness, as inviting women and infectious merrymakers. Thus, from *companions* in myth 3 they change to *seducers* in myth 1. In myth 2 they still behave as human beings, but they now act as *aggressors,* and permit themselves all kinds of rough play. This is even more evident in myth 4, but here the human element vanishes; it is only at the end that we know that ghosts, not crawling insects, are respon-

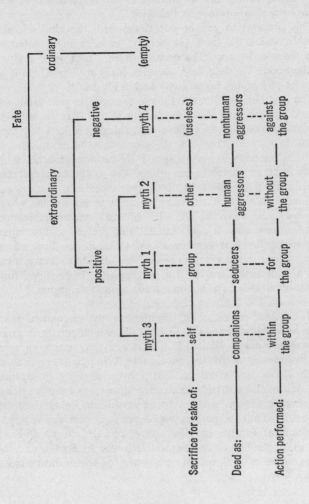

sible for the trials of the hero. We have thus a twofold progression, from a *peaceful* attitude to an *aggressive* one, and from *human* to *nonhuman* behavior.

This progression can be correlated with the kind of relationship which the hero (or heroes) of each myth entertain with the social group. The hero of myth 3 belongs to a ritual brotherhood: he definitely assumes his (privileged) fate as member of a group, he acts with and in his group.

The two heroes of myth 1 have resolved to part from the group, but the text states repeatedly that this is in order to find an opportunity to achieve something beneficial for their fellow tribesmen. They act, therefore, for the group. But in myth 2 the hero is only inspired by his love for his wife. There is no reference to the group. The action is undertaken independently for the sake of another individual.

Finally, in myth 4, the negative attitude toward the group is clearly revealed; the girl dies of her "uncommunicativeness," if one may say so. Indeed she prefers to die rather than speak; death is her "final" exile. As for the boy, he refuses to follow the villagers when they decide to move away and abandon the grave. The segregation is thus willfully sought on all sides; the action unrolls against the group.

The accompanying chart summarizes our discussion. I am quite aware that, in order to be fully convincing, the argument should not be limited to the four myths considered here, but include more of the invaluable Winnebago mythology which Radin has given us. But I hope that by integrating more material the basic structure outlined has become richer and more complex, without being impaired. By singling out one book which its author would perhaps consider a minor contribution, I have intended to emphasize, in an indirect way, the fecundity of the method followed by Radin, and the lasting value of the problems he poses for the anthropologist.

12

History and Dialectic

In the course of this work I have allowed myself, not without ulterior motive, to borrow a certain amount of Sartre's vocabulary. I wanted to lead the reader to face a problem, the discussion of which will serve to introduce my conclusion. The problem is to what extent thought that can and will be both anecdotal and geometrical may yet be called dialectical. The savage mind totalizes. It claims indeed to go very much further in this direction than Sartre allows dialectical reason, for, on the one hand, the latter lets pure seriality escape (and we have just seen how classificatory systems succeed in incorporating it) and, on the other, it excludes schematization, in which these same systems reach their consummation. In my view, it is in this intransigent refusal on the part of the savage mind to allow anything human (or even living) to remain alien to it, that the real principle of dialectical reason is to be found. But my idea of the latter is very different from Sartre's.

In reading the *Critique* it is difficult to avoid feeling that Sartre vacillates between two conceptions of dialectical reason. Sometimes he opposes dialectical and analytical reason as truth and error, if not as God and the devil, while at other times these two kinds of reason are apparently complementary, different routes to the same truths. The first conception not only discredits scientific knowledge and finally even leads to suggesting the impossibility of a science of biology, it also involves a curious paradox; for the work entitled *Critique de*

From *The Savage Mind*, Chicago: The University of Chicago Press, 1966, Chapter 9; © 1962 by Librairie Plon, 8, rue Garanciere, Paris–6e. English translation © 1966 by George Weidenfeld and Nicolson Ltd. Reprinted by permission of the publisher and of the author.

la raison dialectique is the result of the author's exercise of his own analytical reason: he defines, distinguishes, classifies and opposes. This philosophical treatise is no different in kind from the works it examines and with which it engages in discussion, if only to condemn them. It is difficult to see how analytical reason could be applied to dialectical reason and claim to establish it, if the two are defined by mutually exclusive characteristics. The second conception is open to a different objection: if dialectical and analytical reason ultimately arrive at the same results, and if their respective truths merge into a single truth, then, one may ask in what way they are opposed and, in particular, on what grounds the former should be pronounced superior to the latter. Sartre's endeavour seems contradictory in the one case and superfluous in the other.

How is the paradox to be explained, and avoided? Sartre attributes a reality *sui generis* to dialectical reason in both the hypotheses between which he hesitates. It exists independently of analytical reason, as its antagonist or alternatively its complement. Although in both our cases Marx is the point of departure of our thought, it seems to me that the Marxist orientation leads to a different view, namely, that the opposition between the two sorts of reason is relative, not absolute. It corresponds to a tension within human thought which may persist indefinitely *de facto,* but which has no basis *de jure*. In my view dialectical reason is always constitutive: it is the bridge, forever extended and improved, which analytical reason throws out over an abyss; it is unable to see the further shore but it knows that it is there, even should it be constantly receding. The term dialectical reason thus covers the perpetual efforts analytical reason must make to reform itself if it aspires to account for language, society and thought; and the distinction between the two forms of reason in my view rests only on the temporary gap separating analytical reason from the understanding of life. Sartre calls analytical reason reason in repose; I call the same reason dialectical when it is roused to action, tensed by its efforts to transcend itself.

In Sartre's terminology I am therefore to be defined as a transcendental materialist and aesthete. I am a transcendental materialist (p. 124) because I do not regard dialectical reason as *something other than* analytical reason, upon which the absolute originality of a human order would be based, but as *something additional in* analytical reason: the necessary condition for it to venture to undertake the resolution of the human into the non-human. And I count as an aesthete since Sartre applies this term to anyone purporting to study men as if they were ants (p. 183). But apart from the fact that this seems to me just the attitude of any scientist who is an agnostic, there is nothing very compromising about it, for ants with their artificial tunnels, their social life and their chemical messages, already present a sufficiently tough resistance to the enterprises of analytical reason . . . So I accept the characterization of aesthete in so far as I believe the ultimate goal of the human sciences to be not to constitute, but to dissolve man. The pre-eminent value of anthropology is that it represents the first step in a procedure which involves others. Ethnographic analysis tries to arrive at invariants beyond the empirical diversity of human societies; and, as the present work shows, these are sometimes to be found at the most unforeseen points. Rousseau (2, ch. VIII) foresaw this with his usual acumen: 'One needs to look near at hand if one wants to study men; but to study man one must learn to look from afar; one must first observe differences in order to discover attributes'. However, it would not be enough to reabsorb particular humanities into a general one. This first enterprise opens the way for others which Rousseau would not have been so ready to accept and which are incumbent on the exact natural sciences: the reintegration of culture in nature and finally of life within the whole of its physico-chemical conditions.[1]

However, in spite of the intentionally brutal turn given to my thesis, I am not blind to the fact that the verb 'dissolve' does not in any way imply (but even excludes) the destruction of the constituents of the body subjected to the action of another body. The solution of a solid into a liquid alters the disposition of its molecules. It also often provides an efficacious method of putting them by so that they can be

---

[1] The opposition between nature and culture to which I attached much importance at one time (1, ch. 1 and 2) now seems to be of primarily methodological importance.

recovered in case of need and their properties be better stud
ied. The reductions I am envisaging are thus legitimate, o
indeed possible, only if two conditions are satisfied. First, the
phenomena subjected to reduction must not be impoverished
one must be certain that everything contributing to their dis
tinctive richness and originality has been collected aroun
them. For it is pointless to pick up a hammer unless to hit the
nail on the head.

Secondly, one must be ready to accept, as a consequenc
of each reduction, the total overturning of any preconceive
idea concerning the level, whichever it may be, one is strivin
to attain. The idea of some general humanity to which ethno
graphic reduction leads, will bear no relation to any on
may have formed in advance. And when we do finally suc
ceed in understanding life as a function of inert matter, i
will be to discover that the latter has properties very differen
from those previously attributed to it. Levels of reductio
cannot therefore be classed as superior and inferior, for th
level taken as superior must, through the reduction, be ex
pected to communicate retroactively some of its richness t
the inferior level to which it will have been assimilated. Sci
entific explanation consists not in moving from the comple
to the simple but in the replacement of a less intelligibl
complexity by one which is more so.

Seen in this light, therefore, my self is no more oppose
to others than man is opposed to the world: the truths learn
through man are 'of the world', and they are important fc
this reason.[2] This explains why I regard anthropology as th
principle of all research, while for Sartre it raises a proble

[2] This even holds for mathematical truths of which a contemporar
logician, however, says that 'The characteristic of mathematical though
is that it does not convey truth about the external world' (Heytin
pp. 8–9). But mathematical thought at any rate reflects the free func
tioning of the mind, that is, the activity of the cells of the cerebral co
tex, relatively emancipated from any external constraint and obeyin
only its own laws. As the mind too is a thing, the functioning of th
thing teaches us something about the nature of things: even pure reflec
tion is in the last analysis an internalization of the cosmos. It illustrate
the structure of what lies outside in a symbolic form: 'Logic and lc
gistics are empirical sciences belonging to ethnography rather than ps
chology' (Beth, p. 151).

in the shape of a constraint to overcome or a resistance to reduce. And indeed what can one make of peoples 'without history' when one has defined man in terms of dialectic and dialectic in terms of history? Sometimes Sartre seems tempted to distinguish two dialectics: the 'true' one which is supposed to be that of historical societies, and a repetitive, short-term dialectic, which he grants so-called primitive societies whilst at the same time placing it very near biology. This imperils his whole system, for the bridge between man and nature which he has taken such pains to destroy would turn out to be surreptitiously re-established through ethnography, which is indisputably a human science and devotes itself to the study of these societies. Alternatively Sartre resigns himself to putting a 'stunted and deformed' humanity on man's side (p. 203), but not without implying that its place in humanity does not belong to it in its own right and is a function only of its adoption by historical humanity: either because it has begun to internalize the latter's history in the colonial context, or because, thanks to anthropology itself, historical humanity has given the blessing of meaning to an original humanity which was without it. Either way the prodigious wealth and diversity of habits, beliefs and customs is allowed to escape; and it is forgotten that each of the tens or hundreds of thousands of societies which have existed side by side in the world or succeeded one another since man's first appearance, has claimed that it contains the essence of all the meaning and dignity of which human society is capable and, reduced though it may have been to a small nomad band or a hamlet lost in the depths of the forest, its claim has in its own eyes rested on a moral certainty comparable to that which we can invoke in our own case. But whether in their case or our own, a good deal of egocentricity and naïvety is necessary to believe that man has taken refuge in a single one of the historical or geographical modes of his existence, when the truth about man resides in the system of their differences and common properties.

He who begins by steeping himself in the allegedly self-evident truths of introspection never emerges from them. Knowledge of men sometimes seems easier to those who allow themselves to be caught up in the snare of personal identity. But they thus shut the door on knowledge of man: written or unavowed 'confessions' form the basis of all ethnographic research. Sartre in fact becomes the prisoner of his Cogito: Descartes made it possible to attain universality, but conditionally on remaining psychological and individual; by sociologizing the Cogito, Sartre merely exchanges one prison for another. Each subject's group and period now take the place of timeless consciousness. Moreover, Sartre's view of the world and man has the narrowness which has been traditionally credited to closed societies. His insistence on tracing a distinction between the primitive and the civilized with the aid of gratuitous contrasts reflects, in a scarcely more subtle form, the fundamental opposition he postulates between myself and others. Yet there is little difference between the way in which this opposition is formulated in Sartre's work and the way it would have been formulated by a Melanesian savage, while the analysis of the practico-inert quite simply revives the language of animism.[3]

Descartes, who wanted to found a physics, separated Man from Society. Sartre, who claims to found an anthropology, separates his own society from others. A Cogito—which strives to be ingenuous and raw—retreats into individualism and empiricism and is lost in the blind alleys of social psychology. For it is striking that the situations which Sartre uses as a starting point for extracting the formal conditions of social reality—strikes, boxing matches, football matches, bus-stop queues—are all secondary incidentals of life in society; and they cannot therefore serve to disclose its foundations.

This axiomatic, so far removed from the anthropologist's, is all the more disappointing when he feels himself very close to Sartre whenever the latter applies himself, with incomparable artistry, to grasping, in its dialectical movement, a present or past social experience within our own culture. Sartre

[3] It is precisely because all these aspects of the savage mind can be discovered in Sartre's philosophy, that the latter is in my view unqualified to pass judgment on it: he is prevented from doing so by the very fact of furnishing its equivalent. To the anthropologist, on the contrary, this philosophy (like all the others) affords a first-class ethnographic document, the study of which is essential to an understanding of the mythology of our own time.

then does what every anthropologist tries to do in the case of different cultures: to put himself in the place of the men living there, to understand the principle and pattern of their intentions, and to perceive a period or a culture as a significant set. In this respect we can often learn from him, but these are lessons of a practical, not a theoretical, nature. It is possible that the requirement of 'totalization' is a great novelty to some historians, sociologists and psychologists. It has been taken for granted by anthropologists ever since they learned it from Malinowski. But Malinowski's deficiencies have also taught us that this is not where explanation ends. It only begins when we have succeeded in constituting our object. The role of dialectical reason is to put the human sciences in possession of a reality with which it alone can furnish them, but the properly scientific work consists in decomposing and then recomposing on a different plane. With all due respect to Sartrian phenomenology, we can hope to find in it only a point of departure, not one of arrival.

Furthermore, dialectical reason must not let itself be carried away by its own elan, nor must the procedure leading to the comprehension of an *other* reality attribute to it, in addition to its own dialectical features, those appertaining to the procedure rather than to the object: it does not follow from the fact that all knowledge of others is dialectical, that others are wholly dialectical in every respect. By making analytical reason an anti-comprehension, Sartre often comes to refuse it any reality as an integral part of the object of comprehension. This paralogism is already apparent in his manner of invoking history, for one is hard put to it to see whether it is meant to be the history men make unconsciously, history of men consciously made by historians, the philosopher's interpretation of the history of men or his interpretation of the history of historians. The difficulty becomes even greater, however, when Sartre endeavours to explain the life and thought of the present or past members not of his own society but of exotic societies.

He thinks, rightly, that this attempted comprehension stands no chance of succeeding unless it is dialectical; and he concludes, wrongly, that the relationship between native thought and his knowledge of it, is that of a constitutive to a constituted dialectic, and thus, by an unforeseen detour, he repeats all the illusions of theorists of primitive mentality on his own account. It seems even less tolerable to him than to Levy-Bruhl that the savage should possess 'complex understanding' and should be capable of analysis and demonstration. Of the Ambrym native, made famous by Deacon's work, who was able to show the field-worker the functioning of his marriage rules and kinship system by a diagram in the sand (an aptitude in no way exceptional as plenty of similar cases are recorded in ethnographic literature) Sartre says: 'It goes without saying that this construction is not a thought: it is a piece of manual work governed by unexpressed synthetical knowledge' (p. 505). Granted: but then the same must be said of a professor at the Ecole Polytechnique demonstrating a proof on the blackboard, for every ethnographer capable of dialectical comprehension is intimately persuaded that the situation is exactly the same in both cases. So it would follow that all reason is dialectical, which for my part I am prepared to concede, since dialectical reason seems to me like analytical reason in action; but then the distinction between the two forms of reason which is the basis of Sartre's enterprise would become pointless.

I must now confess to having myself unintentionally and unwittingly lent support to these erroneous ideas, by having seemed all too often in *Les structures élémentaires de la parenté* as if I were seeking out an unconscious genesis of matrimonial exchange. I should have made more distinction between exchange as it is expressed spontaneously and forcefully in the *praxis* of groups and the conscious and deliberate rules by which these same groups—or their philosophers—spend their time in codifying and controlling it. If there is anything to be learnt from the ethnographic enquiries of the last twenty years, it is that this latter aspect is much more important than has generally been realized by observers, who labour under the same delusion as Sartre. Thus we must, as Sartre advocates, apply dialectical reason to the knowledge of our own and other societies. But we must not lose sight of the fact that analytical reason occupies a considerable place in all of them and that, as it is present, the approach we adopt must also allow us to rediscover it there.

But even were it not present, Sartre's position would not be improved. For in this case exotic societies would merely confront us, in a more general manner than others, with an unconscious teleology, which, although historical, completely eludes human history: that of which certain aspects are revealed by linguistics and psycho-analysis and which rests on the interplay of biological mechanisms (structure of the brain, lesions, internal secretions) and psychological ones. There, it seems to me, is 'the bone' (to borrow a phrase from Sartre) which his critique does not manage to break, and moreover cares nothing about, which is the most serious charge one could level at it. For language does not consist in the analytical reason of the old-style grammarians nor in the dialectic constituted by structural linguistics nor in the constitutive dialectic of individual *praxis* facing the practico-inert, since all three presuppose it. Linguistics thus presents us with a dialectical and totalizing entity but one outside (or beneath) consciousness and will. Language, an unreflecting totalization, is human reason which has its reasons and of which man knows nothing. And if it is objected that it is so only for a subject who internalizes it on the basis of linguistic theory, my reply is that this way out must be refused, for this subject is one who *speaks:* for the same light which reveals the nature of language to him also reveals to him that it was so when he did not know it, for he already made himself understood, and that it will remain so tomorrow without his being aware of it, since his discourse never was and never will be the result of a conscious totalization of linguistic laws. But if, as speaking subject, man can find his apodictic experience in an *other* totalization, there seems no longer any reason why, as living subject, he should not have access to the same experience in other, not necessarily human, but living beings.

This method could also lay claim to the name 'progressive-regressive'; in fact, what Sartre describes as such is the very method anthropologists have been practising for many years. But Sartre restricts it to its preliminary step. For our method is progressive-regressive not once but twice over. In the first stage, we observe the datum of experience, analyse it in the present, try to grasp its historical antecedents as far as we can delve into the past, and bring all these facts back to the light of day to incorporate them into a meaningful totality. The second stage, which repeats the first on a different plane and at a different level, then begins. This internalized human thing which we have sought to provide with all its wealth and originality, only fixes the distance analytical reason must cover, the leap it must make, to close the gap between the ever unforeseen complexity of this new object and the intellectual means at its disposal. It must therefore transform itself as dialectical reason, in the hope that once flexible, widened and strengthened, by its agency this unforeseen object will be assimilated to others, this novel totality will be merged into other totalities and that thus little by little clambering on to the mass of its conquests, dialectical reason will descry other horizons and other objects. No doubt the procedure would go astray if it were not, at every stage and, above all, when it seemed to have run its course, ready to retrace its steps and to double back on itself to preserve the contact with that experienced totality which serves both as its end and means. This return on itself is in my view a verification, rather than, as Sartre regards it, a demonstration, for, as I see it, a conscious being aware of itself as such poses a problem to which it provides no solution. The discovery of the dialectic subjects analytical reason to an imperative requirement: to account also for dialectical reason. This standing requirement relentlessly forces analytical reason to extend its programme and transform its axiomatic. But dialectical reason can account neither for itself nor for analytical reason.

It will be objected that this expansion is illusory since it is always accompanied by a contraction in meaning, and we should abandon the substance for the shadow, clarity for obscurity, the manifest for the conjectural, truth for science fiction (Sartre, p. 129). Again, Sartre would have to show that he himself avoids this dilemma, inherent in every attempt at explanation. The real question is not whether our endeavour to understand involves a gain or a loss of meaning, but whether the meaning we preserve is of more value than that we have been judicious enough to relinquish. In this respect Sartre seems to have remembered only half of Marx's and Freud's combined lesson. They have taught us that man has meaning only on the condition that he view himself as meaningful. So far I agree with Sartre. But it must be added that *this meaning is never the right one:* superstructures are *faulty acts* which have 'made it' socially. Hence it is vain to go to historical consciousness for the truest meaning. What Sartre calls dialectical reason is only a reconstruction, by what he calls analytical reason, of hypothetical moves about which it is impossible to know—unless one should perform them without thinking them—whether they bear any relation at all to what he tells us about them and which, if so, would be definable in terms of analytical reason alone. And so we end up in the paradox of a system which invokes the criterion of historical consciousness to distinguish the 'primitive' from the 'civilized' but—contrary to its claim—is itself ahistorical. It offers not a concrete image of history but an abstract schema of men making history of such a kind that it can manifest itself in the trend of their lives as a synchronic totality. Its position in relation to history is therefore the same as that of primitives to the eternal past: in Sartre's system, history plays exactly the part of a myth.

Indeed, the problem raised by the *Critique de la raison dialectique* is reducible to the question: under what conditions is the myth of the French Revolution possible? And I am prepared to grant that the contemporary Frenchman must believe in this myth in order fully to play the part of an historical agent and also that Sartre's analysis admirably extracts the set of formal conditions necessary if this result is to be secured. But it does not follow that his meaning, just because it is the richest (and so most suited to inspire practical action), should be the truest. Here the dialectic turns against itself. This truth is a matter of context, and if we place ourselves outside it—as the man of science is bound to do—what appeared as an experienced truth first becomes confused and finally disappears altogether. The so-called men of the Left still cling to a period of contemporary history which bestowed the blessing of a congruence between practical imperatives and schemes of interpretation. Perhaps this golden age of historical consciousness has already passed; and that this eventuality can at any rate be envisaged proves that what we have here is only a contingent context like the fortuitous 'focusing' of an optical instrument when its object-glass and eye-piece move in relation to each other. We are still 'in focus' so far as the French Revolution is concerned, but so we should have been in relation to the Fronde had we lived earlier. The former will rapidly cease to afford a coherent image on which our action can be modelled, just as the latter has already done. What we learn from reading Retz is that thought is powerless to extract a scheme of interpretation from events long past.

At first sight, there seems no doubt: on one side the privileged, on the other the humble and exploited; how could we hesitate? We are Frondeurs. However, the people of Paris were being manoeuvred by noble houses, whose sole aim was to arrange their own affairs with the existing powers, and by one half of the royal family which wanted to oust the other. And now we are already only half Frondeurs. As for the Court, which took refuge at Saint-Germain, it appears at first to have been a faction of good for nothings vegetating on their privileges and growing fat on exactions and usury at the expense of the collectivity. But no, it had a function all the same since it retained military power; it conducted the struggle against foreigners, the Spaniards, whom the Frondeurs invited without hesitation to invade the country and impose their wills on this same Court which was defending the fatherland. The scales, however, tilt the other way again: the Frondeurs and Spaniards together formed the party of peace. The Prince de Condé and the Court only sought warlike adventures. We are pacifists and once again become Frondeurs. But nevertheless did not the military exploits of Mazarin and the Court extend France to its present frontiers, thus founding the state and the nation? Without them we should not be what we are to-day. So here we are on the other side again.

It suffices therefore for history to move away from us in time or for us to move away from it in thought, for it to cease to be internalizable and to lose its intelligibility, a spurious intelligibility attaching to a temporary internality. I am not however suggesting that man can or should sever himself from this internality. It is not in his power to do so and wisdom consists for him in seeing himself live it, while at the same time knowing (but in a different register) that what he lives so completely and intensely is a myth—which will appear as such to men of a future century, and perhaps to himself a few years hence, and will no longer appear at all to men of a future millennium. All meaning is answerable to a lesser meaning, which gives it its highest meaning, and if this regression finally ends in recognizing 'a contingent law of which one can say only: *it is thus,* and not otherwise' (Sartre, p. 128), this prospect is not alarming to those whose thought is not tormented by transcendence even in a latent form. For man will have gained all he can reasonably hope for if, on the sole condition of bowing to this contingent law, he succeeds in determining his form of conduct and in placing all else in the realm of the intelligible.

Sartre is certainly not the only contemporary philosopher to have valued history above the other human sciences and formed an almost mystical conception of it. The anthropologist respects history, but he does not accord it a special value. He conceives it as a study complementary to his own: one of them unfurls the range of human societies in time, the other in space. And the difference is even less great than it might seem, since the historian strives to reconstruct the picture of vanished societies as they were at the points which for them corresponded to the present, while the ethnographer does his best to reconstruct the historical stages which temporally preceded their existing form.

This symmetry between history and anthropology seems to be rejected by philosophers who implicitly or explicitly deny that distribution in space and succession in time afford equivalent perspectives. In their eyes some special prestige seems to attach to the temporal dimension, as if diachrony were to establish a kind of intelligibility not merely superior to that provided by synchrony, but above all more specifically human.

It is easy to explain, if not to justify, this preference. The diversity of social forms, which the anthropologist grasps as deployed in space, present the appearance of a discontinuous system. Now, thanks to the temporal dimension, history seems to restore to us, not separate states, but the passage from one state to another in a continuous form. And as we believe that we apprehend the trend of our personal history as a continuous change, historical knowledge appears to confirm the evidence of inner sense. History seems to do more than describe beings to us from the outside, or at best give us intermittent flashes of insight into internalities, each of which are so on their own account while remaining external to each other: it appears to re-establish our connection, outside ourselves, with the very essence of change.

There would be plenty to say about this supposed totalizing continuity of the self which seems to me to be an illusion sustained by the demands of social life—and consequently a reflection of the external on the internal—rather than the object of an apodictic experience. But there is no need to resolve this philosophical problem in order to perceive that the proposed conception of history corresponds to no kind of reality. As historical knowledge is claimed to be privileged, I feel entitled (as I would not otherwise feel) to make the point that there is a twofold antinomy in the very notion of an historical fact. For, *ex hypothesi,* a historical fact is what really took place, but where did anything take place? Each episode in a revolution or a war resolves itself into a multitude of individual psychic movements. Each of these movements is the translation of unconscious development, and these resolve themselves into cerebral, hormonal or nervous phenomena, which themselves have reference to the physical or chemical order. Consequently, historical facts are no more *given* than any other. It is the historian, or the agent of history, who constitutes them by abstraction and as though under the threat of an infinite regress.

What is true of the constitution of historical facts is no less so of their selection. From this point of view, the historian and the agent of history choose, sever and carve them up, for a truly total history would confront them with chaos. Every corner of space conceals a multitude of individuals each of whom totalizes the trend of history in a manner which cannot be compared to the others; for any one of these individuals, each moment of time is inexhaustibly rich in physical and psychical incidents which all play their part in his totalization. Even history which claims to be universal is still only a juxtaposition of a few local histories within which (and between which) very much more is left out than is put in. And it would be vain to hope that by increasing the number of collaborators and making research more intensive one would obtain a better result. In so far as history aspires to meaning, it is doomed to select regions, periods, groups of men and individuals in these groups and to make them stand out, as discontinuous figures, against a continuity barely good enough to be used as a backdrop. A truly total history would cancel itself out—its product would be nought. What makes history possible is that a sub-set of events is found, for a given period, to have approximately the same significance for a contingent of individuals who have not necessarily experienced the events and may even consider them at an interval of several centuries. History is therefore never history, but history-for.[4] It is partial in the sense of being biased even when it claims not to be, for it inevitably remains partial—that is, incomplete—and this is itself a form of partiality. When one proposes to write a history of the French Revolution one knows (or ought to know) that it cannot, simultaneously and under the same heading, be that of the Jacobin and that of the aristocrat. *Ex hypothesi,* their respective totalizations (each of which is anti-symmetric to the other) are equally true. One must therefore choose between two alternatives. One must select as the principal either one or a third (for there are an infinite number of them) and give up the attempt to find in history a totalization of the set of partial totalizations; or alternatively one must recognize them all as equally real: but only to discover that the French Revolution as commonly conceived never took place.

History does not therefore escape the common obligation of all knowledge, to employ a code to analyse its object, even (and especially) if a continuous reality is attributed to that

[4] Quite so, will be the comment of the supporters of Sartre. But the latter's whole endeavour shows that, though the subjectivity of history-for-me can make way for the objectivity of history-for-us, the 'I' can still only be converted into 'we' by condemning this 'we' to being no more than an 'I' raised to the power of two, itself hermetically sealed off from the other 'we's. The price so paid for the illusion of having overcome the insoluble antinomy (in such a system) between my self and others, consists of the assignation, by historical consciousness, of the metaphysical function of Other to the Papuans. By reducing the latter to the state of means, barely sufficient for its philosophical appetite, historical reason abandons itself to a sort of intellectual cannibalism much more revolting to the anthropologist than real cannibalism.

object.[5] The distinctive features of historical knowledge are due not to the absence of a code, which is illusory, but to its particular nature: the code consists in a chronology. There is no history without dates. To be convinced of this it is sufficient to consider how a pupil succeeds in learning history: he reduces it to an emaciated body, the skeleton of which is formed by dates. Not without reason, there has been a reaction against this dry method, but one which often runs to the opposite extreme. Dates may not be the whole of history, nor what is most interesting about it, but they are its *sine qua non,* for history's entire originality and distinctive nature lie in apprehending the relation between *before* and *after,* which would perforce dissolve if its terms could not, at least in principle, be dated.

Now, this chronological coding conceals a very much more complex nature than one supposes when one thinks of historical dates as a simple linear series. In the first place, a date denotes a moment in a succession: $d\,2$ is after $d\,1$ and before $d\,3$. From this point of view dates only perform the function of ordinal numbers. But each date is also a cardinal number and, as such, expresses a *distance* in relation to the dates nearest to it. We use a large number of dates to code some periods of history; and fewer for others. This variable quantity of dates applied to periods of equal duration are a gauge of what might be called the pressure of history: there are 'hot' chronologies which are those of periods where in the eyes of the historian numerous events appear as differential elements; others, on the contrary, where for him (although not of course for the men who lived through them) very little or nothing took place. Thirdly and most important, a date is a *member* of a class. These classes of dates are definable by the meaningful character each date has within the class in relation to other dates which also belong to it, and by

[5] In this sense too, one can speak of an antinomy of historical knowledge: if it claims to reach the continuous it is impossible, being condemned to an infinite regress; but to render it possible, events must be quantified and thereafter temporality ceases to be the privileged dimension of historical knowledge because as soon as it is quantified each event can, for all useful purposes, be treated as if it were the result of a choice between possible pre-existents.

the absence of this meaningful character with respect to dates appertaining to a different class. Thus the date 1685 belongs to a class of which 1610, 1648 and 1715 are likewise members; but it means nothing in relation to the class composed of the dates: 1st, 2nd, 3rd, 4th millennium, nor does it mean anything in relation to the class of dates: 23 January, 17 August, 30 September, etc.

On this basis, in what would the historian's code consist? Certainly not in dates, since these are not recurrent. Changes of temperature can be coded with the help of figures, because the reading of a figure on the thermometer evokes the return of an earlier situation: whenever I read 0° C, I know that it is freezing and put on my warmest coat. But a historical date, taken in itself, would have no meaning, for it has no reference outside itself: if I know nothing about modern history, the date 1643 makes me none the wiser. The code can therefore consist only of classes of dates, where each date has meaning in as much as it stands in complex relations of correlation and opposition with other dates. Each class is defined by a frequency, and derives from what might be called a corpus or a domain of history. Historical knowledge thus proceeds in the same way as a wireless with frequency modulation: like a nerve, it codes a continuous quantity—and as such an asymbolic one—by frequencies of impulses proportional to its variations. As for history itself, it cannot be represented as an aperiodic series with only a fragment of which we are acquainted. History is a discontinuous set composed of domains of history, each of which is defined by a characteristic frequency and by a differential coding of *before* and *after*. It is no more possible to pass between the dates which compose the different domains than it is to do so between natural and irrational numbers. Or more precisely: the dates appropriate to each class are irrational in relation to all those of other classes.

It is thus not only fallacious but contradictory to conceive of the historical process as a continuous development, beginning with prehistory coded in tens or hundreds of millennia, then adopting the scale of millennia when it gets to the 4th or 3rd millennium, and continuing as history in centuries interlarded, at the pleasure of each author, with slices of

annual history within the century, day to day history within
the year or even hourly history within a day. All these dates
do not form a series: they are of different species. To give just
one example, the coding we use in prehistory is not preliminary to that we employ for modern and contemporary history. Each code refers to a system of meaning which is, at
least in theory, applicable to the virtual totality of human history. The events which are significant for one code are no
longer so for another. Coded in the system of prehistory, the
most famous episodes in modern and contemporary history
cease to be pertinent; except perhaps (and again we know
nothing about it) certain massive aspects of demographic
evolution viewed on a world-wide scale, the invention of the
steam-engine, the discovery of electricity and of nuclear
energy.

Given that the general code consists not in dates which
can be ordered as a linear series but in classes of dates each
furnishing an autonomous system of reference, the discontinuous and classificatory nature of historical knowledge
emerges clearly. It operates by means of a rectangular
matrix:

where each line represents classes of dates, which may be
called hourly, daily, annual, secular, millennial for the purposes of schematization and which together make up a discontinuous set. In a system of this type, alleged historical
continuity is secured only by dint of fraudulent outlines.

Furthermore, although the internal gaps in each class cannot be filled in by recourse to other classes, each class taken
as a whole nevertheless always refers back to another class,
which contains the principle of an intelligibility to which it

could not itself aspire. The history of the 17th century is 'annual' but the 17th century, as a domain of history belongs to another class, which codes it in relation to earlier and later centuries; and this domain of modern times in its turn becomes an element of a class where it appears correlated with and opposed to other 'times': the middle ages, antiquity, the present day, etc. Now, these various domains correspond to histories of different power.

Biographical and anecdotal history, right at the bottom of the scale, is low-powered history, which is not intelligible in itself and only becomes so when it is transferred *en bloc* to a form of history of a higher power than itself; and the latter stands in the same relation to a class above it. It would, however, be a mistake to think that we progressively reconstitute a total history by dint of these dovetailings. For any gain on one side is offset by a loss on the other. Biographical and anecdotal history is the least explanatory; but it is the richest in point of information, for it considers individuals in their particularity and details for each of them the shades of character, the twists and turns of their motives, the phases of their deliberations. This information is schematized, put in the background and finally done away with as one passes to histories of progressively greater 'power'.[6] Consequently, de-

---

[6] Each domain of history is circumscribed in relation to that immediately below it, inscribed in relation to that above it. So each low-powered history of an inscribed domain is complementary to the powerful history of the circumscribed domain and contradictory to the low-powered history of this same domain (in so far as it is itself an inscribed domain). Each history is thus accompanied by an indeterminate number of anti-histories, each complementary to the others: to a history of grade 1, there corresponds an anti-history of grade 2, etc. The progress of knowledge and the creation of new sciences take place through the generation of anti-histories which show that a certain order which is possible only on one plane ceases to be so on another. The anti-history of the French Revolution envisaged by Gobineau is contradictory on the plane on which the Revolution had been thought of before him. It becomes logically conceivable (which does not mean that it is true) if one puts oneself on a new plane, which incidentally Gobineau chose clumsily; that is to say: if one passes from a history of 'annual' or 'secular' grade (which is also political, social and ideological) to a history of 'millennial' or 'multi-millennial' grade (which is also cultural and anthropological), a procedure not invented by Gobineau which might be called: Boulainvilliers' 'transformation'.

pending on the level on which he places himself, the historian loses in information what he gains in comprehension or vice versa, as if the logic of the concrete wished to remind us of its logical nature by modelling a confused outline of Godel's theorem in the clay of 'becoming'. The historian's relative choice, with respect to each domain of history he gives up, is always confined to the choice between history which teaches us more and explains less, and history which explains more and teaches less. The only way he can avoid the dilemma is by getting outside history: either by the bottom, if the pursuit of information leads him from the consideration of groups to that of individuals and then to their motivations which depend on their personal history and temperament, that is to say to an infra-historical domain in the realms of psychology and physiology; or by the top, if the need to understand incites him to put history back into prehistory and the latter into the general evolution of organized beings, which is itself explicable only in terms of biology, geology and finally cosmology.

There is, however, another way of avoiding the dilemma without thereby doing away with history. We need only recognize that history is a method with no distinct object corresponding to it to reject the equivalence between the notion of history and the notion of humanity which some have tried to foist on us with the unavowed aim of making historicity the last refuge of a transcendental humanism: as if men could regain the illusion of liberty on the plane of the 'we' merely by giving up the 'I's that are too obviously wanting in consistency.

In fact history is tied neither to man nor to any particular object. It consists wholly in its method, which experience proves to be indispensable for cataloguing the elements of any structure whatever, human or non-human, in their entirety. It is therefore far from being the case that the search for intelligibility comes to an end in history as though this were its terminus. Rather, it is history that serves as the point of departure in any quest for intelligibility. As we say of certain careers, history may lead to anything, provided you get out of it.

This further thing to which history leads for want of a sphere of reference of its own shows that whatever its value (which is indisputable) historical knowledge has no claim to be opposed to other forms of knowledge as a supremely privileged one. We noted above that it is already found rooted in the savage mind, and we can now see why it does not come to fruition there. The characteristic feature of the savage mind is its timelessness; its object is to grasp the world as both a synchronic and a diachronic totality and the knowledge which it draws therefrom is like that afforded of a room by mirrors fixed on opposite walls, which reflect each other (as well as objects in the intervening space) although without being strictly parallel. A multitude of images forms simultaneously, none exactly like any other, so that no single one furnishes more than a partial knowledge of the decoration and furniture but the group is characterized by invariant properties expressing a truth. The savage mind deepens its knowledge with the help of *imagines mundi*. It builds mental structures which facilitate an understanding of the world in as much as they resemble it. In this sense savage thought can be defined as analogical thought.

But in this sense too it differs from domesticated thought, of which historical knowledge constitutes one aspect. The concern for continuity which inspires the latter is indeed a manifestation, in the temporal order, of knowledge which is interstitial and unifying rather than discontinuous and analogical: instead of multiplying objects by schemes promoted to the role of additional objects, it seems to transcend an original discontinuity by relating objects to one another. But it is this reason, wholly concerned with closing gaps and dissolving differences, which can properly be called 'analytical'. By a paradox on which much stress has recently been laid, for modern thought 'continuity, variability, relativity, determinism go together' (Auger, p. 475).

This analytic, abstract continuity will doubtless be opposed to that of the *praxis* as concrete individuals live it. But this latter continuity seems no less derivative than the former, for it is only the conscious mode of apprehending psychological and physiological processes which are themselves discontinuous. I am not disputing that reason develops and transforms itself in the practical field: man's mode of thought reflects his relations to the world and to men. But in order for *praxis* to be living thought, it is necessary first (in a logical and not a historical sense) for thought to exist: that is to say, its initial conditions must be given in the form of an objective structure of the psyche and brain without which there would be neither *praxis* nor thought.

When therefore I describe savage thought as a system of concepts embedded in images, I do not come anywhere near the *robinsonnades*[7] (Sartre, pp. 642–3) of a constitutive constituent dialectic: all constitutive reason presupposes a constituted reason. But even if one allowed Sartre the circularity which he invokes to dispel the 'suspect character' attaching to the first stages of his synthesis, what he proposes really are 'robinsonnades', this time in the guise of descriptions of phenomena, when he claims to restore the sense of marriage exchange, the potlatch or the demonstration of his tribe's marriage rules by a Melanesian savage. Sartre then refers to a comprehension which has its being in the *praxis* of their organizers, a bizarre expression to which no reality corresponds, except perhaps the capacity which any foreign society presents to anyone looking at it from the outside, and which leads him to project the lacunae in his own observation on to it in the form of positive attributes. Two examples will show what I mean.

No anthropologist can fail to be struck by the common manner of conceptualizing initiation rites employed by the most diverse societies throughout the world. Whether in Africa, America, Australia or Melanesia, the rites follow the same pattern: first, the novices, taken from their parents, are symbolically 'killed' and kept hidden in the forest or bush where they are put to the test by the Beyond; after this they are 'reborn' as members of the society. When they are returned to their natural parents, the latter therefore simulate all the phases of a new delivery, and begin a re-education even in the elementary actions of feeding or dressing. It would be tempting to interpret this set of phenomena as a

---

[7] This term alludes to Robinson Crusoe and the Swiss family Robinson whose 'creation' of civilization was not a genuine invention but merely an application of their pre-existing knowledge. [Trans. note.]

proof that at this stage thought is wholly embedded in *praxis*. But this would be seeing things back to front, for it is on the contrary scientific *praxis* which, among ourselves, has emptied the notions of death and birth of everything not corresponding to mere physiological processes and rendered them unsuitable to convey other meanings. In societies with initiation rites, birth and death provide the material for a rich and varied conceptualization, provided that these notions (like so many others) have not been stripped by any form of scientific knowledge oriented towards practical returns—which they lack—of the major part of a meaning which transcends the distinction between the real and the imaginary: a complete meaning of which we can now hardly do more than evoke the ghost in the reduced setting of figurative language. What looks to us like being embedded in *praxis* is the mark of thought which quite genuinely takes the words it uses seriously, whereas in comparable circumstances we only 'play' on words.

The taboos on parents-in-law furnish the matter for a cautionary tale leading to the same conclusion by a different route. Anthropologists have found the frequent prohibition of any physical or verbal contact between close affines so strange that they have exercised their ingenuity in multiplying explanatory hypotheses, without always making sure that the hypotheses are not rendered redundant by one another. Elkin for instance explains the rarity of marriage with the patrilateral cousin in Australia by the rule that as a man has to avoid any contact with his mother-in-law, he will be wise to choose the latter among women entirely outside his own local group (to which his father's sisters belong). The aim of the rule itself is supposed to be to prevent a mother and daughter from being rivals for the affections of the same man; finally, the taboo is supposed to be extended by contamination to the wife's maternal grandmother and her husband. There are thus four concurrent interpretations of a single phenomenon: as a function of a type of marriage, as the result of a psychological calculation, as protection against instinctive tendencies and as the product of association by contiguity. This, however, still does not satisfy Elkin, for in his view the taboo on the father-in-law rests on a fifth explanation: the father-in-law is the creditor of the man to whom he has given his daughter, and the son-in-law feels himself to be in a position of inferiority in relation to him (Elkin, pp. 66–7, 117–20).

I shall content myself with the last explanation which perfectly covers all the cases considered and renders the others worthless by bringing out their naïvety. But why is it so difficult to put these usages into their proper place? The reason is, I think, that the usages of our own society which could be compared with them and might furnish a landmark to identify them by, are in a dissociated form among ourselves, while in these exotic societies they appear in an associated one which makes them unrecognizable to us.

We are acquainted with the taboo on parents-in-law or at least with its approximate equivalent. By the same token we are forbidden to address the great of this world and obliged to keep out of their way. All protocol asserts it: one does not speak first to the Queen of England or the President of the French Republic; and we adopt the same reserve when unforeseen circumstances create conditions of closer proximity between a superior and ourselves than the social distance between us warrants. Now, in most societies the position of wife-giver is accompanied by social (and sometimes also economic) superiority, that of wife-taker by inferiority and dependence. This inequality between affines may be expressed objectively in institutions as a fluid or stable hierarchy, or it may be expressed subjectively in the system of interpersonal relations by means of privileges and prohibitions.

There is therefore nothing mysterious about these usages which our own experience enables us to see from the inside. We are disconcerted only by their constitutive conditions, different in each case. Among ourselves, they are sharply separated from other usages and tied to an unambiguous context. In exotic societies, the same usages and the same context are as it were embedded in other usages and a different context: that of family ties, with which they seem to us incompatible. We find it hard to imagine that, in private, the son-in-law of the President of the French Republic should regard him as the head of the state rather than as his father-in-law. And although the Queen of England's husband may behave as the first of her subjects in public, there are good reasons for supposing that he is just a husband when they are alone together. It is either one or the other. The superficial strangeness of the taboo on parents-in-law arises from its being both at the same time.

Consequently, and as we have already found in the case of operations of understanding, the system of ideas and attitudes is here presented only as *embodied*. Considered in itself, this system has nothing about it to baffle the anthropologist. My relation to the President of the Republic is made up entirely of negative observances, since, in the absence of other ties, any relations we may have are wholly defined by the rule that I should not speak unless he invites me to do so and that I should remain a respectful distance from him. But this abstract relation need only be clothed in a concrete relation and the attitudes appropriate to each to accumulate, for me to find myself as embarrassed by my family as an Australian aborigine. What appears to us as greater social ease and greater intellectual mobility is thus due to the fact that we prefer to operate with detached pieces, if not indeed with 'small change', while the native is a logical hoarder: he is forever tying the threads, unceasingly turning over all the aspects of reality, whether physical, social or mental. We traffic in our ideas; he hoards them up. The savage mind puts a philosophy of the finite into practice.

This is also the source of the renewed interest in it. This language with its limited vocabulary able to express any message by combinations of oppositions between its constitutive units, this logic of comprehension for which contents are indissociable from form, this systematic of finite classes, this universe made up of meanings, no longer appears to us as retrospective witnesses of a time when: '. . . le ciel sur la terre Marchait et respirait dans un peuple de dieux',[8] and which the poet only evokes for the purpose of asking whether or not it is to be regretted. This time is now restored to us, thanks to the discovery of a universe of information where the laws of savage thought reign once more:

[8] i.e. 'when heaven walked and breathed on earth among a population of Gods'. From A. de Musset 'Rolla' 1833 reprinted in *Poesies Nouvelles*. [Trans. note.]

'heaven' too, 'walking on earth' among a population of transmitters and receivers whose messages, while in transmission, constitute objects of the physical world and can be grasped both from without and from within.

The idea that the universe of primitives (or supposedly such) consists principally in messages is not new. But until recently a negative value was attributed to what was wrongly taken to be a distinctive characteristic, as though this difference between the universe of the primitives and our own contained the explanation of their mental and technological inferiority, when what it does is rather to put them on a par with modern theorists of documentation.[9] Physical science had to discover that a semantic universe possesses all the characteristics of an object in its own right for it to be recognized that the manner in which primitive peoples conceptualize their world is not merely coherent but the very one demanded in the case of an object whose elementary structure presents the picture of a discontinuous complexity.

The false antinomy between logical and prelogical mentality was surmounted at the same time. The savage mind is logical in the same sense and the same fashion as ours, though as our own is only when it is applied to knowledge of a universe in which it recognizes physical and semantic properties simultaneously. This misunderstanding once dispelled, it remains no less true that, contrary to Levy-Bruhl's opinion, its thought proceeds through understanding, not affectivity, with the aid of distinctions and oppositions, not by confusion and participation. Although the term had not yet come into use, numerous texts of Durkheim and Mauss show that they understood that so-called primitive thought is a quantified form of thought.

It will be objected that there remains a major difference

[9] The documentalist neither disallows nor disputes the substance of the works he analyses in order to derive the constitutive units of his code or to adapt them, either by combining them among themselves or, if necessary, decomposing them into finer units. He thus treats the authors as gods whose revelations are written down, instead of being inscribed into beings and things, but which have the same sacred value, which attaches to the supremely meaningful character that, for methodological or ontological reasons, it is *ex hypothesi* necessary to recognize in them in both cases.

between the thought of primitives and our own: Information Theory is concerned with genuine messages whereas primitives mistake mere manifestations of physical determinism for messages. Two considerations, however, deprive this argument of any weight. In the first place, Information Theory has been generalized, and it extends to phenomena not intrinsically possessing the character of messages, notably to those of biology; the illusions of totemism have had at least the merit of illuminating the fundamental place belonging to phenomena of this order, in the internal economy of systems of classification. In treating the sensible properties of the animal and plant kingdoms as if they were the elements of a message, and in discovering 'signatures'—and so signs—in them, men have made mistakes of identification: the meaningful element was not always the one they supposed. But, without perfected instruments which would have permitted them to place it where it most often is—namely, at the microscopic level—they already discerned 'as through a glass darkly' principles of interpretation whose heuristic value and accordance with reality have been revealed to us only through very recent inventions: telecommunications, computers and electron microscopes.

Above all, during the period of their transmission, when they have an objective existence outside the consciousness of transmitters and receivers, messages display properties which they have in common with the physical world. Hence, despite their mistakes with regard to physical phenomena (which were not absolute but relative to the level where they grasped them) and even though they interpreted them as if they were messages, men were nevertheless able to arrive at some of their properties. For a theory of information to be able to be evolved it was undoubtedly essential to have discovered that the universe of information is part of an aspect of the natural world. But the validity of the passage from the laws of nature to those of information once demonstrated, implies the validity of the reverse passage—that which for millennia has allowed men to approach the laws of nature by way of information.

Certainly the properties to which the savage mind has access are not the same as those which have commanded the attention of scientists. The physical world is approached from opposite ends in the two cases: one is supremely concrete, the other supremely abstract; one proceeds from the angle of sensible qualities and the other from that of formal properties. But if, theoretically at least and on condition no abrupt changes in perspective occurred, these two courses might have been destined to meet, this explains that they should have both, independently of each other in time and space, led to two distinct though equally positive sciences: one which flowered in the neolithic period, whose theory of the sensible order provided the basis of the arts of civilization (agriculture, animal husbandry, pottery, weaving, conservation and preparation of food, etc.) and which continues to provide for our basic needs by these means; and the other, which places itself from the start at the level of intelligibility, and of which contemporary science is the fruit.

We have had to wait until the middle of this century for the crossing of long separated paths: that which arrives at the physical world by the detour of communication, and that which as we have recently come to know, arrives at the world of communication by the detour of the physical. The entire process of human knowledge thus assumes the character of a closed system. And we therefore remain faithful to the inspiration of the savage mind when we recognize that the scientific spirit in its most modern form will, by an encounter it alone could have foreseen, have contributed to legitimize the principles of savage thought and to re-establish it in its rightful place.

12 June–16 October 1961

REFERENCES

Auger, P., "Structures et complexités dans l'univers de l'antiquité à nos jours," *Cahiers d'histoire mondiale*, vol. 6, no. 3, Neuchâtel, 1960.

Beth, E. W., *The Foundations of Mathematics*, Amsterdam, 1959.

Elkin, A. P., *The Australian Aborigines*, Sydney-London, 3rd ed., 1961.

Heyting, A., *Les Fondements des Mathématiques*, Paris, 1955.

Rousseau, J. J., (1) *Discours sur l'origine et les fondements de l'inégalité parmi les hommes*, Œuvres mêlées, Tome II, Nouvelle ed., London, 1776.

(2) *Essai sur l'origine des langues*, Œuvres posthumes, Tome II, London, 1783.

Sartre, J. P., *Critique de la raison dialectique*, Paris, 1960.

LOUIS ALTHUSSER

Louis Althusser was born in Algeria in 1918, received a degree in philosophy from the École Normale Supérieure in Paris in 1948, and has taught there ever since. His book *For Marx* is composed primarily of articles which had previously appeared in French Communist Party journals. *Reading Capital,* from which the chapter printed below is taken, appeared in French in 1965, and in 1968 he published *Lenine et la philosophie.* Althusser is a defender and exponent of Marx. His vocabulary, his approach to reading a text, and his interest and emphasis on structure link him closely to other French structuralists, despite the fact that he denies all connection with any "structuralist ideology."

13

Marx's Immense Theoretical Revolution

We can now go back to the past and assess the distance between Marx and his predecessors—and between his *object* and theirs.

From now on we can abandon the issue of anthropology, whose function in Political Economy was to establish both the *economic* nature of economic phenomena (by the theory of the *homo oeconomicus*) and their existence in *the homogeneous space of a given*. Once this anthropological 'given' has been removed, the space remains, which is precisely what interests us. What happens to it, in its being, once it can no longer be based on an anthropology, what effects does this weakness have on it?

Political Economy thought the economic phenomena as deriving from a planar space governed by a transitive mechanical causality, such that a determinate effect could be related to an object-cause, a different phenomenon; such that the necessity of its immanence could be grasped completely in the sequence of a given. The homogeneity of this space, its planar character, its property of givenness, its type of linear causality: these are so many theoretical determinations which, as a system, constitute the structure of a theoretical problematic, i.e., of a certain way of conceiving its object, and at the same time of posing it definite questions (defined by the problematic itself) as to its being, while anticipating the form of its answers (the quantitative schema): in short, an empiricist problematic. Marx's theory is radically opposed to this conception. Not that it is an 'inversion' of it: it is differ-

From *Reading Capital*, chapter 9, by Louis Althusser and Étienne Balibar. Copyright © 1970, by NLB. Reprinted by permission of Pantheon Books, a Division of Random House, Inc.

ent, theoretically unrelated to it, and therefore in rupture with it. Because he defined the economic *by its concept,* Marx does not present economic phenomena to illustrate his thought temporarily with a spatial metaphor, in the infinity of a homogeneous planar space, but rather in *a region* determined by a regional structure and itself inscribed in a site defined by a global structure: therefore as a complex and deep space, itself inscribed in another complex and deep space. But let us abandon this spatial metaphor, since this first opposition exhausts its virtues: everything depends, in fact, on the nature of this depth, or, more strictly speaking, of this *complexity.* To define economic phenomena by their concept is to define them by the concept of this complexity, i.e., by the concept of the (global) *structure* of the mode of production, insofar as it determines the (regional) *structure* which constitutes as economic objects and determines the phenomena of this defined region, located in a defined site in the structure of the whole. At the economic level, strictly speaking, the *structure* constituting and determining economic objects is the *following:* the unity of the productive forces and the relations of production. The concept of this last *structure* cannot be defined without the concept of the global structure of the mode of production.

Once we have simply put Marx's fundamental theoretical concepts in their places and posed them in the unity of a theoretical discourse, a number of important consequences follow.

First: the economic cannot have the qualities of a *given* (of the immediately visible and observable, etc.), because its identification requires the concept of the structure of the economic, which in turn requires the concepts of the structure of the mode of production (its different levels and their specific articulations)—because its identification therefore presupposes the construction of its *concept.* The concept of the economic must be constructed *for each mode of production,* as must the concept of each of the other 'levels' that belong to the mode of production: the political, the ideological, etc. Like every other science, therefore, all economic science depends on the construction of the concept of its object. On this condition, there is no contradiction between the theory of Economics and the theory of History: on the contrary, the theory of economics is a subordinate region of the theory of history, understood of course in the non-historicist, non-empiricist sense in which we have outlined the theory of history. And just as any 'history' which does not work out the concept of its object, but claims to 'read' it immediately in what is visible in the 'field' of historical phenomena, is still willy-nilly tainted with empiricism whether intentionally or no, any 'political economy' which goes to the 'things themselves', i.e., to the 'concrete', the 'given', without constructing the concept of its object, is still willy-nilly caught in the toils of an empiricist ideology and constantly threatened by the re-emergence of its true 'objects', i.e., its objectives (whether these are the ideals of classical liberalism or those of a 'humanism' of labour, even a socialist one).

Second: if the 'field' of economic phenomena no longer has the *homogeneity* of an infinite plane, its objects are no longer *de jure* homogeneous at all points with one another: they are therefore no longer uniformly susceptible to comparison and *measurement.* This by no means excludes from economics the possibility of measurement or of the intervention of the instruments of mathematics and its peculiar modalities, etc., but it does make it from now on subject to a prior conceptual definition of the sites and limits of the measureable, and of the sites and limits to which the other resources of mathematical science (e.g., the instruments of econometrics and other formalization procedures) can be applied. Mathematical formalization must be subordinate to conceptual formalization. Here, too, the limits between political economy and empiricism, even formalistic empiricism, coincide with the boundary between the concept of the (theoretical) object and the 'concrete' object, along with even the 'mathematical' protocols of its manipulation.

The practical consequences of this principle are obvious: e.g., in the solution of the 'technical' problems of planning, in which 'problems' which arise quite simply from the absence of the concept of the object, i.e., from economic empiricism, are frequently treated as real 'technical' problems. The intellectual 'technocracy' lives by this kind of confusion, securing its full-time employment with it; for nothing takes

so long to resolve as a problem which does not exist or has
been badly posed.

Third: if the field of economic phenomena is no longer
this planar space but a deep and complex one, if economic
phenomena are determined by their *complexity* (i.e., their
structure), the concept of linear causality can no longer be
applied to them as it has been hitherto. A different concept
is required in order to account for the new form of causality
required by the new definition of the object of Political Economy, by its 'complexity', i.e., by its peculiar determination:
the determination by a structure.

This third consequence deserves our whole attention, for
it introduces us to an absolutely new theoretical domain. An
object cannot be defined by its immediately visible or sensuous
appearance, it is necessary to make a detour via its concept
in order to grasp it (*begreifen* grasp, *Begriff* concept): these
theses have a familiar ring to them—at least they are the lesson of the whole history of modern science, more or less
reflected in classical philosophy, even if this reflection took
place in the element of an empiricism, whether transcendent
(as in Descartes), transcendental (Kant and Husserl) or
'objective'-idealist (Hegel). It is true that much theoretical
work is needed to deal with all the forms of this empiricism
sublimated in the 'theory of knowledge' which dominates
Western philosophy, to break with its problematic of subject
(*cogito*) and object—and all their variations. But at least all
these philosophical ideologies do 'allude' to a real necessity,
imposed against this tenacious empiricism by the theoretical
practice of the real sciences: i.e., that the knowledge of a
real object is not reached by immediate contact with the
'concrete' but by the production of the *concept* of that object
(in the sense of object of knowledge) as the absolute condition of its *theoretical* possibility. If, *formally*, the task which
Marx has allotted to us in forcing us to produce the concept
of the economic in order to be able to constitute a theory of
political economy, in obliging us to define *by its concept* the
domain, limits and conditions of validity of a mathematiza-
tion of that object, if it does break with all the empiricist-
idealist traditions of Western critical philosophy, then it is in
no sense in rupture with effective scientific practice. On the

contrary, Marx's requirements restate in a new domain the requirements which have long been imposed on the practices of those sciences which have achieved autonomy. These requirements often conflict with the practices that have reigned and still do reign in economic science, practices which are deeply steeped in empiricist ideology, but this is undoubtedly because of the youth of this 'science', and also because 'economic science' is especially exposed to the pressures of ideology: the sciences of society do not have the serenity of the mathematical sciences. As Hobbes put it, geometry unites men, social science divides them. 'Economic science' is the arena and the prize of history's great political battles.

But our third conclusion is quite different, and so is the requirement it imposes on us to think the economic phenomena as *determined by a* (*regional*) *structure* of the mode of production, itself determined by *the* (*global*) *structure* of the mode of production. This requirement poses Marx a problem which is not only a *scientific* problem, i.e., one that arises from the theoretical practice of a definite science (Political Economy or History), but a theoretical, or philosophical problem, since it concerns precisely the production of a concept or set of concepts which necessarily affect the forms of existing scientificity or (theoretical) rationality themselves, the forms which, at a given moment, define the *Theoretical* as such, i.e., the object of philosophy. This problem certainly does involve the production of a theoretical (philosophical) concept which is absolutely indispensable to the constitution of a rigorous discourse in the theory of history and the theory of political economy: the production of an indispensable philosophical concept *which does not exist in the form of a concept*.

Perhaps it is too soon to suggest that the birth of every new science inevitably poses theoretical (philosophical) problems of this kind: Engels thought so—and we have every reason to believe him, if we examine what happened at the time of the birth of mathematics in Greece, at the time of the constitution of Galilean physics, of infinitesimal calculus, at the time of the foundation of chemistry and biology, etc. In several of these conjunctures we find the following remarkable phenomenon: the 'reprise' of a basic scientific discovery in philosophical reflection, and the production by philosophy of *a new form of rationality* (Plato after the discoveries of the mathematicians of the fifth and fourth centuries before Christ, Descartes after Galileo, Leibniz with infinitesimal calculus, etc.). This philosophical 'reprise', this production by philosophy of new theoretical concepts which solve the *theoretical problems* contained 'in the practical state', if not explicitly posed, in the great scientific discoveries in question, mark the great breaks in the history of the Theoretical, i.e., in the history of philosophy. However, it seems that certain scientific disciplines have established themselves or thought themselves established by the mere extension of an existing form of rationality (psycho-physiology, psychology, etc.) which would tend to suggest that not *any* scientific foundation *ipso facto* induces a revolution in the Theoretical, but presumably only a scientific foundation which is obliged to reorganize *practically* the existing problematic in the Theoretical in order to think its object; the philosophy capable of reflecting the upheaval produced by the emergence of such a science by bringing to light a new form of rationality (scientificity, apodicticity, etc.) would then mark by its existence a decisive punctuation, a revolution in the history of the Theoretical.

Bearing in mind what has been said elsewhere of the delay required for the philosophical production of this new rationality and even of the historical repressions to which certain theoretical revolutions may be subjected, it seems that Marx offers us precisely an example of this importance. The epistemological problem posed by Marx's radical modification of Political Economy can be expressed as follows: *by means of what concept is it possible to think the new type of determination which has just been identified as the determination of the phenomena of a given region by the structure of that region?* More generally, *by means of what concept, or what set of concepts, is it possible to think the determination of the elements of a structure, and the structural relations between three elements, and all the effects of those relations, by the effectivity of that structure? And* a fortiori, *by means of what concept of what set of concepts is it possible to think the determination of a subordinate structure by a dominant struc-*

ture? In other words, how is it possible to define the concept of a structural causality?

This simple theoretical question sums up Marx's extraordinary scientific discovery: the discovery of the theory of history and political economy, the discovery of *Capital*. But it sums it up as an extraordinary theoretical question *contained* 'in the practical state' in Marx's scientific discovery, the question Marx 'practiced' in his work, in answer to which he gave his scientific work, without producing *the concept* of it in a philosophical *opus* of the same rigour.

This simple question was so new and unforeseen that it contained enough to smash all the classical theories of causality—or enough to ensure that it would be unrecognized, that it would pass unperceived and be buried even before it was born.

Very schematically, we can say that classical philosophy (the existing Theoretical) had two and only two systems of concepts with which to think effectivity. The mechanistic system, Cartesian in origin, which reduced causality to a *transitive* and analytical effectivity: it could not be made to think the effectivity of a whole on its elements, except at the cost of extraordinary distortions (such as those in Descartes' 'psychology' and biology). But a second system was available, one conceived precisely in order to deal with the effectivity of a whole on its elements: the Leibnizian concept of *expression*. This is the model that dominates all Hegel's thought. But it presupposes in principle that the whole in question be reducible to an *inner essence,* of which the elements of the whole are then no more than the phenomenal forms of expression, the inner principle of the essence being present at each point in the whole, such that at each moment it is possible to write the immediately adequate equation: *such and such an element* (economic, political, legal, literary, religious, etc., in Hegel) = *the inner essence of the whole.* Here was a model which made it possible to think the effectivity of the whole on each of its elements, but if this category inner essence/outer phenomenon was to be applicable everywhere and at every moment to each of the phenomena arising in the totality in question, *it presupposed that the whole had a certain nature, precisely the nature of a 'spiritual' whole in*

which each element was expressive of the entire totality as a
'pars totalis'. In other words, Leibniz and Hegel did have a
category for the effectivity of the whole on its elements or
parts, but on the absolute condition that the whole was not a
structure.

If the whole is posed as *structured*, i.e., as possessing a
type of unity quite different from the type of unity of the
spiritual whole, this is no longer the case: not only does it
become impossible to think the determination of the elements
by the structure in the category of analytical and transitive
causality, *it also becomes impossible to think it in the category
of the global expressive causality of a universal inner essence
immanent in its phenomenon*. The proposal to think the determination of the elements of a whole by the structure of
the whole posed an absolutely new problem in the most theoretically embarrassing circumstances, for there were no
philosophical concepts available for its resolution. The only
theoretician who had had the unprecedented daring to pose
this problem and outline a first solution to it was Spinoza.
But, as we know, history had buried him in impenetrable
darkness. Only through Marx, who, however, had little knowledge of him, do we merely begin to guess at the features of
that trampled face.

This is merely to return, to the most general form, of a
fundamental and dramatic theoretical problem of which the
preceding studies have given us a precise idea. I call it a
fundamental problem because it is clear that by other paths
contemporary theory in psycho-analysis, linguistics, other disciplines such as biology, and perhaps even physics, has had to
confront it, without suspecting that Marx had 'produced' it in
the true sense, long ago. I call it a *dramatic* theoretical problem because although Marx *'produced' this problem he did
not pose it as a problem,* but set out to solve it practically in
the absence of its concept, with extraordinary ingenuity, but
without completely avoiding a relapse into earlier schemata
which were necessarily inadequate to pose and solve this
problem. It is on this problem that Marx is attempting to focus
in the tentative sentences we can read in the *Introduction:*

In all forms of society it is a determinate production and its relations which assign every other production and its relations their rank and influence. It is a general illumination (*Beleuchtung*) in which all the other colours are plunged and which modifies their special tonalities. It is a special ether which defines the specific weight of every existence arising in it. (*Grundrisse der Kritik der Politischen* Ökonomie, Dietz Verlag, 1953, p. 27.)

This text is discussing the determination of certain structures of production which are subordinate to a dominant structure of production, i.e., the determination of one structure by another and of the elements of a subordinate structure by the dominant, and therefore determinant structure. I have previously attempted to account for this phenomenon with the concept of *over-determination*, which I borrowed from psycho-analysis; as one might suppose, this transfer of an analytical concept to Marxist theory was not an arbitrary borrowing but a necessary one, *for the same theoretical problem is at stake in both cases: with what concept are we to think the determination of either an element of a structure by a structure?* It is this same problem that Marx has in view and which he is trying to focus by introducing the metaphor of a variation in the *general illumination*, of the *ether* in which bodies are immersed, and of the subsequent alterations produced by the domination of one particular structure in the localization, function and relations (in his own words: the relations, their rank and influence), in the original colour and the specific weight of the objects. The constant and real presence of this problem in Marx has been demonstrated by the rigorous analysis of his expressions and forms of reasoning in the preceding papers. It can be entirely summed up in the concept of '*Darstellung*', the key epistemological concept of the whole Marxist theory of value, the concept whose object is precisely to designate the mode of *presence* of the structure in its *effects*, and therefore to designate structural causality itself.

The fact that we have isolated the concept of '*Darsellung*' does not mean that it is the only one which Marx uses in order to think the effectivity of the structure: a reading of the first thirty pages of *Capital* shows that he uses at least a dozen different expressions of a metaphorical kind in order to deal

with this specific reality, *unthought before him.* We have retained this term because it is both the least metaphorical and,
at the same time, the closest to the concept Marx is aiming at
when he wants to designate at once both absence and presence, i.e., *the existence of the structure in its effects.*

This is an extremely important point if we are to avoid
even the slightest, in a sense inadvertent relapse into the di-
versions of *the classical conception of the economic object,*
if we are to avoid saying that the Marxist conception of the
economic object is, for Marx, determined *from the outside
by a noneconomic structure.* The structure is not an essence
outside the economic phenomena which comes and alters
their aspect, forms and relations and which is effective on
them as an absent cause, *absent because it is outside them.
The absence of the cause in the structure's 'metonymic causality'*[1] *on its effects is not the fault of the exteriority of the
structure with respect to the economic phenomena; on the
contrary, it is the very form of the interiority of the structure,
as a structure, in its effects.* This implies therefore that the
effects are not outside the structure, are not a pre-existing
object, element or space in which the structure arrives to *imprint its mark:* on the contrary, it implies that the structure
is immanent in its effects, a cause immanent in its effects in
the Spinozist sense of the term, that *the whole existence of the
structure consists of its effects,* in short that the structure,
which is merely a specific combination of its peculiar elements, is nothing outside its effects.

This specification is very important when we have to deal
with the occasionally strange form which the discovery of
this reality and the search for expressions for it take, even in
Marx. To understand these strange forms it is essential to
note that the exteriority of the structure with respect to its
effects can be conceived either as a pure exteriority or as an
interiority on the sole condition that this exteriority of interiority are posed as *distinct from their effects.* In Marx, this
distinction often takes the classical form of the distinction
between the inside and the outside, between the 'intimate essence' of things and their phenomenal 'surface', between the

---

[1] An expression Jacques-Alain Miller has introduced to characterize
a form of structural causality registered in Freud by Jacques Lacan.

'intimate' relations, the 'intimate links' of things and the external relations and links of the same things. And it is well known that this opposition, which derives in principle from the classical distinction between essence and phenomenon, i.e., from a distinction which situates *in being itself, in reality itself, the inner site of its concept,* and therefore opposes it to the 'surface' of concrete appearances; which therefore transposes as a difference of level or of components *in the real object itself,* a distinction which does not belong to that real object since it is a matter of the distinction which separates the concept or knowledge of the real from that real as an existing object;—it is well known that this opposition sometimes leads Marx to the following disarming pleonasm: *if the essence were not different from the phenomena, if the essential interior were not different from the inessential or phenomenal exterior, there would be no need for science.*[2] It is also well known that this singular formula may gain strength from all those arguments of Marx's which present the development of the concepts as the transition from the *abstract* to the *concrete,* a transition understood *as the transition from the essential, in principle abstract interiority to the concrete, visible and palpable outer determinations,* a transition summed up in the transition from Volume One to Volume Three. All these ambiguous arguments depend once again on the confusion between the thought-concrete, which Marx completely isolated from the real-concrete in the *Introduction,* and this same real-concrete—whereas in reality, the concrete of Volume Three, i.e., the *knowledge* of ground rent, profit and interest, is, like all knowledge, *not the empirical concrete but the concept,* and therefore still always an abstraction: what I have been able to and have had to call a 'Generality III', in order to stress that it was still a product of thinking, the *knowledge* of an empirical existence and not that empirical *existence* itself. It is therefore essential to be rigorous and draw the conclusion that *the transition from*

2 *Capital,* Vol. III, p. 797: 'All science would be superfluous if the outward appearance and the essence of things directly coincided'. This re-echoes the old dream which haunted all classical political reflection: all politics would be superfluous if men's passions and reasons coincided.

Volume One to Volume Three of Capital *has nothing to do with the transition from the abstract-in-thought to the real-concrete, with the transition from the abstractions of thought necessary in order to know it to the empirical concrete.* We never leave abstraction on the way from Volume One to Volume Three, i.e., we never leave knowledge, the 'product of thinking and conceiving': *we never leave the concept.* We simply pass within the abstraction of knowledge from the concept of the structure and of its most general effects, to the concepts of the structure's particular effects—never for an instant do we set foot beyond the absolutely impassable frontier which separates the 'development' or specification of the concept from the development and particularity of things —and for a very good reason: *this frontier is impassable in principle because it cannot be a frontier, because there is not common homogeneous space (spirit or real) between the abstract of the concept of a thing and the empirical concrete of this thing which could justify the use of the concept of a frontier.*

I am very insistent on this ambiguity because I want to show clearly the difficulty Marx found when he had to think in a really reflected concept the epistemological problem which he had nevertheless produced: *how was he to account theoretically for the effectivity of a structure on its elements?* This difficulty was not without its consequences. I have pointed out that theoretical reflection before Marx had provided two and only two models for an effectivity in thought: the model of a transitive causality, Galilean and Cartesian in origin, and the model of an expressive causality, Leibnizian in origin and adopted by Hegel. But by playing on the ambiguity of the two concepts, these two models could quite easily find common ground in the classical opposition between *phenomenon and essence.* The ambiguity of these concepts is indeed obvious: the essence does refer to the phenomenon, but at the same time secretly to the *inessential.* The phenomenon does refer to the essence of which it can be the manifestation and expression, but at the same time, and secretly, it refers to what appears to be an empirical subject, to perception, and therefore to the empirical state of mind of a possible empirical subject. It then becomes quite simple to accumulate these ambiguous determinations in reality itself, and *to locate in the real itself* a distinction which is only meaningful as a function of a distinction *outside the real,* since it brings into play a distinction between the real and the knowledge of the real. In his search for a concept with which to think the remarkable reality of the effectivity of a structure on its elements, Marx often slipped into the really almost inevitable use of the *classical* opposition between *essence and phenomenon,* adopting its ambiguities by force rather than merit, and *transposing the epistemological difference between the knowledge of a reality and that reality itself* into reality in the form of the *'inside and the outside',* of the real, of the *'real movement and the apparent movement,'* of the *'intimate essence'* and its concrete, phenomenal determinations, perceived and manipulated by subjects. There are surely consequences in this for his conception of science, as we could have seen when Marx had to provide the concept of what his predecessors had either found or missed—or the concept of the difference between himself and them.

But there were also consequences in this ambiguity for the interpretation of the phenomenon he baptized *'fetishism'.* We have proved that fetishism is not a subjective phenomenon related either to the illusions or to the perceptions of the agents of the economic process, that it cannot be reduced by their place in the process, their site in the structure. But how many of Marx's texts present *fetishism as an 'appearance',* an 'illusion' arising purely in 'consciousness', show us the real, inner movement of the process *'appearing'* in a fetished form to the 'consciousness' of the same subjects in the form of the apparent movement! And yet how many other texts of Marx's assure us that this appearance is not subjective at all, but, on the contrary, objective through and through, the 'illusion' of the 'consciousness' and perceptions being itself secondary, and dislocated by the structure of this primary, purely objective 'illusion'! At this point we see Marx most clearly struggling with reference concepts which are inadequate to their objects, now accepting, now rejecting them in a necessarily contradictory movement.

However, and by virtue of these same contradictory hesitations, Marx often takes the side of what he was actually saying: and he then produces concepts adequate to their object, but it is just as if, producing them in a lightning gesture, he had not marshalled and confronted this production theoretically, had not reflected it in order to impose it on the total field of his analysis. For example, when dealing with the rate of profit, Marx wrote:

In fact, the formula s/c [the rate of profit] expresses the degree of self-expression of the total capital advanced . . . taken in conformity with its inner conceptual connexions (*seinem begrifflichen, innern Zusammenhang entsprechend gefasst*) and the nature of surplus-value (*Capital,* Vol. III, p. 45).

In this passage, and in several others, Marx is unambiguously 'practising' the truth that *interiority* is nothing but the '*concept*', that it is not the *real* 'interior' of the phenomenon, but knowledge of it. If this is true, the reality that Marx studies can no longer be presented as a *two-level reality*, inside and outside, the inside being identified with the pure essence and the outside with a phenomenon, sometimes purely subjective, the state of mind of a 'consciousness', sometimes impure, because it is foreign to the essence, or inessential. *If the 'inside' is the concept,* the 'outside' can only be the specification of the concept, exactly as the effects of the structure of the whole can only be the existence of the structure itself. Here, for example is what Marx says of ground rent:

As important as it may be for a scientific analysis of ground rent —that is, the independent and specific economic form of landed property on the basis of the capitalist mode of production—to study it in *its pure form* free of all distorting and obfuscating irrelevancies, it is just as important for an understanding of the practical effects of landed property—even for *a theoretical comprehension of a multitude of facts* which contradict the *concept* and *nature* of ground-rent and yet appear as *modes of existence of ground-rent*—to learn the sources which give rise to such muddling in theory (Vol. III, p. 610).

Here we have in black and white the double status Marx attributes to his analysis. He is analysing a pure form which is none other than the concept of capitalist ground-rent. He thinks this purity both as the modality and the definition of the concept, and at the same time he thinks it as what he distinguishes from *empirical impurity*. Still, he does at once think this same empirical impurity in a second correcting movement as the *'modes of existence'*, i.e., as theoretical determinations of the concept of ground-rent itself. In this latter conception we leave the empiricist distinction between pure essence and impure phenomenon, we abandon the empiricist idea of a purity which is thus only the result of an empirical *purge* (since it is a purge of the empirical)—we really think the purity as *the purity of the concept*, the purity of a knowledge adequate to its object, and the determinations of this concept as the effective knowledge of the modes of existence of ground-rent. It is clear that this language itself revokes the distinction between inside and outside, and substitutes for it the distinction between the concept and the real, or between the object (of knowledge) and the real object. But if we take this indispensable substitution seriously, it directs us towards a conception of scientific practice and of its object which no longer had anything in common with empiricism.

Marx states unambiguously the principles of this quite different conception of scientific practice in the *1857 Introduction*. But it is one thing to develop this concept and quite another to set it to work in order to solve the unprecedented theoretical problem of the production of the concept of the effectivity of a structure on its elements. We have seen Marx *practising* this concept in the use he makes of the *'Darstellung'*, and trying to pinpoint it in the images of a change in illumination or in the specific weight of objects by the ether in which they are immersed, and it is sometimes directly exposed in Marx's analyses, in passages where it is expressed in a novel but extremely precise language: a language of metaphors which are nevertheless already *almost perfect concepts*, and which are perhaps only incomplete insofar as they have not yet been *grasped*, i.e., retained and elaborated as concepts. This is the case each time Marx presents the capitalist system as a mechanism, a machinery, a machine, a construction (*Triebwerk, Mechanismus, Getriebe* . . . Cf. *Capital* Vol. III, p. 858—Marx-Engels *Werke*, Bd. XXV, p. 887— *Capital* Vol. III, p. 859; Vol. II, p. 216; Vol. II, p. 421; Vol.

II, p. 509); or as the complexity of a 'social metabolism' (*Capital,* Vol. III, p. 793—modified). In every case, the ordinary distinctions between outside and inside disappear, along with the 'intimate' links within the phenomena as opposed to their visible disorder: we find a different image, a new quasi-concept, definitely freed from the empiricist antinomies of phenomenal subjectivity and essential interiority; we find an objective system governed in its most concrete determinations by the laws of its *erection (montage)* and *machinery* by the specifications of its concept. Now we can recall that highly symptomatic term *'Darstellung'*, compare it with this 'machinery' and take it literally, as the very existence of this machinery in its effects: the mode of existence of the stage direction (*mise en scène*) of the theatre which is simultaneously its own stage, its own script, its own actors, the theatre whose spectators can, on occasion, be spectators only because they are first of all forced to be its actors, caught by the constraints of a script and parts whose authors cannot be, since it is in essence *an authorless theatre.*

Need I add one more thing? Marx's repeated efforts to break down the objective limits of the existing Theoretical, in order to forge a way of thinking the question that his scientific discovery has posed philosophy, his failures and even his relapses are a part of the theoretical drama he lived, in absolute solitude, long ago, and we are only just beginning to suspect from the signs in our heavens that *his question is our question,* and will be for a long time, that it commands our whole future. Alone, Marx looked around him for allies and supporters: who can reproach him for allowing himself to lean on Hegel? As for us, we can thank Marx for the fact that we are not alone: our solitude only lies in our ignorance of what he said. We should accuse this ignorance in us and in all those who think they have forestalled him, and I only include the best of them—when they were only on the threshold of the land he discovered and opened for us. We even owe it to him that we can see his weaknesses, his lacunae, his omissions: they concur with his greatness, for, in returning to them we are only returning to the beginnings of a discourse interrupted by death. The reader will know how Volume Three ends. A title: *Classes.* Forty lines, then silence.

MICHEL FOUCAULT

Michel Foucault was born in 1926. Formerly a professor at the Centre Universitaire Expérimental de Vincennes, he presently holds an appointment at the Collège de France. In 1961 he published *Madness and Civilization,* a history of insanity from the sixteenth to the eighteenth centuries, in which he attempts to uncover the structure of the ever-shifting line between reason and madness as one moves from one historical age to another. "An Archaeology of the Human Sciences," the subtitle of his book *The Order of Things* (*Les Mots et les choses,* 1966), suggests his approach to the study of culture from the seventeenth century to the modern age. He attempts "to uncover the deepest strata of Western culture." His discussion of the human sciences, reprinted below, situates them as part of our present-day *episteme* and raises the question of whether man, who "is an invention of recent date," is "perhaps nearing its end." He continues his probing in *L'Archéologie du savoir* (1969), and though he can of course present no definitive answer, his view of science and knowledge is subtle and suggestive.

14

The Human Sciences

THE THREE MODELS

At first glance, one could say that the domain of the human sciences is covered by three 'sciences'—or rather by three epistemological regions, all subdivided within themselves, and all interlocking with one another; these regions are defined by the triple relation of the human sciences in general to biology, economics, and philology. Thus one could admit that the 'psychological region' has found its locus in that place where the living being, in the extension of its functions, in its neuro-motor blueprints, its physiological regulations, but also in the suspense that interrupts and limits them, opens itself to the possibility of representation; in the same way, the 'sociological region' would be situated where the labouring, producing, and consuming individual offers himself a representation of the society in which this activity occurs, of the groups and individuals among which it is divided, of the imperatives, sanctions, rites, festivities, and beliefs by which it is upheld or regulated; lastly, in that region where the laws and forms of a language hold sway, but where, nevertheless, they remain on the edge of themselves, enabling man to introduce into them the play of his representations, in that region arise the study of literature and myths, the analysis of all oral expressions and written documents, in short, the analysis of the verbal traces that a culture or an individual may leave behind them. This division, though very summary,

From *The Order of Things,* by Michel Foucault, translated by Alan Sheridan-Smith. Copyright © 1970 by Random House, Inc. Reprinted by permission of Pantheon Books, a Division of Random House, Inc. Sections III, V, and VI from Chapter 10.

is probably not too inexact. It does, however, leave two fundamental problems unsolved: one concerns the form of positivity proper to the human sciences (the concepts around which they are organized, the type of rationality to which they refer and by means of which they seek to constitute themselves as knowledge); the other is their relation to representation (and the paradoxical fact that even while they take place only where there is representation, it is to unconscious mechanisms, forms, and processes, or at least to the exterior boundaries of consciousness, that they address themselves).

The controversies to which the search for a specific positivity in the field of the human sciences has given rise are only too well known: Genetic or structural analysis? Explanation or comprehension? Recourse to what is 'underneath' or decipherment kept strictly to the level of reading? In fact, all these theoretical discussions did not arise and were not pursued throughout the history of the human sciences because the latter had to deal, in man, with an object so complex that it was not yet possible to find a unique mode of access towards it, or because it was necessary to use several in turn. These discussions were able to exist only in so far as the positivity of the human sciences rests simultaneously upon the transference of three distinct models. This transference is not a marginal phenomenon for the human sciences (a sort of supporting framework, a detour to include some exterior intelligibility, a confirmation derived from sciences already constituted); nor is it a limited episode in their history (a crisis of formation, at a time when they were still so young that they could not fix their concepts and their laws themselves). On the contrary, it is a matter of an ineffaceable fact, which is bound up, forever, with their particular arrangement in the epistemological space. We should, indeed, distinguish between two different sorts of model utilized by the human sciences (leaving aside models of formalization). On the one hand, there were—and often still are—concepts introduced from another domain of knowledge, which, losing all operational efficacity in the process, now play only the role of an image (organic metaphors in nineteenth-century sociology; energy metaphors in Janet; geometrical and dynamic metaphors in Lewin). But there are also constituent models, which are not just techniques of formalization for the human sciences, or simple means of devising methods of operation with less effort; they make it possible to create groups of phenomena as so many 'objects' for a possible branch of knowledge; they ensure their connection in the empirical sphere, but they offer them to experience already linked together. They play the role of 'categories' in the area of knowledge particular to the human sciences.

These constituent models are borrowed from the three domains of biology, economics, and the study of language. It is upon the projected surface of biology that man appears as a being possessing *functions*—receiving stimuli (physiological ones, but also social, interhuman, and cultural ones), reacting to them, adapting himself, evolving, submitting to the demands of an environment, coming to terms with the modifications it imposes, seeking to erase imbalances, acting in accordance with regularities, having, in short, conditions of existence and the possibility of finding average *norms* of adjustment which permit him to perform his functions. On the projected surface of economics, man appears as having needs and desires, as seeking to satisfy them, and therefore as having interests, desiring profits, entering into opposition with other men; in short, he appears in an irreducible situation of *conflict;* he evades these conflicts, he escapes from them or succeeds in dominating them, in finding a solution that will —on one level at least, and for a time—appease their contradictions; he establishes a body of *rules* which are both a limitation of the conflict and a result of it. Lastly, on the projected surface of language, man's behaviour appears as an attempt to say something; his slightest gestures, even their involuntary mechanisms and their failures, have a *meaning;* and everything he arranges around him by way of objects, rites, customs, discourse, all the traces he leaves behind him, constitute a coherent whole and a *system* of signs. Thus, these three pairs of *function* and *norm, conflict* and *rule, signification* and *system* completely cover the entire domain of what can be known about man.

It must not be supposed, however, that any of these pairs of concepts remains localized on the projected surface on which it may have appeared: function and norm are not psychological concepts exclusively; conflict and rule do not have an application limited wholly to the sociological domain; signification and system are not valid solely for phenomena more or less akin to language. All these concepts occur throughout the entire volume common to the human sciences and are valid in each of the regions included within it: hence the frequent difficulty in fixing limits, not merely between the objects, but also between the methods proper to psychology, sociology, and the analysis of literature and myth. Nevertheless, we can say in a general way that psychology is fundamentally a study of man in terms of functions and norms (functions and norms which can, in a secondary fashion, be interpreted on the basis of conflicts and significations, rules and systems); sociology is fundamentally a study of man in terms of rules and conflicts (but these may be interpreted, and one is constantly led to interpret them, in a secondary way, either on the basis of functions, as though they were individuals organically connected to themselves, or on the basis of systems of significations, as though they were written or spoken texts); lastly, the study of literature and myth is essentially the province of an analysis of significations and signifying systems, but we all know that this analysis may be carried out in terms of functional coherence or of conflicts or rules. In this way all the human sciences interlock and can always be used to interpret one another: their frontiers become blurred, intermediary and composite disciplines multiply endlessly, and in the end their proper object may even disappear altogether. But whatever the nature of the analysis and the domain to which it is applied, we have a formal criterion for knowing what is on the level of psychology, what on that of sociology, and what on that of language analysis: this is the choice of the fundamental model and the position of the secondary models, which make it possible to know at what point one begins to 'psychologize' or 'sociologize' in the study of literature and myth, or at what point in psychology one has moved over into the decipherment of texts or into sociological analysis. But this superimposition of several models is not a defect of method. It becomes a defect only if the models have not been precisely ordered and explicitly articulated in relation to one another. As we know, it proved possible to conduct an admirably precise study of the Indo-European mythologies by using the sociological model superimposed upon the basic analysis of significants and significations. We know also, on the other hand, to what syncretic platitudes the still mediocre undertaking of founding a so-called 'clinical' psychology has led.

Whether properly founded and controlled, or carried out in confusion, this interlocking of constituent models explains the discussions of method referred to above. They do not have their origin and justification in a sometimes contradictory complexity which we know as the character proper to man; but in the play of oppositions, which makes it possible to define each of the three models in relation to the two others. To oppose genesis to structure is to oppose function (in its development, in its progressively diversified operations, in the powers of adaptation it has acquired and balanced in time) to the synchronism of conflict and rule, of signification and system; to oppose analysis by means of that which is 'underneath' to analysis on the same level as its object is to oppose conflict (a primary, archaic datum inscribed at the same time as man's fundamental needs) to function and signification as they are deployed in their particular realization; to oppose comprehension to explanation is to oppose the technique that makes it possible to decipher a meaning on the basis of a signifying system to those that make it possible to give an account of a conflict together with its consequences, or of the forms and deformations that a function and its organs may assume or undergo. But we must go further. We know that in the human sciences the point of view of discontinuity (the threshold between nature and culture, the irreducibility one to another of the balances or solutions found by each society or each individual, the absence of intermediary forms, the non-existence of a continuum existing in space or time) is in opposition to the point of view of continuity. The existence of this opposition is to be explained by the bipolar character of the models: analysis in a continuous mode relies upon the permanence of function (which is to be found in the very depths of life in an identity that authorizes and provides roots for succeeding adaptations), upon the interconnection of conflicts (they may take various forms, but they are always present in the background), upon the fabric of significations (which link up with one another and constitute, as it were, the continuous expanse of a discourse); on the contrary, the analysis of discontinuities seeks rather to draw out the internal coherence of signifying systems, the specificity of bodies of rules and the decisive character they assume in relation to what must be regulated, and the emergence of the norm above the level of functional fluctuations.

It might be possible to retrace the entire history of the human sciences, from the nineteenth century onward, on the basis of these three models. They have, in fact, covered the whole of that history, since we can follow the dynasty of their privileges for more than a century: first, the reign of the biological model (man, his psyche, his group, his society, the language he speaks—all these exist in the Romantic period as living beings and in so far as they were, in fact, alive; their mode of being is organic and is analysed in terms of function); then comes the reign of the economic model (man and his entire activity are the locus of conflicts of which they are both the more or less manifest expression and the more or less successful solution); lastly—just as Freud comes after Comte and Marx—there begins the reign of the philological (when it is a matter of interpretation and the discovery of hidden meanings) and linguistic model (when it is a matter of giving a structure to and clarifying the signifying system). Thus a vast shift has led the human sciences from a form more dense in living models to another more saturated with models borrowed from language. But this shift was paralleled by another: that which caused the first term in each of the constituent pairs (function, conflict, signification) to recede, and the second term (norm, rule, system) to emerge with a correspondingly greater intensity and importance: Goldstein, Mauss, Dumezil may be taken to represent, as near as makes no difference, the moment at which the reversal took place within each of the models. Such a reversal has two series of noteworthy consequences: as long as the functional point of view continued to carry more weight than the normative point of view (as long as it was not on the basis of the norm and the interior of the activity determining that norm that the attempt was made to understand how a function was performed), it was of course necessary, *de facto*, to share the normal functions with the non-normal; thus a pathological psychology was accepted side by side with normal psychology, but forming as it were an inverted image of it (hence the importance of the Jacksonian notion of disintegration in Ribot or Janet); in the same way, a pathology of societies (Durkheim), of irrational and quasi-morbid forms of belief (Lévy-Bruhl, Blondel) was also accepted; similarly, as long as the point of view of conflict carried more weight than that of the rule, it was supposed that certain conflicts could not be overcome, that individuals and societies ran the risk of destroying themselves by them; finally, as long as the point of view of signification carried more weight than that of system, a division was made between significant and non-significant: it was accepted that there was meaning in certain domains of human behaviour or certain regions of the social area, but not in others. So that the human sciences laid down an essential division within their own field: they always extended between a positive pole and a negative pole; they always designated an alterity (based, furthermore, on the continuity they were analysing). When, on the other hand, the analysis was conducted from the point of view of the norm, the rule, and the system, each area provided its own coherence and its own validity; it was no longer possible to speak of 'morbid consciousness' (even referring to the sick), of 'primitive mentalities' (even with reference to societies left behind by history), or of 'insignificant discourse' (even when referring to absurd stories, or to apparently incoherent legends). Everything may be thought within the order of the system, the rule, and the norm. By pluralizing itself—since systems are isolated, since rules form closed wholes, since norms are posited in their autonomy—the field of the human sciences found itself unified: suddenly, it was no longer fissured along its former dichotomy of values. And bearing in mind that Freud more than anyone else brought the knowledge of man closer to its philological and linguistic model, and that he was also the first to undertake the radical erasure of the division between positive and negative (between the normal and the pathological, the comprehensible and the incommunicable, the significant and the non-significant), it is easy to see how he prefigures the transition from an analysis in terms of functions, conflicts, and significations to an analysis in terms of norms, rules, and systems: thus all this knowledge, within which Western culture had given itself in one century a certain image of man, pivots on the work of Freud, though without, for all that, leaving its fundamental arrangement. But even so, it is not here—as we shall see later on—that the most decisive importance of psychoanalysis lies.

In any case, this transition to the point of view of the norm, the rule, and the system brings us to a problem that has been left in suspense: that of the role of representation in the human sciences. It might already appear extremely contestable to include the human sciences (as opposed to biology, economics, and philology) within the space of representation: was it not already necessary to point out that a function can be performed, a conflict can develop its consequences, a signification can impose its intelligibility, without passing through the stage of explicit consciousness? And now, is it not necessary to recognize that the peculiar property of the norm, in relation to the function it determines, of the rule in relation to the conflict it regulates, of the system in relation to the signification it makes possible, is precisely that of not being given to consciousness? Are we not forced to add a third historical gradient to the two already isolated, and to say that since the nineteenth century the human sciences have never ceased to approach that region of the unconscious where the action of representation is held in suspense? In fact, representation is not consciousness, and there is nothing to prove that this bringing to light of elements or structures that are never presented to consciousness as such enables the human sciences to escape the law of representation. The role of the concept of signification is, in fact, to show how something like a language, even if it is not in the form of explicit discourse, and even if it has not been deployed for a consciousness, can in general be given to representation; the role of the complementary concept of system is to show how signification is never primary and contemporaneous with itself, but always secondary and as it were derived in relation to a system that precedes it, constitutes its positive origin, and posits itself, little by little, in fragments and outlines through signification; in relation to the consciousness of a signification, the system is indeed always unconscious since it was there before the signification, since it is within it that the signification resides and on the basis of it that it becomes effective; but because the system is always promised to a future consciousness which will perhaps never add it up. In other words, the signification/system pair is what ensures both the representability of language (as text or structure analysed by philology and linguistics) and the near but withdrawn presence of the origin (as it is manifested as man's mode of being by means of the analytic of finitude). In the same way, the notion of conflict shows how need, desire, and interest, even if they are not presented to the consciousness experiencing them, can take form in representation; and the role of the inverse concept of rule is to show how the violence of conflict, the apparently untamed insistence of need, the lawless infinity of desire are in fact already organized by an unthought which not only prescribes their rules, but renders them possible upon the basis of a rule. The conflict/rule pair ensures the representability of need (of the need that economics studies as an objective process in labour and production) and the representability of the unthought that is unveiled by the analytic of finitude. Lastly, the concept of function has the role of showing how the structures of life may give rise to representation (even though they are not conscious), and the concept of norm how function provides its own conditions of possibility and the frontiers within which it is effective.

Thus it can be understood why these broad categories can structure the entire field of the human sciences: it is because they span it from end to end, because they both hold apart and link together the empirical positivities of life, labour, and language (on the basis of which man first detached himself historically as a form of possible knowledge) and the forms of finitude that characterize man's mode of being (as he constituted himself when representation ceased to define the general space of knowledge). These categories are not, therefore, mere empirical concepts of rather broad generality; they are indeed the basis on which man is able to present himself to a possible knowledge; they traverse the entire field of his possibility and articulate it boldly in accordance with the two dimensions that form its frame.

But that is not all: they also permit the dissociation, which is characteristic of all contemporary knowledge about man, of consciousness and representation. They define the manner in which the empiricities can be given to representation but in a form that is not present to the consciousness (function, conflict, and signification are indeed the manner in which life, need, and language are doubled over in representation, but in a form that which may be completely unconscious); on the other hand, they define the manner in which the fundamental finitude can be given to representation in a form both positive and empirical, yet not transparent to the naïve consciousness (neither norm, nor rule, nor system is given in daily experience: they run through it, give rise to partial consciousnesses of themselves, but can never be wholly illumined except by a reflexive form of knowledge). So the human sciences speak only within the element of the representable, but in accordance with a conscious/unconscious dimension, a dimension that becomes more and more marked as one attempts to bring the order of systems, rules, and norms to light. It is as though the dichotomy between normal and pathological were tending to be eclipsed in favour of the bipolarity of consciousness and the unconscious.

It must not be forgotten, therefore, that the increasingly marked importance of the unconscious in no way compromises the primacy of representation. This primacy does, however, raise an important problem. Now that the empirical forms of knowledge, such as those of life, labour, and language, have escaped from its law, now that the attempt to define man's mode of being is being made outside the field of representation, what is representation, if not a phenomenon of an empirical order which occurs within man, and could be analysed as such? And if representation occurs within man, what difference is there between it and consciousness? But representation is not simply an object for the human sciences; it is, as we have just seen, the very field upon which the human sciences occur, and to their fullest extent; it is the general pedestal of that form of knowledge, the basis that makes it possible. Two consequences emerge from this. One is of a historical order: it is the fact that the human sciences, unlike the empirical sciences since the nineteenth century, and unlike modern thought, have been unable to find a way around the primacy of representation; like the whole of Classical knowledge, they reside within it; but they are in no way its heirs or its continuation, for the whole configuration of knowledge has been modified and they came into being only to the degree to which there appeared, with man, a being who did not exist before in the field of the *episteme*. However, it is easy to understand why every time one tries to use the human sciences to philosophize, to pour back into the space of thought what one has been able to learn of man, one finds oneself imitating the philosophical posture of the eighteenth century, in which, nevertheless, man had no place; for by extending the domain of knowledge about man beyond its limits one is similarly extending the reign of representation beyond itself, and thus taking up one's position once more in a philosophy of the Classical type. The other consequence is that the human sciences, when dealing with what is representation (in either conscious or unconscious form), find themselves treating as their object what is in fact their condition of possibility. They are always animated, therefore, by a sort of transcendental mobility. They never cease to exercise a critical examination of themselves. They proceed from that which is given to representation to that which renders representation possible, but which is still representation. So that, unlike other sciences, they seek not so much to generalize themselves or make themselves more precise as to be constantly demystifying themselves: to make the transition from an immediate and non-controlled evidence to less transparent but more fundamental forms. This quasi-transcendental process is always given in the form of an unveiling. It is always by an unveiling that they are able, as a consequence, to become sufficiently generalized or refined to conceive of individual phenomena. On the horizon of any human science, there is the project of bringing man's consciousness back to its real conditions, of restoring it to the contents and forms that brought it into being, and elude us within it; this is why the problem of the unconscious—its possibility, status, mode of existence, the means of knowing it and of bringing it to light—is not simply a problem within the human sciences which they can be thought of as encountering by chance in their steps; it is a problem that is ultimately coextensive with their very existence. A transcendental raising of level that is, on the other side, an unveiling of the nonconscious is constitutive of all the sciences of man.

We may find in this the means of isolating them in their essential property. In any case, we can see that what manifests this peculiar property of the human sciences is not that privileged and singularly blurred object which is man. For the good reason that it is not man who constitutes them and provides them with a specific domain; it is the general arrangement of the *episteme* that provides them with a site, summons them, and establishes them—thus enabling them to constitute man as their object. We shall say, therefore, that a 'human science' exists, not wherever man is in question, but wherever there is analysis—within the dimension proper to the unconscious—of norms, rules, and signifying totalities which unveil to consciousness the conditions of its forms and contents. To speak of 'sciences of man' in any other case is simply an abuse of language. We can see, then, how vain and idle are all those wearisome discussions as to whether such and such forms of knowledge may be termed truly scientific, and to what conditions they ought to be subjected in order to become so. The 'sciences of man' are part of the modern *episteme* in the same way as chemistry or medicine or any other such science; or again, in the same way as grammar and natural history were part of the Classical *episteme*. But to say that they are part of the epistemological field means simply that their positivity is rooted in it, that that is where they find their condition of existence, that they are therefore not merely illusions, pseudo-scientific fantasies motivated at the level of opinions, interests, or beliefs, that they are not what others call by the bizarre name of 'ideology'. But that does not necessarily mean that they are sciences.

Although it is true that any science, any science whatever, when it is questioned on the archaeological level and when an attempt is made to clear the ground of its positivity, always reveals the epistemological configuration that made it possible, any epistemological configuration, on the other hand, even if it is completely assignable in its positivity, may very well not be a science: it does not thereby reduce itself, *ipso facto,* to the status of an imposture. We must distinguish carefully between three things: there are themes with scientific pretensions that one may encounter at the level of opinion and that are not (or are no longer) part of a culture's epistemological network: from the seventeenth century, for example, natural magic ceased to belong to the Western *episteme,* but it persisted for a long time in the interaction of beliefs and affective valorizations. Then there are epistemological figures whose outline, position, and function can be reconstituted in their positivity by means of an analysis of the archaeological type; and these, in turn, may obey two different organizations: some present characteristics of objectivity and systematicity which make it possible to define them as sciences; others do not answer to those criteria, that is, their form of coherence and their relation to their object are determined by their positivity alone. The fact that these latter do not possess the formal criteria of a scientific form of knowledge does not prevent them from belonging, nevertheless, to the positive domain of knowledge. It would thus be as futile and unjust to analyse them as phenomena of opinion as to contrast them historically or critically with scientific formations proper; it would be more absurd still to treat them as a combination which mixes together in variable proportions 'rational elements' and other elements that are not rational. They must be replaced on the level of positivity that renders them possible and necessarily determines their form. Archaeology, then, has two tasks with regard to these figures: to determine the manner in which they are arranged in the *episteme* in which they have their roots; and to show, also, in what respect their configuration is radically different from that of the sciences in the strict sense. There is no reason to treat this peculiar configuration of theirs as a negative phenomenon: it is not the presence of an obstacle nor some internal deficiency which has left them stranded across the threshold of scientific forms. They constitute, in their own form, side by side with the sciences and on the same archaeological ground, *other* configurations of knowledge.

We have already encountered examples of such configurations in general grammar or in the Classical theory of value; they possessed the same ground of positivity as Cartesian mathematics, but they were not sciences, at least for the majority of those who were their contemporaries. Such is also the case with what we today call the human sciences; when analysed archaeologically, they provide the outlines of completely positive configurations; but as soon as these configurations and the way in which they are arranged within the modern *episteme* are determined, we understand why they cannot be sciences: what renders them possible, in fact, is a certain situation of 'vicinity' with regard to biology, economics, and philology (or linguistics); they exist only in so far as they dwell side by side with those sciences—or rather beneath them, in the space of their projections. However, they maintain a relationship with those sciences that is radically different from that which can be established between two 'related' or 'germane' sciences: this relationship presupposes, in fact, the transposition of external models within the dimension of the unconscious and consciousness, and the flowing back of critical reflection towards the very place from which those models come. It is useless, then, to say that the 'human sciences' are false sciences; they are not sciences at all; the configuration that defines their positivity and gives them their roots in the modern *episteme* at the same time makes it impossible for them to be sciences; and if it is then asked why they assumed that title, it is sufficient to recall that it pertains to the archaeological definition of their roots that they summon and receive the transference of models borrowed from the sciences. It is therefore not man's irreducibility, what is designated as his invincible transcendence, nor even his excessively great complexity, that prevents him from becoming an object of science. Western culture has constituted, under the name of man, a being who, by one and the same interplay of reasons, must be a positive domain of *knowledge* and cannot be an object of *science*.

PSYCHOANALYSIS AND ETHNOLOGY

Psychoanalysis and ethnology occupy a privileged position in our knowledge—not because they have established the foundations of their positivity better than any other human science, and at last accomplished the old attempt to be truly scientific; but rather because, on the confines of all the branches of knowledge investigating man, they form an undoubted and inexhaustible treasure-hoard of experiences and concepts, and above all a perpetual principle of dissatisfaction, of calling into question, of criticism and contestation of what may seem, in other respects, to be established. Now, there is a reason for this that concerns the object they respectively give to one another, but concerns even more the position they occupy and the function they perform within the general space of the *episteme*.

Psychoanalysis stands as close as possible, in fact, to that critical function which, as we have seen, exists within all the human sciences. In setting itself the task of making the discourse of the unconscious speak through consciousness, psychoanalysis is advancing in the direction of that fundamental region in which the relations of representation and finitude come into play. Whereas all the human sciences advance towards the unconscious only with their back to it, waiting for it to unveil itself as fast as consciousness is analysed, as it were backwards, psychoanalysis, on the other hand, points directly towards it, with a deliberate purpose—not towards that which must be rendered gradually more explicit by the progressive illumination of the implicit, but towards what is there and yet is hidden, towards what exists with the mute solidity of a thing, of a text closed in upon itself, or of a blank space in a visible text, and uses that quality to defend itself. It must not be supposed that the Freudian approach is the combination of an interpretation of meaning and a dynamics of resistance or defence; by following the same path as the human sciences, but with its gaze turned the other way, psychoanalysis moves towards the moment—by definition inaccessible to any theoretical knowledge of man, to any continuous apprehension in terms of signification, conflict, or function—at which the contents of consciousness articulate themselves, or rather stand gaping, upon man's finitude. This means that, unlike the human sciences, which, even while turning back towards the unconscious, always remain within the space of the representable, psychoanalysis advances and leaps over representation, overflows it on the side of finitude, and thus reveals, where one had expected functions bearing their norms, conflicts burdened with rules, and significations forming a system, the simple fact that it is possible for there to be system (therefore signification), rule (therefore conflict), norm (therefore function). And in this region where representation remains in suspense, on the edge of itself, open, in a sense, to the closed boundary of finitude, we find outlined the three figures by means of which life, with its function and norms, attains its foundation in the mute repetition of Death, conflicts and rules their foundation in the naked opening of Desire, significations and systems their foundation in a language which is at the same time Law. We know that psychologists and philosophers have dismissed all this as Freudian mythology. It was indeed inevitable that this approach of Freud's should have appeared to them in this way; to a knowledge situated within the representable, all that frames and defines, on the outside, the very possibility of representation can be nothing other than mythology. But when one follows the movement of psychoanalysis as it progresses, or when one traverses the epistemological space as a whole, one sees that these figures are in fact—though imaginary no doubt to the myopic gaze—the very forms of finitude, as it is analysed in modern thought. Is death not that upon the basis of which knowledge in general is possible—so much so that we can think of it as being, in the area of psychoanalysis, the figure of that empirico-transcendental *duplication* that characterizes man's mode of being within finitude? Is Desire not that which remains always *unthought* at the heart of thought? And the law-language (at once word and word-system) that psychoanalysis takes such pains to make speak, is it not that in which all signification assumes an *origin* more distant than itself, but also that whose return is promised in the very act of analysis? It is indeed true that neither this Death, nor this Desire, nor this Law can ever meet within the knowledge that traverses in its positivity the empirical domain of man; but the reason for this is that they designate the conditions of possibility of all knowledge about man.

And precisely when this language emerges in all its nudity, yet at the same time eludes all signification as if it were a vast and empty despotic system, when Desire reigns in the wild state, as if the rigour of its rule had levelled all opposition, when Death dominates every psychological function and stands above it as its unique and devastating norm—then we recognize madness in its present form, madness as it is posited in the modern experience, as its truth and its alterity. In this figure, which is at once empirical and yet foreign to (and in) all that we can experience, our consciousness no longer finds —as it did in the sixteenth century—the trace of another world; it no longer observes the wandering of a straying reason; it sees welling up that which is, perilously, nearest to us—as if, suddenly, the very hollowness of our existence is outlined in relief; the finitude upon the basis of which we are, and think, and know, is suddenly there before us: an existence at once real and impossible, thought that we cannot think, an object for our knowledge that always eludes it. This is why psychoanalysis finds in that madness *par excellence*—which psychiatrists term schizophrenia—its intimate, its most invincible torture: for, given in this form of madness, in an absolutely manifest and absolutely withdrawn form, are the forms of finitude towards which it usually advances unceasingly (and interminably) from the starting-point of that which is voluntarily-involuntarily offered to it in the patient's language. So psychoanalysis 'recognizes itself' when it is confronted with those very psychoses which nevertheless (or rather, for that very reason) it has scarcely any means of reaching: as if the psychosis were displaying in a savage illumination, and offering in a mode not too distant but just too close, that towards which analysis must make its laborious way.

But this relation of psychoanalysis with what makes all knowledge in general possible in the sphere of the human sciences has yet another consequence—namely, that psychoanalysis cannot be deployed as pure speculative knowledge or as a general theory of man. It cannot span the entire field of representation, attempt to evade its frontiers, or point towards what is more fundamental, in the form of an empirical science constructed on the basis of careful observation; that breakthrough can be made only within the limits of a praxis in which it is not only the knowledge we have of man that is involved, but man himself—man together with the Death that is at work in his suffering, the Desire that has lost its object, and the language by means of which, through which, his Law is silently articulated. All analytic knowledge is thus invincibly linked with a praxis, with that strangulation produced by the relation between two individuals, one of whom is listening to the other's language, thus freeing his desire from the object it has lost (making him understand he has lost it), liberating him from the ever-repeated proximity of death (making him understand that one day he will die). This is why nothing is more alien to psychoanalysis than anything resembling a general theory of man or an anthropology.

Just as psychoanalysis situates itself in the dimension of the unconscious (of that critical animation which disturbs from within the entire domain of the sciences of man), so ethnology situates itself in the dimension of historicity (of that perpetual oscillation which is the reason why the human sciences are always being contested, from without, by their own history). It is no doubt difficult to maintain that ethnology has a fundamental relation with historicity since it is traditionally the knowledge we have of peoples without histories; in any case, it studies (both by systematic choice and because of the lack of documents) the structural invariables of cultures rather than the succession of events. It suspends the long 'chronological' discourse by means of which we try to reflect our own culture within itself, and instead it reveals synchronological correlations in other cultural forms. And yet ethnology itself is possible only on the basis of a certain situation, of an absolutely singular event which involves not only our historicity but also that of all men who can constitute the object of an ethnology (it being understood that we can perfectly well apprehend our own society's ethnology): ethnology has its roots, in fact, in a possibility that properly belongs to the history of our culture, even more to its fundamental relation with the whole of history, and enables it to link itself to other cultures in a mode of pure theory. There is a certain position of the Western ratio that was constituted in its history and provides a foundation for the relation it can have with all other societies, even with the society in which it historically appeared. Obviously, this does not mean that the colonizing situation is indispensable to ethnology: neither hypnosis, nor the patient's alienation within the fantasmatic character of the doctor, is constitutive of psychoanalysis; but just as the latter can be deployed only in the calm violence of a particular relationship and the transference it produces, so ethnology can assume its proper dimensions only within the historical sovereignty—always restrained, but always present—of European thought and the relation that can bring it face to face with all other cultures as well as with itself.

But this relation (in so far as ethnology does not seek to efface it, but on the contrary deepens it by establishing itself definitively within it) does not imprison it within the circular system of actions and reactions proper to historicism; rather, it places it in a position to find a way round that danger by inverting the movement that gave rise to it: in fact, instead of relating empirical contents—as revealed in psychology, sociology, or the analysis of literature and myth—to the historical positivity of the subject perceiving them, ethnology places the particular forms of each culture, the differences that contrast it with others, the limits by which it defines itself and encloses itself upon its own coherence, within the dimension in which its relations occur with each of the three great positivities (life, need and labour, and language) : thus, ethnology shows how, within a given culture, there occur the normalization of the broad biological functions, the rules that render possible or obligatory all the forms of exchange, production, and consumption, and the systems that are organized around or on the model of linguistic structures. Ethnology, then, advances towards that region where the human sciences are articulated upon that biology, that economics, and that philology and linguistics which, as we have seen, dominate the human sciences from such a very great height: this is why the general problem of all ethnology is in fact that of the relations (of continuity or discontinuity) between nature and culture. But in this mode of questioning, the problem of history is found to have been reversed: for it then becomes a matter of determining, according to the symbolic systems employed, according to the prescribed rules, according to the functional norms chosen and laid down, what sort of historical development each culture is susceptible of; it is seeking to re-apprehend, in its very roots, the mode of historicity that may occur within that culture, and the reasons why its history must inevitably be cumulative or circular, progressive or subjected to regulating fluctuations, capable of spontaneous adjustments or subject to crises. And thus is revealed the foundation of that historical flow within which the different human sciences assume their validity and can be applied to a given culture and upon a given synchronological area.

Ethnology, like psychoanalysis, questions not man himself, as he appears in the human sciences, but the region that makes possible knowledge about man in general; like psychoanalysis, it spans the whole field of that knowledge in a movement that tends to reach its boundaries. But psychoanalysis makes use of the particular relation of the transference in order to reveal, on the outer confines of representation, Desire, Law, and Death, which outline at the extremity of analytic language and practice, the concrete figures of finitude; ethnology, on the other hand, is situated within the particular relation that the Western *ratio* establishes with all other cultures; and from that starting-point it avoids the representations that men in any civilization may give themselves of themselves, of their life, of their needs, of the significations laid down in their language; and it sees emerging behind those representations the norms by which men perform the functions of life, although they reject their immediate pressure, the rules through which they experience and maintain their needs, the systems against the background of which all signification is given to them. The privilege of ethnology and psychoanalysis, the reason for their profound kinship and symmetry, must not be sought, therefore, in some common concern to pierce the profound enigma, the most secret part of human nature; in fact, what illuminates the space of their discourse is much more the historical *a priori* of all the sciences of man—those great caesuras, furrows, and dividing-lines which traced man's outline in the Western *episteme* and made him a possible area of knowledge. It was quite inevitable, then, that they should both be sciences of the unconscious: not because they reach down to what is below consciousness in man, but because they are directed towards that which, outside man, makes it possible to know, with a positive knowledge, that which is given to or eludes his consciousness.

On this basis, a certain number of decisive facts become comprehensible. And the first is this: that psychoanalysis and ethnology are not so much two human sciences among others, but that they span the entire domain of those sciences, that they animate its whole surface, spread their concepts throughout it, and are able to propound their methods of decipherment and their interpretations everywhere. No human science can be sure that it is out of their debt, or entirely independent of what they may have discovered, or certain of not being beholden to them in one way or another. But their development has one particular feature, which is that, despite their quasi-universal 'bearing', they never, for all that, come near to a general concept of man: at no moment do they come near to isolating a quality in him that is specific, irreducible, and uniformly valid wherever he is given to experience. The idea of 'psychoanalytic anthropology', and the idea of a 'human nature' reconstituted by ethnology, are no more than pious wishes. Not only are they able to do without the concept of man, they are also unable to pass through it, for they always address themselves to that which constitutes his outer limits. One may say of both of them what Lévi-Strauss said of ethnology: that they dissolve man. Not that there is any question of revealing him in a better, purer, and as it were more liberated state; but because they go back towards that which foments his positivity. In relation to the 'human sciences', psychoanalysis and ethnology are rather 'counter-sciences'; which does not mean that they are less 'rational' or 'objective' than the others, but that they flow in the opposite direction, that they lead them back to their epistemological basis, and that they ceaselessly 'unmake' that very man who is creating and re-creating his positivity in the human sciences. Lastly, we can understand why psychoanalysis and ethnology should have been constituted in confrontation, in a fundamental correlation: since *Totem and taboo*, the establishment of a common field for these two, the possibility of a discourse that could move from one to the other without discontinuity, the double articulation of the history of individuals upon the unconscious of culture, and of the historicity of those cultures upon the unconscious of individuals, have opened up, without doubt, the most general problems that can be posed with regard to man.

One can imagine what prestige and importance ethnology could possess if, instead of defining itself in the first place —as it has done until now—as the study of societies without history, it were deliberately to seek its object in the area of the unconscious processes that characterize the system of a given culture; in this way it would bring the relation of historicity, which is constitutive of all ethnology in general, into play within the dimension in which psychoanalysis has always been deployed. In so doing it would not assimilate the mechanisms and forms of a society to the pressure and repression of collective hallucinations, thus discovering—though on a larger scale—what analysis can discover at the level of the individual; it would define as a system of cultural unconsciousness the totality of formal structures which render mythical discourse significant, give their coherence and necessity to the rules that regulate needs, and provide the norms of life with a foundation other than that to be found in nature, or in pure biological functions. One can imagine the similar importance that a psychoanalysis would have if it were to share the dimension of an ethnology, not by the establishment of a 'cultural psychology', not by the sociological explanation of phenomena manifested at the level of individuals, but by the discovery that the unconscious also possesses, or rather that it *is* in itself, a certain formal structure. By this means, ethnology and psychoanalysis would succeed, not in superimposing themselves on one another, nor even perhaps in coming together, but in intersecting like two lines differently oriented: one proceeding from the apparent elision of the signified in a neurosis to the lacuna in the signifying system through which the neurosis found expression; the other proceeding from the analogy between the multiple things signified (in mythologies, for example) to the unity of a structure whose formal transformations would yield up the diversity existing in the actual stories. It would thus not be at the level of the relations between the individual and society, as has often been believed, that psychoanalysis and ethnology could be articulated one upon the other; it is not because the individual is a part of his group, it is not because a culture is reflected and expressed in a more or less deviant manner in the individual, that these two forms of knowledge are neighbours. In fact, they have only one point in common, but it is an essential and inevitable one: the one at which they intersect at right angles; for the signifying chain by which the unique experience of the individual is constituted is perpendicular to the formal system on the basis of which the significations of a culture are constituted: at any given instant, the structure proper to individual experience finds a certain number of possible choices (and of excluded possibilities) in the systems of the society; inversely, at each of their points of choice the social structures encounter a certain number of possible individuals (and others who are not)—just as the linear structure of language always produces a possible choice between several words or several phonemes at any given moment (but excludes all others).

Whereupon there is formed the theme of a pure theory of language which would provide the ethnology and the psychoanalysis thus conceived with their formal model. There would thus be a discipline that could cover in a single movement both the dimension of ethnology that relates the human sciences to the positivities in which they are framed and the dimension of psychoanalysis that relates the knowledge of man to the finitude that gives it its foundation. In linguistics, one would have a science perfectly founded in the order of positivities exterior to man (since it is a question of pure language), which, after traversing the whole space of the human sciences, would encounter the question of finitude (since it is through language, and within it, that thought is able to think: so that it is in itself a positivity with the value of a fundamental). Above ethnology and psychoanalysis, or, more exactly, interwoven with them, a third 'counter-science' would appear to traverse, animate, and disturb the whole constituted field of the human sciences; and by overflowing it both on the side of positivities and on that of finitude, it would form the most general contestation of that field. Like the two other counter-sciences, it would make visible, in a discursive mode, the frontier-forms of the human sciences; like them, it would situate its experience in those enlightened and dangerous regions where the knowledge of man acts out, in the form of the unconscious and of historicity, its relation with what renders them possible. In 'exposing' it, these three counter-sciences threaten the very thing that made it possible for man to be known. Thus we see the destiny of man being spun before our very eyes, but being spun backwards; it is being led back, by those strange bobbins, to the forms of its birth, to the homeland that made it possible. And is that not one way of bringing about its end? For linguistics no more speak of man himself than do psychoanalysis and ethnology.

It may be said that, in playing this role, linguistics is doing no more than resuming the functions that had once been those of biology or of economics, when, in the nineteenth and early twentieth centuries, an attempt was made to unify the human sciences under concepts borrowed from biology or economics. But linguistics may have a much more fundamental role. And for several reasons. First, because it permits—or it in any case strives to render possible—the structuration of contents themselves; it is therefore not a theoretical reworking of knowledge acquired elsewhere, the interpretation of an already accomplished reading of phenomena; it does not offer a 'linguistic version' of the facts observed in the human sciences, it is rather the principle of a primary decipherment; to a gaze forearmed by linguistics, things attain to existence only in so far as they are able to form the elements of a signifying system. Linguistic analysis is more a perception than an explanation: that is, it is constitutive of its very object. Moreover, we find that by means of this emergence of structure (as an invariable relation within a totality of elements) the relation of the human sciences to mathematics has been opened up once more, and in a wholly new dimension; it is no longer a matter of knowing whether one can quantify results, or whether human behaviour is susceptible of being introduced into the field of a measurable probability; the question that arises is that of knowing whether it is possible without a play on words to employ the notion of structure, or at least whether it is the same structure that is referred to in mathematics and in the human sciences: a question that is central if one wishes to know the possibilities and rights, the conditions and limitations, of a justified formalization; it will be seen that the relation of the sciences of man to the axis of the formal and *a priori* discipline—a relation that had not been essential till then, and as long as the attempt was made to identify it with the right to measure—returns to life and perhaps becomes fundamental now that within the space of the human sciences there emerges their relation both to the empirical positivity of language and to the analytic of finitude; the three axes which define the volume proper to the sciences of man thus become visible, and almost simultaneously so, in the questions they pose. Lastly, as a result of the importance of linguistics and of its application to the knowledge of man, the question of the being of language, which, as we have seen, is so intimately linked with the fundamental problems of our culture, reappears in all its enigmatic insistence. With the continually extended use of linguistic categories, it is a question of growing importance, since we must henceforth ask ourselves what language must be in order to structure in this way what is nevertheless not in itself either word or discourse, and in order to articulate itself on the pure forms of knowledge. By a much longer and much more unexpected path, we are led back to the place that Nietzsche and Mallarmé signposted when the first asked: Who speaks?, and the second saw his glittering answer in the Word itself. The question as to what language is in its being is once more of the greatest urgency.

At this point, where the question of language arises again with such heavy over-determination, and where it seems to lay siege on every side to the figure of man (that figure which had once taken the place of Classical Discourse), contemporary culture is struggling to create an important part of its present, and perhaps of its future. On the one hand, suddenly very near to all these empirical domains, questions arise which before had seemed very distant from them: these questions concern a general formalization of thought and knowledge; and at a time when they were still thought to be dedicated solely to the relation between logic and mathematics, they suddenly open up the possibility, and the task, of purifying the old empirical reason by constituting formal languages, and of applying a second critique of pure reason on the basis of new forms of the mathematical *a priori*. However, at the other extremity of our culture, the question of language is entrusted to that form of speech which has no doubt never ceased to pose it, but which is now, for the first time, posing it to itself. That literature in our day is fascinated by the being of language is neither the sign of an imminent end nor proof of a radicalization: it is a phenomenon whose necessity has its roots in a vast configuration in which the whole structure of our thought and our knowledge is traced. But if the question of formal languages gives prominence to the possibility or impossibility of structuring positive contents, a literature dedicated to language gives prominence, in all their empirical vivacity, to the fundamental forms of finitude. From within language experienced and traversed as language, in the play of its possibilities extended to their furthest point, what emerges is that man has 'come to an end', and that, by reaching the summit of all possible speech, he arrives not at the very heart of himself but at the brink of that which limits him; in that region where death prowls, where thought is extinguished, where the promise of the origin interminably recedes. It was inevitable that this new mode of being of literature should have been revealed in works like those of Artaud or Roussel—and by men like them; in Artaud's work, language, having been rejected as discourse and re-apprehended in the plastic violence of the shock, is referred back to the cry, to the tortured body, to the materiality of thought, to the flesh; in Roussel's work, language, having been reduced to powder by a systematically fabricated chance, recounts interminably the repetition of death and the enigma of divided origins. And as if this experiencing of the forms of finitude in language were insupportable, or inadequate (perhaps its very inadequacy was insupportable), it is within madness that it manifested itself—the figure of finitude thus positing itself in language (as that which unveils itself within it), but also before it, preceding it, as that formless, mute, unsignifying region where language can find its freedom. And it is indeed in this space thus revealed that literature, first with surrealism (though still in a very much disguised form), then, more and more purely, with Kafka, Bataille, and Blanchot, posited itself as experience: as experience of death (and in the element of death), of unthinkable thought (and in its inaccessible presence), of repetition (of original innocence, always there at the nearest and yet always the most distant limit of language); as experience of finitude (trapped in the opening and the tyranny of that finitude).

It is clear that this 'return' of language is not a sudden interruption in our culture; it is not the irruptive discovery of some long-buried evidence; it does not indicate a folding back of thought upon itself, in the movement by which it emancipates itself from all content, or a narcissism occurring within a literature freeing itself at last from what it has to say in order to speak henceforth only about the fact that it is language stripped naked. It is, in fact, the strict unfolding of Western culture in accordance with the necessity it imposed upon itself at the beginning of the nineteenth century. It would be false to see in this general indication of our experience, which may be termed 'formalism', the sign of a drying up, of a rarefaction of thought losing its capacity for re-apprehending the plenitude of contents; it would be no less false to place it from the outset upon the horizon of some new thought or new knowledge. It is within the very tight-knit, very coherent outlines of the modern *episteme* that this contemporary experience found its possibility; it is even that *episteme* which, by its logic, gave rise to such an experience, constituted it through and through, and made it impossible for it not to exist. What occurred at the time of Ricardo, Cuvier, and Bopp, the form of knowledge that was established with the appearance of economics, biology, and philology, the thought of finitude laid down by the Kantian critique as philosophy's task—all that still forms the immediate space of our reflection. We think in that area.

And yet the impression of fulfilment and of end, the muffled feeling that carries and animates our thought, and perhaps lulls it to sleep with the facility of its promises, and makes us believe that something new is about to begin, something we glimpse only as a thin line of light low on the horizon—that feeling and that impression are perhaps not ill founded. It will be said that they exist, that they have never ceased to be formulated over and over again since the early nineteenth century; it will be said that Hölderlin, Hegel, Feuerbach, and Marx all felt this certainty that in them a thought and perhaps a culture were coming to a close, and that from the depths of a distance which was perhaps not invincible, another was approaching—in the dim light of dawn, in the brilliance of noon, or in the dissension of the falling day. But this close, this perilous imminence whose promise we fear today, whose danger we welcome, is probably not of the same order. Then, the task enjoined upon thought by that annunciation was to establish for man a stable sojourn upon this earth from which the gods had turned away or vanished. In our day, and once again Nietzsche indicated the turning-point from a long way off, it is not so much the absence or the death of God that is affirmed as the end of man (that narrow, imperceptible displacement, that recession in the form of identity, which are the reason why man's finitude has become his end); it becomes apparent, then, that the death of God and the last man are engaged in a contest with more than one round: is it not the last man who announces that he has killed God, thus situating his language, his thought, his laughter in the space of that already dead God, yet positing himself also as he who has killed God and whose existence includes the freedom and the decision of that murder? Thus, the last man is at the same time older and yet younger than the death of God; since he has killed God, it is he himself who must answer for his own finitude; but since it is in the death of God that he speaks, thinks, and exists, his murder itself is doomed to die; new gods, the same gods, are already swelling the future Ocean; man will disappear. Rather than the death of God—or, rather, in the wake of that death and in a profound correlation with it—what Nietzsche's thought heralds is the end of his murderer; it is the explosion of man's face in laughter, and the return of masks; it is the scattering of the profound stream of time by which he felt himself carried along and whose pressure he suspected in the very being of things; it is the identity of the Return of the Same with the absolute dispersion of man. Throughout the nineteenth century, the end of philosophy and the promise of an approaching culture were no doubt one and the same thing as the thought of finitude and the appearance of man in the field of knowledge; in our day, the fact that philosophy is still—and again—in the process of coming to an end, and the fact that in it perhaps, though even more outside and against it, in literature as well as in formal reflection, the question of language is being posed, prove no doubt that man is in the process of disappearing.

For the entire modern *episteme*—that which was formed towards the end of the eighteenth century and still serves as the positive ground of our knowledge, that which constituted man's particular mode of being and the possibility of knowing him empirically—that entire *episteme* was bound up with the disappearance of Discourse and its featureless reign, with the shift of language towards objectivity, and with its reappearance in multiple form. If this same language is now emerging with greater and greater insistence in a unity that we ought to think but cannot as yet do so, is this not the sign that the whole of this configuration is now about to topple, and that man is in the process of perishing as the being of language continues to shine ever brighter upon our horizon? Since man was constituted at a time when language was doomed to dispersion, will he not be dispersed when language regains its unity? And if that were true, would it not be an error—a profound error, since it could hide from us what should now be thought—to interpret our actual experience as an application of the forms of language to the human order? Ought we not rather to give up thinking of man, or, to be more strict, to think of this disappearance of man—and the ground of possibility of all the sciences of man—as closely as possible in correlation with our concern with language? Ought we not to admit that, since language is here once more, man will return to that serene non-existence in which he was formerly maintained by the imperious unity of Discourse? Man had been a figure occurring between two modes of language; or, rather, he was constituted only when language, having been situated within representation and, as it were, dissolved in it, freed itself from that situation at the cost of its own fragmentation: man composed his own figure in the interstices of that fragmented language. Of course, these are not affirmations; they are at most questions to which it is not possible to reply; they must be left in suspense, where they pose themselves, only with the knowledge that the possibility of posing them may well open the way to a future thought.

IN CONCLUSION

One thing in any case is certain: man is neither the oldest nor the most constant problem that has been posed for human knowledge. Taking a relatively short chronological sample within a restricted geographical area—European culture since the sixteenth century—one can be certain that man is a recent invention within it. It is not around him and his secrets that knowledge prowled for so long in the darkness. In fact, among all the mutations that have affected the knowledge of things and their order, the knowledge of identities, differences, characters, equivalences, words—in short, in the midst of all the episodes of that profound history of the *Same*—only one, that which began a century and a half ago and is now perhaps drawing to a close, has made it possible for the figure of man to appear. And that appearance was not the liberation of an old anxiety, the transition into luminous consciousness of an age-old concern, the entry into objectivity of something that had long remained trapped within beliefs and philosophies: it was the effect of a change in the fundamental arrangements of knowledge. As the archaeology of our thought easily shows, man is an invention of recent date. And one perhaps nearing its end.

If those arrangements were to disappear as they appeared, if some event of which we can at the moment do no more than sense the possibility—without knowing either what its form will be or what it promises—were to cause them to crumble, as the ground of Classical thought did, at the end of the eighteenth century, then one can certainly wager that man would be erased, like a face drawn in sand at the edge of the sea.

JACQUES LACAN

Jacques Lacan was born in 1901 in Paris. He received his medical degree in Paris and is a specialist in psychiatry, neuropsychiatry, and psychoanalysis. Since 1963 he has been Chargé de Conférences at the École Pratique des Hautes Études. He is the founder of the École Freudienne de Paris. The massive volume *Écrits*, a collection of his major papers, appeared in 1966, and *The Language of the Self: The Function of Language in Psychoanalysis* appeared in English translation in 1968. In the article reprinted below (a lecture he gave at the Sorbonne on May 9, 1957) Lacan develops the theme that "what the psychoanalytic experience discovers in the unconscious is the whole structure of language." He freely acknowledges his debt to both Freud and Saussure in his attempt to develop a scientific study of the unconscious by adopting the methodology of linguistic analysis.

15

The Insistence of the Letter
in the Unconscious

Of Children in Swaddling Clothes
O cities of the sea, I behold in you your citizens, women as well
as men tightly bound with stout bonds around their arms and legs
by folk who will have no understanding of our speech; and you
will only be able to give vent to your griefs and sense of loss of
liberty by making tearful complaints, and sighs, and lamentations
one to another; for those who bind you will not have understanding of your speech nor will you understand them.

—LEONARDO DA VINCI

If the nature of this contribution has been set by the theme
of this volume of *La Psychanalyse,* I yet owe to what will
be found in it to insert it at a point somewhere between the
written and spoken word—it will be halfway between the two.

A written piece is in fact distinguished by a prevalence of
the "text" in the sense which that factor of speech will be
seen to take on in this essay, a factor which makes possible
the kind of tightening up that I like in order to leave the reader
no other way out than the way in, which I prefer to be difficult. In that sense, then, this will not be a written work.

The priority I accord to the nourishing of my seminars each
time with something new has until now prevented my drawing
on such a text, with one exception, not outstanding in the context of the series, and I refer to it at all only for the general
level of its argument.

From *Structuralism*, edited with an introduction by Jacques Ehrmann,
copyright © 1966 by Yale French Studies. Reprinted by permission of
Doubleday & Company, Inc.

For the urgency which I now take as a pretext for leaving aside such an aim only masks the difficulty that, in trying to maintain this discourse on the level at which I ought in these writings to present my teaching, I might push it too far from the spoken word which, with its own measures, differs from writing and is essential to the instructive effect I am seeking.

That is why I have taken the expedient offered me by the invitation to lecture to the philosophy group of the union of humanities students[1] to produce an adaptation suitable to my talk; its necessary generality having to accommodate itself to the exceptional character of the audience, but its sole object encountering the collusion of their common preparation, a literary one, to which my title pays homage.

How should we forget in effect that until the end of his life Freud constantly maintained that such a preparation was the first requisite in the formation of analysts, and that he designated the eternal *universitas litterarum* as the ideal place for its institution.[2]

And thus my recourse to the movement of this speech, feverishly restored, by showing whom I meant it for, marks even more clearly those for whom it is not meant. I mean that it is not meant for those who for any reason, psychoanalytic or other, allow their discipline to parade under a false identity; a fault of habit, but its effect on the mind is such that the true identity may appear as simply one alibi among others, a sort of refined reduplication whose implications will not be missed by the most acute.

So one observes the curious phenomenon of a whole new tack concerning language and symbolization in the *International Journal of Psychoanalysis,* buttressed by many sticky fingers in the pages of Sapir and Jespersen—amateurish exercises so far, but it is even more the tone which is lacking. A certain seriousness is cause for amusement from the standpoint of veracity.

And how could a psychoanalyst of today not realize that his realm of truth is in fact the word, when his whole experi-

[1] The lecture took place on 9th May 1957 in the Descartes Amphitheatre of the Sorbonne.
[2] *Die Frage der Laienanalyse, G.W., XIV,* pp. 281-283.

ence must find in the word alone its instrument, its framework, its material, and even the static of its uncertainties.

I. THE MEANING OF THE LETTER

As our title suggests, beyond what we call "the word," what the psychoanalytic experience discovers in the unconscious is the whole structure of language. Thus from the outset we have alerted informed minds to the extent to which the notion that the unconscious is merely the seat of the instincts will have to be rethought.

But this "letter," how are we to take it here? How indeed but literally.

By "letter" we designate that material support which concrete speech borrows from language.

This simple definition assumes that language not be confused with the diverse psychic and somatic functions which serve it in the individual speaker.

For the primary reason that language and its structure exist prior to the moment at which each individual at a certain point in his mental development makes his entry into it.

Let us note, then, that aphasia, although caused by purely anatomical lesions in the cerebral apparatus which supplies the mental center for these linguistic functions, produces language deficiencies which divide naturally between the two poles of the signifying effect of what we call here "the letter" in the creation of meaning.[3] A point which will be clarified later.

The speaking subject, if he seems to be thus a slave of language, is all the more so of a discourse in the universal moment of which he finds himself at birth, even if only by dint of his proper name.

---

[3] This aspect of aphasia, very suggestive in the direction of an overthrow of the concept of "psychological function," which only obscures every aspect of the question, appears in its proper luminosity in the purely linguistic analysis of the two major forms of aphasia worked out by one of the leaders of modern linguistics, Roman Jakobson. See the most available of his works, the *Fundamentals of Language*, with Morris Halle (Mouton and Co., 'S-Gravenhage), part II, Chs. 1 to 4.

Reference to the "experience of the community" as the substance of this discourse settles nothing. For this experience has as its essential dimension the tradition which the discourse itself founds. This tradition, long before the drama of history gets written into it, creates the elementary structures of culture. And these structures reveal an ordering of possible exchanges which, even unconscious, is inconceivable outside the permutations authorized by language.

With the result that the ethnographic duality of nature and culture is giving way to a ternary conception of the human condition: nature, society, and culture, the last term of which could well be equated to language, or that which essentially distinguishes human society from natural societies.

But we shall not make of this distinction either a point or a point of departure, leaving to its own obscurity the question of the original relation between work and the signifier. We shall be content, for our little jab at the general function of *praxis* in the genesis of history, to point out that the very society which wished to restore, along with the privileges of the producer, the causal hierarchy of the relations between production and the ideological superstructure to their full political rights, has nonetheless failed to give birth to an esperanto in which the relations of language to socialist realities would have rendered any literary formalism radically impossible.[4]

As for us, we shall have faith only in those assumptions which have already proven their value by virtue of the fact that language through them has attained the status of an object of scientific investigation.

For it is by dint of this fact that linguistics[5] is seen to occupy the key position in this domain, and the reclassification

[4] We may recall that the discussion of the necessity for a new language in the communist society did in fact take place, and Stalin, much to the relief of those depending on his philosophy, cut off the discussion with the decision: language is not a superstructure.

[5] By "linguistics" we understand the study of existing languages in their structure and in the laws revealed therein; this leaves out any theory of abstract codes sometimes included under the heading of communication theory, as well as the theory, originating in the physical sciences, called information theory, or any semiology more or less hypothetically generalized.

of sciences and regrouping of them around it points up, as is the rule, a revolution in knowledge; only the necessities of communication made us call this volume and this grouping the "human sciences" given the confusion that this term can be made to hide.

To pinpoint the emergence of linguistic science we may say that, as in the case of all sciences in the modern sense, it is contained in the constitutive moment of a formula which is its foundation. This formula is the following:

$$\frac{S}{s}$$

which is read as: the signifier over the signified, "over" corresponding to the line separating the two levels.

This sign should be attributed to Ferdinand de Saussure although it is not found in exactly this form in any of the numerous schemas which none the less express it in the printed version of his lectures of the years 1906-07, 1908-09, and 1910-11, which the piety of a group of his disciples caused to be published under the title, *Cours de linguistique générale,* a work of prime importance for the transmission of a teaching worthy of the name, that is, that one can come to terms with only in its own terms.

That is why it is legitimate for us to give him credit for the formulation $\frac{S}{s}$ by which, in spite of the differences among schools, the beginning of modern linguistics can be recognized.

The thematics of this science is henceforth suspended, in effect, at the primordial placement of the signifier and the signified as being distinct orders separated initially by a barrier resisting signification. And that is what was to make possible an exact study of the relations proper to the signifier, and of the breadth of their function in the birth of the signified.

For this primordial distinction goes way beyond the debates on the arbitrariness of the sign which have been elaborated since the earliest reflections of the ancients, and even beyond the impasse which, through the same period, has been encountered in every discussion of the bi-univocal correspondence between the word and the thing, even in the mere act of naming. All this, of course, is quite contrary to the appearances suggested by the importance often imputed to the role of the index finger pointing to an object in the learning process of the infant subject learning his mother tongue, or the use in foreign language teaching of methods sometimes called "concrete."

One cannot and need not go further along this line of thought than to demonstrate that no meaning is sustained by anything other than reference to another meaning;[6] in its extreme form this is tantamount to the proposition that there is no language in existence for which there is any question of its inability to cover the whole field of the signified, it being an effect of its existence as a language that it necessarily answer all needs. Should we try to grasp in the realm of language the constitution of the object, how can we help but notice that the object is to be found only at the level of concept, a very different thing from a simple nominative, and that the thing, to take it at its word reduces to two divergent factors: the cause in which it has taken shelter in the French word *chose*, and the nothing (*rien*) to which it has abandoned its Latin dress (*rem*).

These considerations, however stimulating they may seem to philosophers, turn us aside from the area in which language questions us on its very nature. And one will fail even to keep the question in view as long as one has not got rid of the illusion that the signifier answers to the function of representing the signified, or better, that the signifier has to answer for its existence in the name of any signification whatever.

For even reduced to this latter formulation, the heresy is the same, the heresy that leads logical positivism in search of the "meaning of meaning" as its object is called in the language its disciples like to wallow in. Whence we can observe that even a text charged with meaning reduces itself, through this sort of analysis, to meaningless bagatelles, all that sur-

---

[6] Cf. the *De Magistro* of Saint Augustine, especially the chapter "De significatione locutionis" which I analysed in my seminar of 23rd June 1954.

vives being mathematical formulas which are, of course, meaningless.[7]

To return to our formula $\frac{S}{s}$: if we could infer nothing from it beyond the notion of the parallelism of its upper and lower terms, each one taken in its globality, it would remain only the enigmatic sign of a total mystery. Which of course is not the case.

In order to grasp its function I shall begin by reproducing the classical, yet faulty illustration by which its usage is normally presented. It is:

TREE

and one can see already how it seems to favor the sort of erroneous interpretation just mentioned.

I replaced this in my lecture with another, which has no greater claim to correctness than that it has been transplanted into that incongruous dimension which the psychoanalyst has not yet altogether renounced because of his quite justified

[7] So, Mr. I. A. Richards, author of a work precisely in accord with such an objective, has in another work shown us its application. He took for his purposes a page from Mong-tse (Mencius to the Jesuits) and called the piece, *Mencius on the Mind*. The guarantees of the purity of the experiment are nothing to the luxury of the approaches. And our expert on the traditional Canon which contains the text is found right on the spot in Peking where our demonstration-model mangle has been transported regardless of cost.

But we shall be no less transported, if less expensively, to see a bronze which gives out bell-tones at the slightest contact with true thought, transformed into a rag to wipe the blackboard of the most dismaying British psychologism. And not without eventually being identified with the meninx of the author himself—all that remains of him or his object after having exhausted the meaning of meaning of the latter and the good sense of the former.

feeling that his conformism takes its value entirely from it. Here is the other diagram:

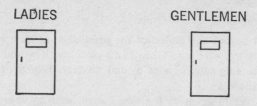

LADIES   GENTLEMEN

where we see that, without greatly extending the scope of the signifier concerned in the experiment, that is, by doubling a noun through the mere juxtaposition of two terms whose complementary meanings ought apparently to reinforce each other, a surprise is produced by an unexpected precipitation of meaning: the image of twin doors symbolizing, through the solitary confinement offered Western Man for the satisfaction of his natural needs away from home, the imperative that he seems to share with the great majority of primitive communities which submits his public life to the laws of urinary segregation.

It is not only with the idea of silencing the nominalist debate with a low blow that I use this example, but rather to show how in fact the signifier intrudes into the signified, namely in a form which, not being immaterial, raises the very question of its place in reality. For the blinking gaze of a near-sighted person would be quite justified in doubting whether this was indeed the signifier as he peered closely at the little enamel signs which bore it, a signifier of which the signified received its final honors from the double and solemn procession from the upper nave.

But no contrived example can equal the sharpness of the encounter with a lived truth. And so I am happy to have invented the above since it awoke in the person whose word I most trust this memory of childhood which having thus happily come to my knowledge could well be inserted here.

A train arrives at a station. A little boy and a little girl, brother and sister, are seated in a compartment face to face next to the window through which the buildings along the station platform can be seen passing as the train pulls to a stop. "Look," says the brother, "we're at Ladies!" "Idiot," replies his sister, "can't you see we're at Gentlemen."

Besides the fact that the rails in this story offer a material counterpart to the line in the Saussurian formula (and in a form designed to suggest that its resistance may be other than dialectical), we should add that only someone who didn't have his eyes in front of the holes (it's the appropriate image here) could possibly confuse the place of the signifier and the signified in this story, or not see from what shining center the signifier goes forth to reflect its light into the shadow of incomplete meanings. For this signifier will now carry a purely animal Dissension, meant for the usual oblivion of natural mists, to the unbridled power of ideological Warfare, relentless for families, a torment to the Gods. Ladies and Gentlemen will be henceforth for these children two countries towards which each of their souls will strive on divergent wings, and between which a cessation of hostilities will be the more impossible since they are in truth the same country and neither can compromise on its own superiority without detracting from the glory of the other.

But enough. It begins to sound like the history of France. Which it is more human, as it ought to be, to evoke here than that of England, destined to tumble from the Large to the Small End of Dean Swift's egg.

It remains to be conceived what steps, what corridor, the S of the signifier, visible here in the plurals in which it focuses its welcome beyond the window, must take in order to rest its elbows on the ventilators through which, like warm and cold air, scorn and indignation come hissing out below.

One thing is certain: if the formula $\frac{S}{s}$ with its line is appropriate, access from one to the other cannot in any case have a meaning. For the formula, insofar as it is itself only pure function of the signifier, can reveal only the structure of a signifier in the transfer.

Now the structure of the signifier is, as it is commonly said of language itself, that it be articulated.

This means that no matter where one starts from in order to describe the zones of reciprocal infringement and the areas of expanding inclusiveness of its units, these units are submitted to the double condition of reducing to ultimate distinctive features and of combining according to the laws of a closed order.

These units, one of the decisive discoveries of linguistics, are *phonemes;* but we must not expect to find any *phonetic* constancy in the modulatory variability to which this term applies, but rather the synchronic system of distinguishing connections necessary for the discernment of sounds in a given language. Through this, one sees that an essential element of the word itself was predestined to slide down into the mobile characters which—in a scurry of lower-case Didots or Garamonds—render validly present what we call the "letter," namely the essentially localized structure of the signifier.

With the second property of the signifier, that of combining according to the laws of a closed order, is affirmed the necessity of the topological substratum of which the term I ordinarily use, namely, the signifying chain, gives an approximate idea: rings of a necklace that is a ring in another necklace made of rings.

Such are the conditions of structure which define grammar as the order of constitutive infringements of the signifier up to the level of the unit immediately superior to the sentence, and lexicology as the order of constitutive inclusions of the signifier to the level of the verbal locution.

In examining the limits by which these two exercises in the understanding of linguistic usage are determined, it is easy to see that only the correlations between signifier and signifier supply the standard for all research into meaning, as is indicated in fact by the very notion of "usage" of a taxeme or semanteme which in fact refers to the context just above that of the units concerned.

But it is not because the undertakings of grammar and lexicology are exhausted within certain limits that we must think that beyond those limits meaning reigns supreme. That would be an error.

For the signifier, by its very nature, always anticipates on meaning by unfolding its dimension before it. As is seen at the level of the sentence when it is interrupted before the significant term: "I shall never . . . ," "All the same it is . . . ,"

"And yet there may be . . .". Such sentences are not without meaning, a meaning all the more oppressive in that it is content to make us wait for it.[8]

But the phenomenon is no different which by the mere recoil of a "but" brings to the light, comely as the Shulamite, honest as the dew, the negress adorned for the wedding and the poor woman ready for the auction-block.[9]

From which we can say that it is in the chain of the signifier that the meaning "insists" but that none of its elements "consists" in the meaning of which it is at the moment capable.

We are forced, then, to accept the notion of an incessant sliding of the signified under the signifier—which F. de Saussure illustrates with an image resembling the wavy lines of the upper and lower Waters in miniatures from manuscripts of Genesis; a double flow in which the guidelines of fine streaks of rain, vertical dotted lines supposedly confining segments of correspondence, seem too slight.

All our experience runs counter to this linearity, which made me speak once, in one of my seminars on psychosis, of something more like spaced upholstery buttons as a schema for taking into account the dominance of the letter in the dramatic transformation which the dialogue can bring about in a subject.[10]

The linearity which F. de Saussure holds to be constitutive of the chain of discourse, in conformity with its emission by a single voice and with its horizontal position in our writing—if this linearity is necessary in fact, it is not sufficient. It applies to the chain of discourse only in the direction in which it is oriented in time, being taken as a signifying factor in all lan-

---

[8] To which verbal hallucination, when it takes this form, opens a communicating door with the Freudian structure of psychosis—a door until now unnoticed.

[9] The allusions are to the "I am black, but comely . . ." of the *Song of Solomon,* and to the nineteenth-century cliché of the "poor but honest" woman. (Trans.)

[10] We spoke in our seminar of 6th June 1956, of the first scene of *Athalie,* incited by an allusion—tossed off by a high-brow critic in the *New Statesman and Nation*—to the "high whoredom" of Racine's heroines, to renounce reference to the savage dramas of Shakespeare, which have become compulsional in analytic milieux where they play the role of status-symbol for the Philistines.

guages in which "Peter hits Paul" reverses its time when the terms are inverted.

But one has only to listen to poetry, which perhaps Saussure was not in the habit of doing, to hear a true polyphony emerge, to know in fact that all discourse aligns itself along the several staves of a score.

There is in effect no signifying chain which does not have attached to the punctuation of each of its units a whole articulation of relevant contexts suspended "vertically" from that point.

Let us take our word "tree" again, this time not as an isolated noun, but at the point of one of these punctuations, and see how it crosses the line of the Saussurian formula.

For even broken down into the double spectre of its vowels and consonants, it can still call up with the robur and the plane tree the meanings it takes on, in the context of our flora, of strength and majesty. Drawing on all the symbolic contexts suggested in the Hebrew of the Bible, it erects on a barren hill the shadow of the cross. Then reduces to the capital Y, the sign of dichotomy which, except for the illustration used by heraldry, would owe nothing to the tree however genealogical we may think it. Circulatory tree, tree of life of the cerebellum, tree of Saturn, tree of Diana, crystals formed in a tree struck by lightning, is it your figure which traces our destiny for us in the tortoise-shell cracked by the fire, or your lightning which causes that slow shift in the axis of being to surge up from an unnamable night into the "Εν Παντα of language:

> No! says the Tree, it says No! in the shower of sparks
> Of its superb head

lines which require the harmonics of the tree just as much as their continuation:

> Which the storm treats as universally
> As it does a blade of grass.[11]

[11] "Non! dit l'Arbre, il dit: Non! dans l'étincellement
 De sa tête superbe
Que la tempête traite universellement
 Comme elle fait une herbe."
Lines from Valéry's "Au Platane" in *Les Charmes*. (Trans.)

For this modern verse is ordered according to the same law of the parallelism of the signifier which creates the harmony governing the primitive Slavic epic or the most refined Chinese poetry.

As is seen in the fact that the tree and the blade of grass are chosen from the same mode of the existent in order for the signs of contradiction—saying "No!" and "treat as"—to affect them, and also so as to bring about, through the categorical contrast of the particularity of "superb" with the "universally" which reduces it, in the condensation of the "head" and the "storm", the indiscernible shower of sparks of the eternal instant.

But this whole signifier can only operate, someone may object, if it is present in the subject. It is this objection that I answer by supposing that it has passed over to the level of the signified.

For what is important is not that the subject know anything whatsoever. (If LADIES and GENTLEMEN were written in a language unknown to the little boy and girl, their quarrel would simply be the more exclusively a quarrel over words, but none the less ready to take on meaning.)

One thing this structure of the signifying chain makes evident is the possibility I have, precisely insofar as I have this language in common with other subjects, that is insofar as it exists as a language, to use it in order to say something quite other than what it says. This function of the word is more worth pointing out than that of "disguising the thought" (more often than not indefinable) of the subject; it is no less than the function of indicating the place of the subject in the search for the truth.

I have only to plant my tree in a locution: climb the tree, indeed illuminate it by playing on it the light of a descriptive context; plant it firm so as not to let myself be trapped in some sort of *communiqué,* however official, and if I know the truth, let it be heard, in spite of all the between-the-lines censures, by the only signifier I know how to create with my acrobatics among the branches of the tree, tantalizing to the point of burlesque, or sensible only to the experienced eye, according to whether I wish to be heard by the mob or the few.

The properly signifying function thus described in language has a name. We learned this name in some grammar of our childhood, on the last page, where the shade to Quintilian, relegated to a phantom chapter of "ultimate considerations on style," seemed in a hurry to get his word in as though threatened with the hook.

It is among the figures of style, or tropes, that we find the word: the name is *metonymy*.

We shall recall only the example given there: thirty sails. For the anxiety we felt over the fact that the word 'boat' lurking in the background was only part of the craft employed in this example did less to veil these illustrious sails than did the definition they were supposed to illustrate.

The part taken for the whole, we said to ourselves, and if we take it seriously, we are left with very little idea of the importance of this fleet, which "thirty sails" is precisely supposed to give us: for each boat to have just one sail is in fact the least likely possibility.

By which we see that the connection between boat and sail is nowhere but in the signifier, and that it is in the word-to-word connection that metonymy is based.[12]

We shall designate as metonymy, then, the one slope of the effective field of the signifier in the constitution of meaning.

Let us name the other: it is *metaphor*. Let us find again an illustration; Quillet's dictionary seemed an appropriate place to find a sample which would not seem to be chosen for my own purposes, and for an appropriate dressing I didn't have to go any further than the well known line of Victor Hugo:

[12] We give homage here to the works of Roman Jakobson—to which we owe much of this formulation; works to which a psychoanalyst can constantly refer in order to structure his own experience, and which render superfluous the "personal communications" of which we could boast as much as the next fellow.

Let us thank also, in this context, the author [R. M. Loewenstein] of "Some remarks on the role of speech in psycho-analytic technique" (I.J.P., Nov.-Dec., 1956, XXXVII, 6, p. 467) for taking the trouble to point out that his remarks are "based on" work dating from 1952. This is no doubt the explanation for the fact that he has learned nothing from work done since then, yet which he is not ignorant of, as he cites me as their editor (sic).

His sheaves were not miserly nor spiteful[13]

under which aspect I presented metaphor to my seminar on psychosis.

Let us admit that modern poetry and especially the surrealist school have taken us quite far in this domain by showing that any conjunction of two signifiers would be equally sufficient to constitute a metaphor, except for the additional requirement of the greatest possible disparity of the images signified, needed for the production of the poetic spark, or in other words for there to be metaphoric creation.

It is true this radical position is based on the experiment known as automatic writing which would not have been tried if its pioneers had not been reassured by the Freudian discovery. But it remains a position branded with confusion because the doctrine behind it is false.

The creative spark of the metaphor does not spring from the conjunction of two images, that is of two signifiers equally actualized. It springs from two signifiers one of which has taken the place of the other in the signifying chain, the hidden signifier then remaining present through its (metonymic) relation to the rest of the chain.

One word for another: that is the formula for the metaphor and if you are a poet you will produce for your own delight a continuous stream, a dazzling tissue of metaphors. If the result is the sort of intoxication of the dialogue that Jean Tardieu wrote under this title, that is only because he was giving us a demonstration of the radical superfluousness of all meaning to a perfectly convincing representation of a bourgeois comedy.

It is manifest that in the line of Hugo cited above, not the slightest spark of light springs from the proposition that his sheaves were neither miserly nor spiteful, for the reason that there is no question of the sheaves' having either the merit or demerit of these attributes, since the attributes, as the sheaves, belong to Booz who exercises the former in disposing of the latter and without informing the latter of his sentiments in the case.

[13] "Sa gerbe n'etait pas avare ni haineuse," a line from "Booz endormi." (Trans.)

If, however, his sheaves do refer us to Booz, and this is indeed the case, it is because they have replaced him in the signifying chain at the very spot where he was to be exalted by the sweeping away of greed and spite. But now Booz himself has been swept away by the sheaves, and hurled into the outer darkness where greed and spite harbor him in the hollow of their negation.

But once *his* sheaves have thus usurped his place, Booz can no longer return there; the slender thread of the little word *his* which binds him to it is only one more obstacle to his return in that it links him to the notion of possession which retains him in the very zone of greed and spite. So *his* generosity, affirmed in the passage, is yet reduced to less than nothing by the munificence of the sheaves which, coming from nature, know not our caution or our casting out, and even in their accumulation remain prodigal by our standards.

But if in this profusion, the giver has disappeared along with his gift, it is only in order to rise again in what surrounds this figure by which he was annihilated. For it is the figure of the burgeoning of fecundity, and this it is which announces the surprise which the poem sings, namely the promise which the old man will receive in a sacred context of his accession to paternity.

So, it is between the signifier in the form of the proper name of a man, and the signifier which metaphorically abolishes him that the poetic spark is produced, and it is in this case all the more effective in realizing the meaning of paternity in that it reproduces the mythic event in terms of which Freud reconstructed the progress, in the individual unconscious, of the mystery of the father.

Modern metaphor has the same structure. So this ejaculation:

Love is a pebble laughing in the sunlight,

recreates love in a dimension that seems to me most tenable in the face of its imminent lapse into the mirage of narcissistic altruism.

We see, then, that metaphor occurs at the precise point at which sense comes out of non-sense, that is, at that frontier which, as Freud discovered, when crossed the other way produces what we generally call "wit" (*Witz*); it is at this frontier that we can glimpse the fact that man tempts his very destiny when he derides the signifier.

But to draw back from that place, what do we find in metonymy other than the power to bypass the obstacles of social censure? This form which lends itself to the truth under oppression, doesn't it show the very servitude inherent in its presentation?

One may read with profit a book by Leo Strauss, of the land which traditionally offers asylum to those who chose freedom, in which the author gives his reflections on the relation between the art of writing and persecution.[14] By pushing to its limits the sort of connaturality which links that art to that condition, he lets us glimpse a certain something which in this matter imposes its form, in the effect of the truth on desire.

But haven't we felt for some time now that, having followed the path of the letter in search of the truth we call Freudian, we are getting very warm indeed, that it is burning all about us?

Of course, as it is said, the letter killeth while the spirit giveth life. We can't help but agree, having had to pay homage elsewhere to a noble victim of the error of seeking the spirit in the letter; but we should like to know, also, how the spirit could live without the letter. Even so, the claims of the spirit would remain unassailable if the letter had not in fact shown us that it can produce all the effects of truth in man without involving the spirit at all.

It is none other than Freud who had this revelation, and he called his discovery the Unconscious.

II. THE LETTER IN THE UNCONSCIOUS

One out of every three pages in the complete works of Freud is devoted to philological references, one out of every two pages to logical inferences, and everywhere the apprehension

---

[14] Leo Strauss, *Persecution and the Art of Writing,* The Free Press, Glencoe, Ill.

of experience is dialectical, with the proportion of linguistic analysis increasing just insofar as the unconscious is directly concerned.

Thus in *The Interpretation of Dreams* every page deals with what we are calling the letter of the discourse, in its texture, its usage, its immanence in the matter in question. For it is with this work that the work of Freud begins to open the royal road to the unconscious. And Freud gave us notice of this; his confidence at the time of launching this book in the early days of this century[15] only confirms what he continued to proclaim to the end: that his whole message was at stake in this, the whole of his discovery.

The first sentence of the opening chapter announces what for the sake of the exposition could not be postponed: that the dream is a rebus. And Freud goes on to stipulate what I have said from the start, that it must be understood literally. This derives from the persistence in the dream of that same literal (or phonematic) structure through which the signifier in ordinary discourse is articulated and analyzed. So the unnatural images of the boat on the roof, or the man with a comma for a head which are specifically mentioned by Freud, are examples of dream-images which have importance only as signifiers, that is, insofar as they allow us to spell out the "proverb" presented by the rebus of the dream. The structure of language which enables us to read dreams is the very principle of the "meaning of dreams," the *Traumdeutung*.

Freud shows us in every possible way that the image's value as signifier has nothing whatever to do with what it signifies, giving as an example Egyptian hieroglyphics in which it would be sheer buffoonery to pretend that in a given text the frequency of a vulture which is an *aleph*, or of a chick which is a *vau*, and which indicate a form of the verb "to be" or a plural, prove that the text has anything at all to do with these ornithological specimens. Freud finds in this script certain uses of the signifier which are lost in ours, such as the use of determinatives, where a categorical figure is added to the literal figuration of a verbal term; but this is only to show us that even in this script, the so-called "ideogram" is a letter.

---

[15] See the correspondence, namely letters 107 and 109.

But the current confusion on this last term was not needed for there to prevail in the minds of psychoanalysts lacking linguistic training the prejudice in favor of a symbolism by natural analogy, that is of the image as fitted to the instinct. And to such an extent that, outside of the French school which has been alerted, one must draw the line between reading coffee grounds and reading hieroglyphics, by recalling to its own principles a technique which nothing could possibly justify except the very aim and content of the unconscious.

It must be said that this truth is admitted only with difficulty and that the bad mental habits denounced above enjoy such favor that today's psychoanalyst can be expected to say that he decodes before he will come around to taking the necessary tour with Freud (turn at the statue of Champollion, says the guide) which will make him understand that he deciphers; the distinction is that a cryptogram takes on its full dimension only when it is in a lost language.

Taking the tour is nothing other than continuing in the *Traumdeutung.*

Entstellung, translated as distortion, is what Freud shows to be the general precondition for the functioning of dreams, and it is what we described above, following Saussure, as the sliding of the signified under the signifier which is always active in speech (its action, let us note, is unconscious).

But what we called the two slopes of the incidence of the signifier on the signified are also found here.

The *Verdichtung,* or condensation, is the structure of the superimposition of signifiers which is the field of metaphor, and its very name, condensing in itself the word *Dichtung,* shows how the process is connatural with the mechanism of poetry to the point that it actually envelops its properly traditional function.

In the case of *Verschiebung,* displacement, the German term is closer to the idea of that veering off of meaning that we see in metonymy, and which from its first appearance in Freud is described as the main method by which the unconscious gets around censorship.

What distinguishes these two mechanisms which play such a privileged role in the dream-work (*Traumarbeit*), from their homologous functions in speech? Nothing except a condition imposed on the signifying material by the dream, called *Rücksicht auf Darstellbarkeit,* translated as Considerations of Representability. But this condition constitutes a limitation operating *within* the system of notation; it is a long way from dissolving the system into a figurative semiology on a level with certain phenomena of natural expression. This fact could perhaps shed light on the problems involved in certain modes of pictography which, simply because they have been abandoned by writing systems as imperfect, are not therefore to be considered as mere evolutionary stages. Let us say, then, that the dream is like the parlor-game in which one is put on the spot to cause a group of spectators to guess some known utterance or variant of it by means solely of a silent performance. That the dream uses words makes no difference since for the unconscious they are but one among several elements of the performance. It is exactly the fact that both the game and the dream run up against a lack of taxematic material for the representation of such logical articulations as causality, contradiction, hypothesis, etc., that proves they are both writing systems rather than pantomime. The subtle processes which dreams are seen to use to represent these logical articulations, in a much less artificial way than the game brings to bear, are the object of a special study in Freud in which we see once more confirmed that dream-work follows the laws of the signifier.

The rest of the dream-elaboration is designated as secondary by Freud, the nature of which indicates its value: they are fantasies or day-dreams (*Tagtraum*) to use the term Freud prefers in order to emphasize their function of wish-fulfillment (*Wunscherfüllung*). Given the fact that these fantasies can remain unconscious, their distinctive trait is in this case their meaning. Now concerning these fantasies, Freud tells us that their place in dreams is either to be taken up and used as signifying elements in the message of the dream-thought (*Traumgedanke*), or else to be used in the secondary elaboration just mentioned, that is in a function not to be distinguished from our waking thought (*von unserem wachen Denken nicht zu unterschieden*). No better idea of this function can be got than by comparing it to splotches of color which when applied here and there to a stencil would create for our view in a topical painting the pictures, rather grim in themselves, of the rebus or hieroglyph.

Excuse me if I seem to have to spell out the text of Freud; I do it not only to show how much is to be gained by not cutting or abridging it, but also in order to situate the development of psychoanalysis according to its first guide-lines, which were fundamental and never revoked.

Yet from the beginning there was a general failure to recognize the formative role of the signifier in the status which Freud from the first assigned to the unconscious and in the most precise formal manner. And for a double reason, of which the least obvious, naturally, is that this formalization was not sufficient in itself to bring about a recognition of the insistence of the signifier because the time of the appearance of the *Traumdeutung* was well ahead of the formalizations of linguistics for which one could no doubt show that it paved the way by the sheer weight of its truth.

And the second reason, which is after all only the underside of the first, is that if psychoanalysts were fascinated exclusively by the meanings revealed in the unconscious, that is because the secret attraction of these meanings arises from the dialectic which seems to inhere in them.

I showed in my seminars that it is the necessity of counteracting the continuously accelerating effects of this bias which alone explains the apparent sudden changes, or rather changes of tack, which Freud, through his primary concern to preserve for posterity both his discovery and the fundamental revisions it effected in our other knowledge, felt it necessary to apply to his doctrine.

For, I repeat: in the situation in which he found himself, having nothing which corresponded to the object of his discovery which was at the same level of scientific development —in this situation, at least he never failed to maintain this object on the level of its proper ontological dignity.

The rest was the work of the gods and took such a course that analysis today takes as its basis those imaginary forms which I have just shown to be written on the margin of the text they mutilate—and analysis tries to accommodate its goal according to them, in the interpretation of dreams confusing them with the visionary liberation of the hieroglyphic apiary, and seeking generally the control of the exhaustion of the analysis in a sort of scanning process[16] of these forms whenever they appear, with the idea that, just as they are a sign of the exhaustion of regressions, they are also signs of the re-modeling of the "object-relation" which characterizes the subject.

The technique which is based on such positions can be fertile in its diverse results, and under the aegis of therapy, difficult to criticize. But an internal criticism must none the less arise from the flagrant disparity between the mode of operation by which the technique is justified—namely the analytic rule, all the instruments of which, from "free association" on up, depend on the conception of the unconscious of their inventor—and on the other hand the general ignorance which reigns regarding this conception of the unconscious. The most peremptory champions of this technique think themselves freed of any need to reconcile the two by the simplest pirouette: the analytic rule (they say) must be all the more religiously observed since it is only the result of a lucky accident. In other words, Freud never knew what he was doing.

A return to Freud's text shows on the contrary the absolute coherence between his technique and his discovery, and at the same time this coherence allows us to put all his procedures in their proper place.

That is why the rectification of psychoanalysis must inevitably involve a return to the truth of that discovery which, taken in its original moment, is impossible to mistake.

For in the analysis of dreams, Freud intends only to give us the laws of the unconscious in the most general extension. One of the reasons why dreams were most propitious for this demonstration is exactly, Freud tells us, that they reveal the same laws whether in the normal person or in the neurotic.

But in the one case as in the other, the efficacy of the uncon-

---

[16] That is the process by which the results of a piece of research are assured through a mechanical exploration of the entire extent of the field of its object.

scious does not cease in the waking state. The psychoanalytic experience is nothing other than the demonstration that the unconscious leaves none of our actions outside its scope. The presence of the unconscious in the psychological order, in other words in the relation-functions of the individual, should, however, be more precisely defined: it is not coextensive with that order, for we know that if unconscious motivation is manifest in conscious psychic effects, as well as in unconscious ones, conversely it is only elementary to recall to mind that a large number of psychic effects which are quite legitimately designated as unconscious, in the sense of excluding the characteristic of consciousness, never the less are without any relation whatever to the unconscious in the Freudian sense. So it is only by an abuse of the term that unconscious in that sense is confused with psychic, and that one may thus designate as psychic what is in fact an effect of the unconscious, as on the somatic for instance.

It is a matter, therefore, of defining the locus of this unconscious. I say that it is the very locus defined by the formula $\frac{S}{s}$. What we have been able to unfold concerning the incidence of the signifier on the signified suggests its transformation into:

$$f(S)\frac{1}{s}$$

We have shown the effects not only of the elements of the horizontal signifying chain, but also of its vertical dependencies, divided into two fundamental structures called metonymy and metaphor. We can symbolize them by, first:

$$f(S...S') \ S \sim S \ (-)s$$

that is, the metonymic structure, indicating that it is the connection between signifier and signifier which alone permits the elision in which the signifier inserts the lack of being into the object relation, using the reverberating character of meaning to invest it with the desire aimed at the very lack it supports. The sign — placed between ( ) represents here the retention of the line — which in the original formula marked the irreducibility in which, in the relations between signifier and signified, the resistance of meaning is constituted.[17]

Secondly,

$$f\left(\frac{S'}{S}\right) S \sim S \; (+)s$$

the metaphoric structure, indicates that it is in the substitution of signifier for signifier that an effect of signification is produced which is creative or poetic, in other words which is the advent of the signification in question.[18] The sign $+$ between ( ) represents here the leap over the line — and the constitutive value of the leap for the emergence of meaning.

This leap is an expression of the condition of passage of the signifier into the signified which I pointed out above, although provisionally confusing it with the place of the subject. It is the function of the subject, thus introduced, which we must now turn to as it is the crucial point of our problem.

Je pense, donc je suis (*cogito ergo sum*) is not merely the formula in which is constituted, along with the historical apogee of reflection on the conditions of knowledge, the link between the transparence of the transcendental subject and his existential affirmation.

Perhaps I am only object and mechanism (and so nothing more than phenomenon), but assuredly insofar as I think so, I am—absolutely. No doubt philosophers have made important corrections on this formulation, notably that in that which thinks (*cogitans*), I can never pose myself as anything but object (*cogitatum*). None the less it remains true that by way of this extreme purification of the transcendental subject, my existential link to its project seems irrefutable, at least in its present form, and that:

"cogito ergo sum" ubi cogito, ibi sum,

overcomes this objection.

Of course this confines me to being there in my being only insofar as I think that I am in my thought; just how far I ac-

[17] The sign $\sim$ here represents congruence.
[18] (S' i.e. prime) designating here the term productive of the signifying effect (or significance); one can see that the term is latent in metonymy, patent in metaphor.

tually think this concerns only myself and if I say it, interests no one.[19]

To elude this problem on the pretext of its philosophical pretensions is simply to show our inhibition. For the notion of subject is indispensable even to the operation of a science such as strategy (in the modern sense) whose calculations exclude all subjectivism.

It is also to deny oneself access to what we may call the Freudian universe—in the way that we speak of the Copernican universe. It was in fact the so-called Copernican revolution to which Freud himself compared his discovery, emphasizing that it was once again a question of the place man assigns to himself at the center of a universe.

The place that I occupy as the subject of a signifier: is it, in relation to the place I occupy as subject of the signified, concentric or ex-centric?—that is the question.

It is not a question of knowing whether I speak of myself in a way that conforms to what I am, but rather of knowing whether I am the same as that of which I speak. And it is not at all inappropriate to use the word "thought" here. For Freud uses the term to designate the elements involved in the unconscious, that is the signifying mechanisms which we now recognize as being there.

It is none the less true that the philosophical *cogito* is at the center of that mirage which renders modern man so sure of being himself even in his uncertainties about himself, or rather in the mistrust he has learned to erect against the traps of self-love.

Likewise, if I charge nostalgia with being in the service of metonymy and refuse to seek meaning beyond tautology; if in the name of "war is war" and "a penny's a penny" I determine to be only what I am, yet how even here can I eliminate the obvious fact that in that very act I am?

And it is no less true if I take myself to the other, metaphorical pole in my quest for meaning, and if I dedicate myself to becoming what I am, to coming into being, I cannot

[19] It is quite otherwise if by posing a question such as "Why philosophers?" I become more candid than nature, for then I am asking the question which philosophers have been asking themselves for all time and also the one in which they are in fact the most interested.

doubt that even if I lose myself in the process, in that process, I am.

Now it is on these very points where evidence will be subverted by the empirical, that the trick of the Freudian conversion lies.

This meaningful game between metonymy and metaphor up to and including the active edge which splits my desire between a refusal of meaning or a lack of being and links my fate to the question of my destiny, this game, in all its inexorable subtlety, is played until the match is called, there where I am not because I cannot locate myself there.

That is, what is needed is more than these words with which I disconcerted my audience: I think where I am not, therefore I am where I think not. Words which render sensible to an ear properly attuned with what weasling ambiguity the ring of meaning flees from our grasp along the verbal thread.

What one ought to say is: I am not, wherever I am the plaything of my thought; I think of what I am wherever I don't think I am thinking.

This two-faced mystery is linked to the fact that the truth can be evoked only in that dimension of alibi in which all "realism" in creative works takes its virtue from metonymy; it is likewise linked to this other fact that we accede to meaning only through the double twist of metaphor when we have the unique key: the S and the s of the Saussurian formula are not on the same level, and man only deludes himself when he believes his true place is at their axis, which is nowhere.

Was nowhere, that is, until Freud discovered it; for if what Freud discovered isn't that, it isn't anything.

The content of the unconscious with all its disappointing ambiguities gives us no reality in the subject more consistent than the immediate; its force comes from the truth and in the dimension of being: *Kern unseres Wesen* are Freud's own terms.

The double-triggered mechanism of metaphor is in fact the very mechanism by which the symptom, in the analytic sense, is determined. Between the enigmatic signifier of a sexual trauma and its substitute term in a present signifying chain there passes the spark which fixes in a symptom the meaning inaccessible to the conscious subject in which is its resolution —a symptom which is in effect a metaphor in which flesh or function are taken as signifying elements.

And the enigmas which desire seems to pose for a "natural philosophy"—its frenzy mocking the abyss of the infinite, the secret collusion by which it obscures the pleasure of knowing and of joyful domination, these amount to nothing more than that derangement of the instincts that comes from being caught on the rails—eternally stretching forth towards the desire for something else—of metonymy. Wherefore its "perverse" fixation at the very suspension-point of the signifying chain where the memory-screen freezes and the fascinating image of the fetish petrifies.

There is no other way to conceive the indestructibility of unconscious desire, when there is no natural need which, when prevented from satisfying itself, isn't dissipated even if it means the destruction of the organism itself. It is in a memory, comparable to what they call by that name in our modern thinking-machines (which are in turn based on an electronic realization of the signifying compound), it is in this sort of memory that is found that chain which insists on reproducing itself in the process of transference, and which is the chain of dead desire.

It is the truth of what this desire was in its history which the patient cries out through his symptom, as Christ said that the stones themselves would have cried out if the children of Israel had not lent them their voice.

And that is why only psychoanalysis allows us to differentiate within memory the function of recall. Rooted in the signifier, it resolves the Platonic puzzles of reminiscence through the ascendancy of the historic in man.

One has only to read the "Three Essays on Sexuality" to observe, in spite of the pseudo-biological glosses with which it is decked out for popular consumption, that Freud there derives any accession to the object from the dialectic of the return.

Starting from Hölderlin's νοστος Freud will arrive less than twenty years later at Kierkegaard's repetition; that is, through submitting his thought solely to the humble but inflexible consequences of the talking cure, he was unable ever to escape the living servitudes which led him from the regal principle of the Logos to re-thinking the mortal Empedoclean antinomies.

And how else are we to conceive the recourse of a man of science to a *Deus ex machina* than on that other stage of which he speaks as the dream place, a *Deus ex machina* only less derisory for the fact that it is revealed to the spectator that the machine directs the director? How else can we imagine that a scientist of the nineteenth century, unless we realize that he had to bow before the force of evidence that overwhelmed his prejudices, put more stock in his *Totem and Taboo* than in all his other works, with its obscene and ferocious figure of the primordial father, not to be exhausted in the expiation of Oedipus' blindness, and before which the ethnologists of today bow as before the growth of an authentic myth?

So that imperious proliferation of particular symbolic creations, such as what are called the sexual theories of the child, which supply the motivation down to the smallest detail of neurotic compulsions, these reply to the same necessities as do myths.

Likewise, to speak of the precise point we are treating in my seminars on Freud, little Hans, left in the lurch at the age of five by his symbolic environment, and suddenly forced to face the enigma of his sex and his existence, under the direction of Freud and of his father, Freud's disciple, developed in a mythic form, around the signifying crystal of his phobia, all the permutations possible on a limited number of signifiers.

The operation shows that even on the individual level the solution of the impossible is brought within man's reach by the exhaustion of all possible forms of the impossibilities encountered in solution by recourse to the signifying equation. It is a striking demonstration for the clarifying of this labyrinth of observation which so far has only been used as a source of demolished fragments. We should be struck also with the fact that the coextensivity of the unfolding of the symptom and of its curative resolution shows the true nature of neurosis: whether phobic, hysterical or obsessive, a neurosis is a question which being poses for the subject "from the place where it was before the subject came into the world" (Freud's phrase which he used in explaining the Oedipal complex to little Hans).

The "being" referred to is that which appears in a lightning moment in the void of the verb "to be" and I said that it poses its question for the subject. What does that mean? It does not pose it *before* the subject, since the subject cannot come to the place where it is posed, but it poses it *in place* of the subject, that is, in that place it poses the question *with* the subject, as one poses a problem *with* a pen, or as man in antiquity thought *with* his soul.

It is only in this way that Freud fits the ego into his doctrine. Freud defined the ego by the resistances which are proper to it. They are of an imaginary nature much in the same sense as those adaptational activities which the ethology of animal behavior shows us in courting-pomp or combat. Freud showed their reduction in man to a narcissistic relation, which I elaborated in my essay on the mirror-stage. And he grouped within it the synthesis of the perceptive functions in which the sensori-motor selections are integrated which determine for man what he calls reality.

But this resistance, essential for the solidifying of the inertias of the imaginary order which obstruct the message of the unconscious, is only secondary in relation to the specific resistances of the journey in the signifying order of the truth.

That is the reason why an exhaustion of the mechanisms of defence, which Fenichel the practitioner shows us so well in his studies of technique (while his whole reduction on the theoretical level of neuroses and psychoses to genetic anomalies in libidinal development is pure platitude), manifests itself, without Fenichel's accounting for it or realizing it himself, as simply the underside or reverse aspect of the mechanisms of the unconscious. Periphrasis, hyperbaton, ellipsis, suspension, anticipation, retraction, denial, digression, irony, these are the figures of style (Quintilian's *figurae sententiarum*); as catachresis, litotes, antonomasia, hypotyposis are the tropes, whose terms impose themselves as the most proper for the labelling of these mechanisms. Can one really see these as mere figures of speech when it is the figures themselves which are the active principle of the rhetoric of the discourse which the patient in fact utters?

By the obstinacy with which today's psychoanalysts reduce

to a sort of emotional police station the reality of the resistance of which the patient's discourse is only a cover, they have sunk beneath one of the fundamental truths which Freud rediscovered through psychoanalysis. One is never happy making way for a new truth, for it always means making our way into it: the truth demands that we bestir ourselves. We cannot even manage to get used to the idea most of the time. We get used to reality. But the truth we repress.

Now it is quite specially necessary to the scientist and the magician, and even the quack, that he be the only one to *know*. The idea that deep in the simplest (and even sick) souls there is something ready to blossom—perish the thought! but if someone seems to know as much as the savants about what we ought to make of it . . . come to our aid, categories of primitive, prelogical, archaic, or even magical thought, so easy to impute to others! It is not right that these nibblers keep us breathless with enigmas which turn out to be only malicious.

To interpret the unconscious as Freud did, one would have to be as he was, an encyclopedia of the arts and muses, as well as an assiduous reader of the *Fliegende Blätter*.[20] And the task is made no easier by the fact that we are at the mercy of a thread woven with allusions, quotations, puns, and equivocations. And is that our profession; to be antidotes to trifles?

Yet that is what we must resign ourselves to. The unconscious is neither primordial nor instinctual; what it knows about the elementary is no more than the elements of the signifier.

The three books that one might call canonical with regard to the unconscious—the *Traumdeutung*, the *Psychopathology of Everyday Life*, and *Wit in its Relation to the Unconscious* —are but a web of examples whose development is furnished by the formulas of connection and substitution (though carried to the tenth degree by their particular complexity—the rundown of them is sometimes given by Freud outside the text); these are the formulas we give to the signifier in its *transference*-function. For in the *Traumdeutung* it is in the sense of such a function that the term *Ubertragung*, or transference, is introduced, which only later will give its name to

[20] A German comic newspaper of the late nineteenth and early twentieth centuries. (Trans.)

the mainspring of the intersubjective link between analyst and analyzed.

Such diagrams (of the various transfers of the signifier) are not only constitutive of each of the symptoms in a neurosis, but they alone make possible the understanding of the thematic of its course and resolution. The great observations of analyses which Freud gave amply demonstrate this.

To fall back on data that are more limited but more apt to furnish us with the final seal to bind up our proposition, let me cite the article on fetishism of 1927,[21] and the case Freud reports there of a patient who, to achieve sexual satisfaction, needed something shining on the nose (*Glanz auf der Nase*); analysis showed that his early, English-speaking years had seen the displacement of the burning curiosity which he felt for the phallus of his mother, that is for that eminent failure-to-be the privileged signification of which Freud revealed to us, into a *glance at the nose* in the forgotten language of his childhood, rather than a *shine on the nose*.

That a thought makes itself heard in the abyss, that is an abyss open before all thought—and that is what provoked from the outset resistance to psychoanalysis. And not, as is commonly said, the emphasis on man's sexuality. This latter is after all the dominant object in the literature of the ages. And in fact the more recent evolution of psychoanalysis has succeeded by a bit of comical legerdemain in turning it into a quite moral affair, the cradle and trysting-place of attraction and oblativity. The Platonic setting of the soul, blessed and illuminated, rises straight to paradise.

The intolerable scandal in the time before Freudian sexuality was sanctified was that it was so "intellectual." It was precisely in that that it showed itself to be the worthy ally of the terrorists plotting to ruin society.

At a time when psychoanalysts are busy remodeling psychoanalysis into a right-thinking movement whose crowning expression is the sociological poem of the autonomous ego, and by this I mean what will identify, for those who understand me, bad psychoanalysts, this is the term they use to deprecate all technical or theoretical research which carries forward

[21] *Fetischismus*, G.W., XIV, p. 311.

the Freudian experience along its authentic lines: *intellectualization* is the word—execrable to all those who, living in fear of being tried and found wanting by the wine of truth spit on the bread of men, although their slaver can no longer have any effect other than that of leavening.

III. BEING, THE LETTER AND THE OTHER

Is what thinks in my place then another I? Does Freud's discovery represent the confirmation on the psychological level of Manicheism?[22]

In fact there is no confusion on this point: what Freud's researches led us to is not a few more or less curious cases of split personality. Even at the heroic epoch we were talking about, when, like the animals in fairy stories, sexually talked, the demonic atmosphere that such an orientation might have given rise to never materialized.[23]

The end which Freud's discovery proposes for man was defined by him at the apex of his thought in these moving terms: *Wo es war, soll Ich werden.* I must come to the place where that (id) was.

The goal is one of reintegration and harmony, I could even say of reconciliation (*Versöhnung*).

But if we ignore the self's radical ex-centricity to itself with which man is confronted, in other words, the truth discovered by Freud, we shall falsify both the order and methods of psychoanalytic mediation; we shall make of it nothing more than the compromise operation which it has effectively become, namely just what the letter as well as the spirit of Freud's work most repudiates. For since he constantly invoked the notion of compromise as the main support of all the miseries which analysis is meant to help, we can say that any recourse

[22] One of my Colleagues went so far in this direction as to wonder if the Id of the last phase wasn't in fact the "bad Ego."

[23] Note, none the less, the tone with which one spoke in that period of the "elfin pranks" of the unconscious; a work of Silberer's is called, *Der Zufall und die Koboldstreiche des Unbewussten*—completely anachronistic in the context of our present soul-managers.

to compromise, explicit or implicit, will necessarily disorient psychoanalytic action and plunge it into darkness.

Neither does it suffice, moreover, to associate oneself with the moralistic tartufferies of our times or to be forever spouting something about the "total personality" in order to have said anything articulate about the possibility of mediation.

The radical heteronomy which Freud's discovery shows gaping within man can never again be covered over without whatever is used to hide it being fundamentally dishonest.

Then who is this other to whom I am more attached than to myself, since, at the heart of my assent to my own identity it is still he who wags me?

Its presence can only be understood at a second degree of otherness which puts it in the position of mediating between me and the double of myself, as it were with my neighbor.

If I have said elsewhere that the unconscious is the discourse of the Other (with a capital O), I meant by that to indicate the beyond in which the recognition of desire is bound up with the desire of recognition.

In other words this other is the Other which my lie invokes as a gage of the truth in which it thrives.

By which we can also see that the dimension of truth emerges only with the appearance of language.

Prior to this point, we can recognize in psychological relations which can be easily isolated in the observation of animal behavior the existence of subjects, not on account of any projective mirage, the phantoms of which a certain type of psychologist delights in hacking to pieces, but simply on account of the manifest presence of intersubjectivity. In the animal hidden in his lookout, in the well-laid trap of certain others, in the feint by which an apparent straggler leads a bird of prey away from a fugitive band, we see something more emerge than in the fascinating display of mating or combat ritual. Yet there is nothing even there which transcends the function of decoy in the service of a need, nor which affirms a presence in that Beyond where we think we can question the designs of Nature.

For there even to be a question (and we know that it is one Freud himself posed in *Beyond the Pleasure Principle*), there must be language.

For I can decoy my adversary by means of a movement contrary to my actual plan of battle, and this movement will have its deceiving effect only insofar as I produce it in reality and for my adversary.

But in the propositions with which I open peace negotiations with him, what my negotiations propose to him is situated in a third place which is neither my words nor my interlocutor.

This place is none other than the area of signifying convention, of the sort revealed in the comedy of the sad plaint of the Jew to his crony: "Why do you tell me you are going to Cracow so I'll believe you are going to Lvov, when you are really going to Cracow?"

Of course the troop-movement I just spoke of could be understood in the conventional context of game-strategy where it is in function of a rule that I deceive my adversary, but in that case my success is evaluated within the connotation of betrayal, that is, in relation to the Other who is the guarantee of Good Faith.

Here the problems are of an order the basic heteronomy of which is completely misunderstood if it is reduced to an "awareness of the other" by whatever name we call it. For the "existence of the other" having once upon a time reached the ears of the Midas of psychoanalysis through the partition which separates him from the Privy Council of phenomenology, the news is now bruited through the reeds: "Midas, King Midas is the other of his patient. He himself has said it."

What sort of breakthrough is that? The other, what other?

The young André Gide, defying the landlady to whom his mother had confided him to treat him as a responsible being, opening with a key (false only in that it opened all locks of the same make) the lock which this lady took to be a worthy signifier of her educational intentions, and doing it with ostentation in her sight—what "other" was he aiming at? She who was supposed to intervene and to whom he would then say: "Do you think my obedience can be secured with a ridiculous lock?" But by remaining out of sight and holding her peace until that evening in order, after primly greeting his return, to lecture him like a child, she showed him not just another with the face of anger, but another André Gide who is no longer sure, either then or later in thinking back on it, of just what he really meant to do—whose own truth has been changed by the doubt thrown on his good faith.

Perhaps it would be worth our while pausing a moment over this dominion of confusion which is none other than that in which the whole human opera-buffa plays itself out, in order to understand the ways in which analysis can proceed not just to restore an order but to found the conditions for the possibility of its restoration.

Kern unseres Wesen, the nucleus of our being, but it is not so much that Freud commands us to seek it as so many others before him have with the empty adage "Know thyself"—as to reconsider the ways which lead to it, and which he shows us.

Or rather that which he proposes for us to attain is not that which can be the object of knowledge, but that (doesn't he tell us as much?) which creates our being and about which he teaches us that we bear witness to it as much and more in our whims, our aberrations, our phobias and fetishes, as in our vaguely civilized personalities.

Folly, you are no longer the object of the ambiguous praise with which the sage decorated the impregnable burrow of his terror; and if after all he finds himself tolerably at home there, it is only because the supreme agent forever at work digging its galleries and labyrinths is none other than reason, the very Logos which he serves.

So how do you imagine that a scholar with so little talent for the *"engagements"* which solicited him in his age (as they do in all ages), that a scholar such as Erasmus held such an eminent place in the revolution of a Reformation in which man has much of a stake in each man as in all men?

The answer is that the slightest alteration in the relation between man and the signifier, in this case in the procedures of exegesis, changes the whole course of history by modifying the lines which anchor his being.

It is in precisely this way that Freudianism, however misunderstood it has been, and confused the consequences, to anyone capable of perceiving the changes we have lived through in our own lives, is seen to have founded an intangible but radical revolution. No need to collect witnesses to the

fact:[24] everything involving not just the human sciences, but
the destiny of man, politics, metaphysics, literature, art, advertising, propaganda, and through these even the economy,
everything has been affected.

Is all this anything more than the unharmonized effects of
an immense truth in which Freud traced for us a clear path?
What must be said, however, is that any technique which bases
its claim on the mere psychological categorization of its object is not following this path, and this is the case of psychoanalysis today except insofar as we return to the Freudian discovery.

Likewise the vulgarity of the concepts by which it recom-
mends itself to us, the embroidery of Freudery which is no
longer anything but decoration, as well as the bad repute in
which it seems to prosper, all bear witness to its fundamental
denial of its founder.

Freud, by his discovery, brought within the circle of science
the boundary between being and the object which seemed before to mark its outer limit.

That this is the symptom and the prelude of a reexamination
of the situation of man in the existent such as has been assumed up to the present by all our postulates of knowledge—
don't be content, I beg of you, to write this off as another case
of Heideggerianism, even prefixed by a neo- which adds nothing to the trashcan style in which currently, by the use of his
ready-made mental jetsam, one excuses oneself from any real
thought.

When I speak of Heidegger, or rather when I translate him,
I at least make the effort to leave the word he proffers us its
sovereign significance.

If I speak of being and the letter, if I distinguish the other
and the Other, it is only because Freud shows me that they are

[24] To pick the most recent in date, Francois Mauriac, in the *Figaro
Litteraire* of May 25, excuses himself for not "narrating his life." If no
one these days can undertake to do that with the old enthusiasm, the
reason is that, "a half century since, Freud, whatever we think of him"
has already passed that way. And after being briefly tempted by the old
saw that this is only the "history of our body," Mauriac returns to the
truth that his sensitivity as a writer makes him face: to write the history
of oneself is to write the confession of the deepest part of our neighbors'
souls as well.

the terms to which must be referred the effects of resistance and transfer against which, in the twenty years I have engaged in what we all call after him the impossible practice of psychoanalysis, I have done unequal battle. And it is also because I must help others not to lose their way there.

It is to prevent the field of which they are the inheritors from becoming barren, and for that reason to make it understood that if the symptom is a metaphor, it is not a metaphor to say so, no more than to say that man's desire is a metonymy. For the symptom *is* a metaphor whether one likes it or not, as desire *is* a metonymy for all that men mock the idea.

Finally, if I am to rouse you to indignation that, after so many centuries of religious hypocrisy and philosophical bravado, nothing valid has yet been articulated on what links metaphor to the question of being and metonymy to its lack, there must be an object there to answer to that indignation both as its provocator and its victim: it is humanistic man and the credit, affirmed beyond reparation, which he has drawn on his intentions.

T.t.y.m.u.p.t. 14-26 May, 1957.

INDEX